I am delighted to welcome the publication of *Hebrew* which is an excellent basic introducti essentials of Hebrew grammar in a clear and simple manner and helps students to read and understand well-known sections of the Bible in the original Hebrew much earlier than is usually attempted. After some shorter extracts earlier on, the final four lessons guide the student through a reading of the whole biblical story of Jonah, an inspired choice! Several other features make this a most enjoyable and effective textbook, such as some Hebrew songs (with music!). The approach and its outworking have been tested and refined in over thirty years of Dr. Baker's own teaching, which began in Indonesia, where the original edition was published in 1988. Literally tens of thousands of students have benefited from this valuable guide and the launch of an English edition will give thousands more across the world access to it.

Graham I. Davies, DD
Emeritus Professor of Old Testament Studies,
University of Cambridge, UK

This book is a winner! A clearly written, affordable Hebrew grammar with straightforward grammatical explanations, exercises, readings of Biblical texts, songs, conversations, and dramatic readings all in one volume. Road-tested in a global context over many years, David Baker's textbook will be invaluable for students and teachers of introductory Hebrew.

Rev. Jill Firth, PhD
Lecturer in Hebrew and Old Testament,
Ridley College Melbourne, Australia

Success in teaching biblical Hebrew is not only a matter of teacher qualification, but it also requires an appropriate textbook. During my teaching Hebrew at seminary level, the seminal edition of Dr. David Baker's book on Hebrew in Indonesian has been my faithful companion since 2008. My Hebrew students enthusiastically sing Jewish songs from the textbook. As the fruit of his many dedicated years of teaching in Indonesia and the UK, I believe that the present textbook, which has been refined from its original version, is surely user-friendly for classroom setting, both for lecturers and students. Welcome to this Hebrew for beginners to be used worldwide!

Yonky Karman, PhD
Lecturer in Old Testament,
Jakarta Theological Seminary, Indonesia

The strength of this introductory grammar lies in its concision, readability, accessibility and teachability. Baker's years of teaching experience come through in his helpful hints, examples, layout, summaries, and teaching strategies. He touches on a wide range of topics (grammatical, historical, exegetical, theological, discourse analysis), yet navigates through the potential convolution, bringing awareness and reassuring his learners with the essentials. His simple, straightforward approach echoes throughout the book as constant reassurance. All this creates confidence and encourages the learner to enjoy the process, making successful language learning and biblical interpretation attainable.

Crystal L. Melara
Hebrew Instructor,
University of California, Los Angeles, USA

David's book combines three great strengths. First, the grammar of Hebrew is presented with the utmost simplicity and clarity, stripping away extraneous detail. Second, the focus from the very beginning is on reading, translating, and interpreting the biblical text itself, and David does not shy away from drawing out some of the historical and theological implications of the passages studied. This focus culminates in a series of guided readings from the book of Jonah, which skillfully support the student as they begin to immerse themselves in the biblical text. Finally, the inclusion of Hebrew songs throughout the book enlivens the learning experience while simultaneously reinforcing much of the grammar and vocabulary. The result is a rich and rewarding course, by the end of which the student will be able to begin to engage with much of the Hebrew prose of the Old Testament. May this book deepen the church's worship as it enables pastors to go deeper into the riches of his word!

Kim Phillips, PhD
Affiliated Lecturer of Hebrew,
Faculty of Divinity, University of Cambridge, UK

I remember vividly my impression of learning biblical Hebrew using the Indonesian version of this book years ago in North Sumatra. Though quite intimidating initially, it turned out to be an enjoyable experience due to the book's carefully graded lessons. As it is now available in English, students from diverse backgrounds and interests worldwide will surely benefit from its gradual approach to learning the ancient language. The basic grammar and vocabulary studied are immediately applied to reading and understanding simple sentences in biblical Hebrew. It doesn't take very long before one can read the actual texts of the Hebrew Bible. No doubt, the book will provide a solid foundation for doing exegetical work as well as for more advanced study of the language. Highly recommended for theological students and Bible translators alike.

Anwar Tjen, PhD
Head of Translation Department,
Indonesian Bible Society

Getting to Grips with Biblical Hebrew

Revised Edition

Langham
GLOBAL LIBRARY

Getting to Grips with Biblical Hebrew

An Introductory Textbook

Revised Edition

David L. Baker

© 2022 David L. Baker

Published 2020 by Langham Global Library; revised edition 2022
An imprint of Langham Publishing
www.langhampublishing.org

Langham Publishing and its imprints are a ministry of Langham Partnership

Langham Partnership
PO Box 296, Carlisle, Cumbria, CA3 9WZ, UK
www.langham.org

ISBNs:
978-1-83973-673-5 Print
978-1-83973-712-1 PDF

British Library Cataloguing-in-Publication Data
A catalogue record for this book is available from the British Library.

ISBN: 978-1-83973-673-5

Cover & Book Design: projectluz.com

Contents

Preface xiii

Note for Teachers xv

Abbreviations xvii

Lesson 1: Introduction 1
  1.1 Hebrew in Context 1
  1.2 The Invention of Writing 2
  1.3 Historical Development 3
  1.4 Comparison of Hebrew and English 4
  1.5 Hebrew Song 1 (*Shalom Kh^averim*) 5

Lesson 2: Alphabet 6
  2.1 Writing 6
  2.2 Pronunciation 8
  2.3 Final Letters 10
  2.4 Gutturals 10

Lesson 3: Vowels 13
  3.1 Vowel Letters 13
  3.2 Vowel Signs 13
  3.3 Shewa 16
  3.4 Syllables and Stress 16

Lesson 4: Signs 19
  4.1 Silent Shewa 19
  4.2 Weak Dagesh 20
  4.3 Strong Dagesh 21
  4.4 Mappiq 22
  4.5 Hyphen 22
  4.6 Punctuation 23

Lesson 5: Words 26
  5.1 Nouns and Adjectives 26
  5.2 Verbs 28
  5.3 Particles 28
  5.4 The Name of God 29
  5.5 Hebrew Song 2 (*Lo V^ekhayil*) 30

Lesson 6: Sentences 1 32
  6.1 Nominal Sentences 32

6.2 Adjectives 33
6.3 Gender 34
6.4 Personal Pronouns 34
6.5 Waw Conjunction 35

Lesson 7: Sentences 2 39
7.1 Verbal Sentences 39
7.2 Definite Article 39
7.3 Object Marker 41
7.4 Questions 41
7.5 Demonstratives 42

Lesson 8: Prepositions 46
8.1 Prefix Prepositions 46
8.2 Prefix Prepositions with Definite Article 47
8.3 The Preposition מִן 47
8.4 Hebrew Song 3 (*Hinne Mattov*) 48

Lesson 9: Verbs 1 51
9.1 Perfect – Forms 51
9.2 Perfect – Meaning 52
9.3 Subjects 53
9.4 Strong and Weak Verbs 54

Lesson 10: Reading 1 *Genesis 1:1–2* 57
10.1 The Beginning (Gen 1:1a) 57
10.2 The Universe (Gen 1:1b) 58
10.3 Darkness (Gen 1:2a) 59
10.4 The Spirit (Gen 1:2b) 60

Lesson 11: Nouns 63
11.1 The Suffix הָ 63
11.2 The Prefix מ 64
11.3 The Construct (Genitive) 65

Lesson 12: Plurals and Numbers 69
12.1 Masculine Plurals 69
12.2 Feminine Plurals 70
12.3 Irregular Plurals 70
12.4 Duals 71
12.5 Plurals of Adjectives 72
12.6 Numbers 73

Lesson 13: Verbs 2 76
13.1 Imperfect – Forms 76
13.2 Imperfect – Meaning 77

13.3 Weak Verbs 78
13.4 Analysis 79

Lesson 14: Reading 2 *Genesis 1:3–5* 82
14.1 Light (Gen 1:3) 82
14.2 Goodness (Gen 1:4) 83
14.3 Day and Night (Gen 1:5) 84

Lesson 15: Roots 87
15.1 Weak Initial Letters 87
15.2 Hollow Verbs 88
15.3 Key Characteristics 89
15.4 Hebrew Song 4 (*Barukh Habba*) 90

Lesson 16: Suffix Pronouns 93
16.1 Forms 93
16.2 Possessive Suffixes 94
16.3 Objective Suffixes 95
16.4 Suffix Pronouns with אֶל and אֵת 96

Lesson 17: Reading 3 *Exodus 20:1–3* 100
17.1 Accents 100
17.2 Introduction (Exod 20:1) 101
17.3 Theology and History (Exod 20:2) 102
17.4 First Commandment (Exod 20:3) 103

Lesson 18: Verbs 3 106
18.1 Imperative 106
18.2 Active Participle 108
18.3 Passive Participle 109

Lesson 19: Verbs 4 113
19.1 Infinitive Absolute 114
19.2 Infinitive Construct – Forms 115
19.3 Infinitive Construct – Meaning 117

Lesson 20: Conversation 121
20.1 Jacob and the Angel (Gen 32:28, 30) 121
20.2 Jonah and the Sailors (Jonah 1:8–9) 122
20.3 Hebrew Song 5 (*Adonay Yishmorkha*) 125

Lesson 21: Complex Stems 1 128
21.1 Niphal 128
21.2 Hiphil 129
21.3 Hophal 130
21.4 Perfect 131

Lesson 22: Complex Stems 2 135
   22.1 Imperfect 135
   22.2 Imperative 136
   22.3 Participle 137
   22.4 Infinitives 139

Lesson 23: Complex Stems 3 142
   23.1 Piel 142
   23.2 Pual 143
   23.3 Hithpael 143
   23.4 Conjugations 144
   23.5 Summary of Stems 145

Lesson 24: Reading 4 *Jeremiah 31:31–34* 149
   24.1 A New Covenant (Jer 31:31) 149
   24.2 Old Covenant Broken (Jer 31:32) 150
   24.3 Relationship with God (Jer 31:33) 150
   24.4 Knowing God (Jer 31:34) 151

Lesson 25: Summary of Word Forms 155
   25.1 Verbs 155
   25.2 Nouns and Adjectives 156
   25.3 Numbers 157
   25.4 Hebrew Song 6 (*Hevenu Shalom*) 159

Lesson 26: Dictionaries. 162
   26.1 Using a Hebrew Dictionary 162
   26.2 Summary of Prefixes 163
   26.3 Summary of Suffixes 165
   26.4 Homonyms 167

Lesson 27: Reading 5 *Jonah 1:1–7* 171
   27.1 Jonah's Call (Jonah 1:1–3) 171
   27.2 The Great Storm (Jonah 1:4–5) 173
   27.3 Jonah Found Guilty (Jonah 1:6–7) 174

Lesson 28: Reading 6 *Jonah 1:8–2:2* 178
   28.1 Confession of Faith (Jonah 1:8–9) 178
   28.2 Confession of Sin (Jonah 1:10–12) 178
   28.3 Salvation for the Sailors (Jonah 1:13–15) 179
   28.4 Repentance of the Sailors (Jonah 1:16) 180
   28.5 Lesson from the Fish (Jonah 2:1–2) 180

Lesson 29: Reading 7 *Jonah 2:11–3:10* 183
   29.1 Salvation for Jonah (Jonah 2:11) 183
   29.2 Jonah's Second Call (Jonah 3:1–3) 183
   29.3 Repentance of Nineveh (Jonah 3:4–5) 184

29.4 The King's Command (Jonah 3:6–9) 184

29.5 Salvation for Nineveh (Jonah 3:10) 185

Lesson 30: Reading 8 *Jonah 4:1–11* 188

30.1 Jonah's Anger (Jonah 4:1–3) 188

30.2 Jonah Leaves the City (Jonah 4:4–5) 189

30.3 Lesson from the Plant (Jonah 4:6–8) 190

30.4 God's Love (Jonah 4:9–11) 191

30.5 Hebrew Song 7 (*Hava Nagila*) 192

Appendix 194

Dramatic Reading 197

Mini Dictionary 201

Mini Songbook 211

Bibliography 219

List of Figures

Figure 1. Semitic Language Family.. 1

Figure 2. Cuneiform Tablet 5

Figure 3. Gezer Calendar 12

Figure 4. The Great Isaiah Scroll... 25

Figure 5. Printed Hebrew Bible (BHS)... 45

Figure 6. Road Signs in Hebrew, Arabic, and English 50

Figure 7. Ketef Hinnom Amulet (KH2).. 56

Figure 8. The Ancient of Days... 62

Figure 9. Tel Dan Inscription... 68

Figure 10. Traditional Jew Reading Hebrew Book in Jerusalem 75

Figure 11. Seal of Jaazaniah 99

Figure 12. Manhole Cover in English, Hebrew, Arabic, and Russian 127

Figure 13. Seal of Shema (replica)... 134

Figure 14. Jewish Prayer Shawl (*Tallit*).................................... 148

Figure 15. The Story of Jonah 177

Figure 16. Jonah in the Belly of the Fish 182

Figure 17. Jonah Preaches in Nineveh 187

Preface

Hebrew? Oh no! I came to theological college to learn about God and the relevance of the Christian message in the twenty-first century. Do I really have to learn an ancient language to understand the Bible?

A simple answer to this student's question is of course 'No.' There are many excellent translations into modern English, and most other major languages, so it is perfectly possible to understand the Bible today without learning Hebrew or Greek. For most people, including students who only have a year or two for theological study, learning the original languages of the Bible is not a high priority. Nevertheless, for those who wish to dig deeper and can give the time, there are great benefits in learning the languages in which the core texts of our faith were written. To give an example, it is possible to read and enjoy Shakespeare's plays in French, Spanish, Arabic, or Chinese; but a student of literature is more likely to read them in the original English, in order to understand the finer points and appreciate them fully. So, my answer to the question above is, 'No, it is not essential to learn Hebrew, but it is definitely worthwhile.'

This introduction to biblical Hebrew will not make you fluent in the language within days or weeks. My aim is less ambitious but more realistic. After completing this course, you will know the Hebrew alphabet, many of the most common words, and the essential points of grammar. You will be able to read selected passages from the Bible in Hebrew. You will understand how translation works and be better equipped to interpret Old Testament texts in the twenty-first century. Along the way, you will have learnt some Hebrew songs and experimented with simple conversation in Hebrew.

The thirty lessons are designed to be spread over one academic year, though they can be completed in a few weeks of intensive study if preferred. Either way, each lesson should be studied with a teacher for an hour, then students need to spend three or four hours reviewing the lesson, learning twelve new words, and doing the exercise. The teacher should mark the exercise and go through it in class before progressing to the next lesson. That adds up to about six hours of study per lesson, or 180 hours for the whole course.

I wrote the first draft of this book in 1981, when teaching at the HKBP Theological Seminary in North Sumatra, Indonesia. This material was revised and expanded each year, with input from students and colleagues, then published in Jakarta by BPK Gunung Mulia in 1988. It is now in its twenty-ninth printing, having sold about 37,000 copies, and will shortly be republished in a completely new edition. Meanwhile, I have translated the material into English and am using it to teach Hebrew at All Nations Christian College, England. The enthusiastic response of students has been very encouraging, and I am delighted that Langham Publishing is making the book available to a much wider group of students throughout the world.

Many students, colleagues, and friends have contributed to this work in various ways, and it is impossible to acknowledge them all. I wish to record my gratitude to each and every one, because without them the book would never have been published.

David L. Baker
All Nations Christian College
Pentecost 2020

The revised edition is substantially the same as the first, but there are small corrections and improvements throughout:

- Misprints have been corrected;
- Some points have been rephrased to make them clearer or more precise, and others have been reshaped into tables;
- Several footnotes have been added to exercises to explain difficult points;
- Four sentences in the exercises have been modified or replaced: Exercise 9 sentence o, Exercise 12 sentence g, and Exercise 16 sentences a and n.

David L. Baker
April 2022

Note for Teachers

This book provides thirty lessons for teaching and learning biblical Hebrew, starting with the history and nature of the language, then gradually introducing letters and sounds, words, and sentences. The Hebrew verbal system is taught systematically, beginning with the perfect (because it is easier), and later introducing the imperfect, imperative, participles, and infinitives. I focus on regular forms first, so students understand the way the language works, before explaining irregular forms. Complex stems are introduced later in the book. A whole lesson is spent on learning to use a Hebrew dictionary effectively, including tables of Hebrew prefixes and suffixes to help students identify the dictionary form of a word. I assume only a minimal knowledge of English grammar and explain key concepts as the course progresses, so it can be used by students whose knowledge of English is limited and those who have never learnt a foreign language before.

There are eight lessons that focus on reading biblical texts, to reinforce the grammar learnt in other lessons and give insights into interpreting Old Testament texts in their original language. There is one lesson on Hebrew conversation, to help students appreciate that this was the everyday language of Israel in biblical times. It is not expected that students will be able to hold conversations in Hebrew, but they learn enough to experiment. Hebrew songs are taught throughout the course and have proved popular.

After each lesson, students are expected to memorize twelve Hebrew words and complete an exercise. These words are mostly chosen on the basis of their frequency in the Hebrew Bible, though some are included because they occur in the readings or songs. Sentences in the exercises are almost all taken from the Old Testament, so students are reading and understanding authentic biblical Hebrew as they practise the grammatical points studied and words that are memorized. A distinctive feature of this course is the analysis of verb forms that is introduced in Lesson 13 and used in most of the following exercises. It is very helpful if teachers mark each exercise and go through it in class before progressing to the next lesson. Regular vocabulary tests are also important.

There are many other textbooks for learning biblical Hebrew, and you may wonder what this book offers that is new or different. I have used twelve of these books and have learnt something from all of them. However, some are unnecessarily complicated, in my view, and others are very expensive or hard to obtain. Three have innovative approaches, but they are inadequate for a basic introduction to the language. This book provides a simple introduction to Hebrew for beginners, focusing on basic grammar and vocabulary, while introducing students to reading and understanding biblical texts as soon as possible. None of the others do this, so I believe my book makes a unique contribution.

There are four larger Hebrew introductions that can be recommended for teachers and students who wish to go into more detail. They are listed in the bibliography at the end of this book, together with Hebrew Bibles, dictionaries, and resources for advanced study.

Abbreviations

General

abs.	absolute
adj.	adjective
c.	common
cf.	compare
cstr.	construct
e.g.	for example
f.	feminine
i.e.	that is
impf.	imperfect
impv.	imperative
inf.	infinitive
lit.	literally
m.	masculine
mod.	Modern Hebrew
pf.	perfect
pl.	plural
pt.	participle
sg.	singular
v.	verse
vv.	verses

Bible Texts and Translations

BFBS	Hebrew Old Testament (British & Foreign Bible Society, 1958)
BHS	Biblia Hebraica Stuttgartensia (1997)
CEB	Common English Bible (2011)
CEV	Contemporary English Version (1995)
ESV	English Standard Version (2001; updated 2016)
GNT	Good News Translation (2nd ed, 1992)
KJV	King James Version ('Authorised Version,' 1611)

MHT   Modern Hebrew New Testament (translated from Greek, rev. ed, 2010)
NET   New English Translation (2006)
NIV   New International Version (updated Anglicised ed, 2011)
NJB   New Jerusalem Bible (1985)
NJPS   New Jewish Publication Society translation (2nd ed, 1999)
NLT   New Living Translation (2nd edn, 2004)
NRSV   New Revised Standard Version (1989; Anglicised ed, 1995)

For more abbreviations of Hebrew Bibles and dictionaries, see the bibliography at the end of this book.

Introduction

1.1 Hebrew in Context

World languages may be divided into several groups, for example *Indo-European* (languages in Europe, Iran, and India), *Austronesian* (languages in Indonesia, Philippines, and Oceania), and *Afroasiatic* (languages in Africa and western Asia). The Afroasiatic group is further divided into several families, one of which is the Semitic language family.

The Semitic family gets its name from Shem, son of Noah, traditionally considered the ancestor of Middle Eastern nations (Gen 10). It has several branches:

- Akkadian (including Babylonian and Assyrian)
- Northwest Semitic (including Hebrew and Aramaic)
- Arabian (primarily Arabic)
- Ethiopian (including Amharic and Tigrinya).

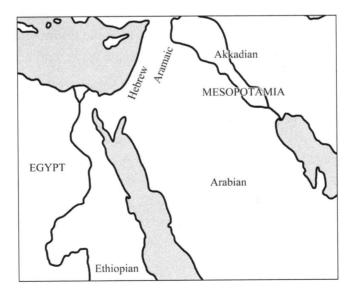

Figure 1. Semitic Language Family

Two of these languages are used in the Old Testament. Most is written in Hebrew (*ivrit*), while a few later sections are in Aramaic (*ªramit*): Ezra 4:8–6:18; 7:12–26; Jeremiah 10:11; and Daniel 2:4–7:28.

Hebrew was the main language of Israel until the sixth century BC. However, since the ninth century onwards Aramaic had become the major international language in that part of the world (cf. 2 Kgs 18:26) and gradually Israelites began to speak it alongside Hebrew. Eventually Aramaic became the everyday language in Israel, and Hebrew was only used for reading the Bible and religious purposes.

1.2 The Invention of Writing

The idea of writing seems to have originated in Mesopotamia around 3200 BC. The first language to be written down was probably Sumerian, an ancient language used in southern Mesopotamia. Sumerian used pictures to represent words. For example, a picture of the sun meant 'sun,' and covered related ideas like 'day' and 'light.' A picture of a foot could mean 'foot,' 'walk,' or 'carry.' The system gradually became more complex, and signs were added to represent syllables and letters. It was called cuneiform (from Latin *cuneus* 'wedge') because each sign consisted of a distinctive set of wedges made by pressing the corner of a square-ended stylus into soft clay.

In due course, other languages made use of cuneiform, modifying the Sumerian system for their own purposes, including Akkadian, Hittite, and Ugaritic. It was not long before the idea found its way to Egypt, where another kind of picture language was developed (hieroglyphics). These writing systems enabled many documents from ancient Mesopotamia and Egypt to be preserved, so we can read and study them today. However, they were very complicated and the number of people who could read and write was inevitably limited.

This changed radically with the invention of the alphabet in the early second millennium BC. It was probably a scribe in Canaan who realized that languages could be written down much more easily by focusing on the pronunciation instead of the meaning. This is because most languages have thousands of words with different meanings, but they are pronounced with combinations of a small number of sounds. For example, there are only twenty or so consonants in Canaanite languages plus an even smaller number of vowels. A selection of signs was chosen from the older picture language to represent consonants, according to the first letter of key words (see table for examples).

Picture	Meaning	Pronunciation	Latin	Hebrew
	'house'	*bet*	*b*	בּ
	'fish'	*dag*	*d*	ד
	'water'	*ma̲yim*	*m*	מ
	'head'	*rosh*	*r*	ר

The idea developed over the following centuries and was used for writing Hebrew, Aramaic, Moabite, and Edomite. The Phoenicians learnt from the Canaanites and passed it on to the Greeks. They called it the 'alphabet' after the first two letters (*alpha = a; bet = b*). Though the name of its inventor is unknown, the alphabet is one of the most important inventions of all time and is used for most modern languages, except those that use Chinese characters and their derivatives.

1.3 Historical Development

There seem to have been four main stages in the development of the Hebrew language, though the dates are very approximate:

- Before 1200 BC: There are insufficient examples to determine the exact nature of the language in this period.
- 1200–400 BC: The language of this period is called 'Classical Hebrew' or 'Biblical Hebrew'. It is known primarily from the Old Testament (Hebrew Bible), plus a few inscriptions. During the exile and Persian period, the language changed significantly and is often called 'Late Biblical Hebrew.'
- 400 BC–AD 1900: Hebrew declined as an everyday language but was still used by Jews as the language of religion for over two thousand years. During this period, Jewish scholars ('Masoretes') improved the Hebrew writing system, carefully copied manuscripts of the Hebrew Bible, and established the standard text that is still used today.
- Modern Hebrew: Hebrew was revived as a spoken language in some parts of the Holy Land in 1881 and became the official language of the state of Israel in 1948. Modern Hebrew is essentially the same as biblical Hebrew, but its grammar and pronunciation have been simplified, and many new words formed or borrowed

from other languages.[1] This book follows the modern simplified pronounciation.

1.4 Comparison of Hebrew and English

Hebrew is different in many ways from English and other European languages, not least in the way it is written, so it may seem quite difficult to begin with. After some initial hurdles, however, it is no more difficult than most other languages and easier than many.

The most obvious difference between Hebrew and English is the alphabet. There are twenty-two letters to learn, most of which are consonants, and they are written from right to left instead of left to right. There are also distinctive ways of marking vowels and punctuation.

The basic structure of the language is not very different. There are nouns, verbs, adjectives, prepositions, and other kinds of word that function in a similar way to those in English, though the word order is sometimes different. For example, Hebrew verbs generally come before their subjects, so the English phrase 'God created' is the equivalent of 'created God' in Hebrew.

The most difficult thing to learn is the verbal system, where one verb takes different forms depending on person, gender, number, tense, mood, and whether it is active or passive. However, most other words are relatively straightforward. Some Hebrew words and names will be familiar because they are also used in English. For example:

shal*o*m	'peace'
shal*e*m	'Salem'
y*e*rushal*ai*m	'Jerusalem'
sh*e*lom*o*	'Solomon'
bet-*e*l	'Bethel' (= house of God)
imm*a*nu *e*l	'Immanuel' (= God with us)
el*i* el*i*	'my God, my God'
hal*e*lu-y*a*h	'praise the LORD'
am*e*n	'amen'
ben-kh*u*r	'Ben-Hur' (= son of Hur)
bat-sh*e*va	'Bathsheba' (= daughter of Sheba)
sar*a*f	'seraph'
s*e*raf*i*m	'seraphs'
mash*i*akh	'messiah'
shabb*a*t	'sabbath'

The correct stress is marked by the underlined vowels above.

---

1. For example, there is no tea or coffee in the Bible, so Modern Hebrew has borrowed the French words *thé* and *café*. The latter is linked with the biblical word *bet* ('house') to make *bet qafe* 'coffee house.'

1.5 Hebrew Song 1 (*Shalom Kh^averim*)

Shal<u>o</u>m kh^aver<u>i</u>m, shal<u>o</u>m kh^aver<u>o</u>t, shal<u>o</u>m, shal<u>o</u>m;
l^ehitra'<u>o</u>t, l^ehitra'<u>o</u>t, shal<u>o</u>m, shal<u>o</u>m.
Peace brothers, peace sisters, peace, peace;
till we meet again, till we meet again, peace, peace.

See mini
songbook at
end of book
for music

Exercise (1)

1. Memorize the pronunciation and meaning of the fifteen Hebrew words in the table above.

2. Study the above words carefully, noting similarities between the first four words and between the next three words. Work out the Hebrew for 'son' and 'daughter,' and how the plural is formed in Hebrew.

3. Read the Prologue to Sirach and an extract from one of Luther's writings about the biblical languages (see appendix). Reflect on what we can learn from them today.

4. Practise the Hebrew song *Shalom Kh^averim*.

Figure 2. Cuneiform Tablet. First-millennium BC example of cuneiform writing from Mesopotamia, containing the 'Hymn of Marduk' (chief god of Babylon).[2]

---

2. Photo 'Cuneiform tablet: hymn to Marduk' by the Metropolitan Museum of Art. Public Domain.

Alphabet

2.1 Writing

a. Here are the twenty-two letters of the Hebrew alphabet:

Printed	Handwriting	Pronunciation	Name	Number
א		’	_a_lef	1
ב		b, v	bet	2
ג		g	g_i_mel	3
ד		d	d_a_let	4
ה		h	he	5
ו		w	waw	6
ז		z	z_a_yin	7
ח		kh	khet	8

ט			t	tet	9
י			y	yod	10
כ			k, kh	kaf	20
ל			l	lamed	30
מ			m	mem	40
נ			n	nun	50
ס			s	samekh	60
ע			'	ayin	70
פ			p, f	pe	80
צ			ts	tsade	90
ק			q	qof	100
ר			r	resh	200
ש			s, sh	shin	300
ת			t	taw	400

The letters are mostly square-shaped, and it is important to remember this when writing Hebrew. In terms of height, there are three exceptions: one letter has a head (ל), one has a tail (ק), and one is shorter ('). There are also four narrow letters (ג ו ג ז). Every letter should be written beginning from the top left, as shown above by the number ¹, except for the letter ט. Then the remaining lines are drawn following the numbers ² and ³. To practise Hebrew writing, it will be helpful to use lined paper and to leave alternate lines blank to allow space for the heads and tails.

b. Several letters should be written carefully to avoid confusion with similar letters:

- ד (d*a*let)   and   ר (resh)

- ב (bet)   and   כ (kaf)

- ה (he)   and   ח (khet)   and   ת (taw)

- ע (*a*yin)   and   צ (ts*a*de)

c. Roman letters are sometimes used to write numbers in English (I, II, III, IV, …) and there is a similar system in Hebrew (… 'ד 'ג 'ב 'א). The numerical equivalents are listed in the right-hand column of the table above, and the heading of each lesson in this book has the appropriate number in both Hebrew and Arabic numerals. However, numbers in the Hebrew Bible are written with words rather than letters, so it is not necessary to memorize the number-letter equivalents.

2.2 Pronunciation

a. While Hebrew writing is relatively difficult to learn, the pronunciation is quite straightforward. Ten of the letters are pronounced in a similar way to their English equivalents:

- ר ק נ מ ל י ז ה ד ג (= g d h z y l m n q r)

b. Ten more letters need clarification:

Letter	Pronunciation	Notes	Name
ח	kh	Like 'ch' in Scottish 'loch'	*khet*
ו	w	Sometimes pronounced 'v'	*waw*
ב	b, v	בּ = *b* ; ב = *v*	*bet*
כ	k, kh	כּ = *k* ; כ = *kh*	*kaf*
פ	p, f	פּ = *p* ; פ = *f* (or *ph*)	*pe*
ס	s	Ordinary 's'	*samekh*
צ	ts	Strong 's' like 'ts' in 'bits'	*tsade*
שׁ	s, sh	שׂ = Ordinary 's' שׁ = Like 'sh' in 'sheep'	*shin*
ט	t	Ordinary 't'	*tet*
ת	t	Ordinary 't'	*taw*

The remaining two letters (א and ע) will be explained below (2.4).

c. There were probably more pronunciation distinctions in classical Hebrew, so that ח was pronounced differently from כ, ט differently from ת, and so on. Some scholars continue to make these distinctions, but most Hebrew speakers today use the simplified pronunciation given above. Now ח and כ are pronounced the same (= *kh*), likewise ס and שׂ (= *s*), and ט and ת (= *t*). The letter ו is often pronounced 'v' in Modern Hebrew, but the traditional pronunciation 'w' is kept here, as in many books, because it is then easier to distinguish ו and ב.

d. The system of transliteration in this book is only intended to help with pronunciation and does not provide an exact equivalent for each Hebrew letter in Roman script. Some scholars use a more precise system with exact equivalents, but we do not study that here.

2.3 Final Letters

Hebrew does not have capital letters at the beginning of names and sentences as in English, but five letters have a different form at the end of a word:

Final letter	Handwriting	Pronunciation	Name	Regular letter
ך		kh	kaf	כ
ם		m	mem	מ
ן		n	nun	נ
ף		f	pe	פ
ץ		ts	tsade	צ

For example, the word *mym* is written מים in Hebrew letters. These final letters are also written from the top left, moving to the right, then downwards, and so on. All the final letters, except ם, have tails. Other Hebrew letters have only one form. At the end of words, *kaf* is pronounced *kh* and *pe* is *f*. Final *mem* looks similar to *samekh* but is more square.

Tip: *When writing Hebrew, it is important to ensure that all the letters are the same height, except one short letter (י) and six long letters (ל ק ך ן ף ץ).*

2.4 Gutturals

a. There are four letters called 'gutturals' (from Latin *guttur* 'throat') because they are pronounced in the throat:

- א (*alef* = ')
- ה (*he* = h)
- ח (*khet* = kh)
- ע (*ayin* = ').

The letter ר (*resh*) often behaves like a guttural too. Later we will learn some of the characteristics of these letters.

b. Two of the gutturals (א and ע) need explanation because there is no exact equivalent in English, either in writing or pronunciation. Formerly they each had a distinct pronunciation, but now they both represent a glottal stop (stoppage of sound before or after a vowel):

- At the *beginning and end of a word*, they may be treated as silent letters, like the silent 'h' at the beginning of 'honest' and end of 'hurrah' that is seen when written but not heard when spoken. There is no need to mark them when Hebrew is transliterated into Roman script.
- In the *middle of a word*, however, א and ע indicate a stoppage of sound between two vowels, as in some English dialects where 'butter' is pronounced 'bu'er' (i.e. 'butter'). It is important to mark them in the middle of words because they distinguish between two separate vowels (as in 'bu'er') and a diphthong (as in 'fuel'). To give a Hebrew example, the word *ba'al* has two syllables whereas *ruakh* has only one (diphthong).

c. There is one exception to the preceding rule. Sometimes א is silent in the middle of a word if it has no vowel of its own. In this case, it is not marked in transliteration. This will become clearer after studying vowels in the following lessons.

Exercise (2)

1. Memorize the Hebrew alphabet, so that you can give the name of each letter when seeing it written down.

2. Copy each Hebrew letter at least twenty-five times, until you can write it fluently. Use lined paper and leave one line blank between each row of letters to allow space for the heads and tails.

3. Copy each of the five final letters at least twenty-five times.

4. What are the four gutturals in Hebrew, and which letter is often like a guttural?

5. Which four Hebrew letters have two different pronunciations? Explain how readers can recognize which of the two is intended.

6. See next page.

6. Transliterate the following words into Roman script. The Hebrew is written from right to left, but the Roman equivalent should be written from left to right. Transliteration should be <u>underlined</u> (if handwritten) or in *italics* (if typed).

a מים	b בית	c בן	d יבל
e קדש	f הר	g הלך	h יד
i נאם	j כל	k חיל	l ישראל
m בעל	n צדק	o מלך	p ושם
q קטן	r סלח	s שמר	t נתן

Figure 3. Gezer Calendar. The oldest inscription found to date, on a tenth century BC limestone tablet, containing an agricultural calendar in early Hebrew script.[1]

1. Photo 'The Gezer Calendar tablet' by Dr Shukir Muhammed Amin / CC BY-SA 4.0.

Vowels

3.1 Vowel Letters

All the letters studied so far are consonants. Vowels were not written in early Hebrew, but later it became clear that writing consisting only of consonants can be confusing. For example, the word **יָם** (*ym*) could be pronounced *yam* (= 'sea') or *yom* (= 'day'). The problem was overcome in Aramaic by using a few letters with weaker pronunciation to represent vowels, and this system began to be used in Hebrew as well. To distinguish the two words just mentioned, the letter **ו** was added to represent the vowel *o* in the word *yom* (**יום**), while the word *yam* continued to be written with just consonants (**ים**). Three Hebrew consonants are used as vowel letters:

Letter	As a consonant		As a vowel	
	Sound	Example		Sound	Example
ה	*h*	הר *hr*	*a*	מה *ma*
ו	*w*	ו *w*	*o, u*	טוב *tov*
י	*y*	יד *yd*	*e, i*	מי *mi*

The letter **ה** only represents a vowel at the end of a word. It is usually *a*, but occasionally *e* or *o*.

3.2 Vowel Signs

a. When Hebrew was no longer spoken as an everyday language, people began to find it difficult to read because of its incomplete writing system. Some vowels were represented by consonants and others not written at all. As a result, Jewish scholars in the eighth century AD supplemented Hebrew writing with signs to indicate the vowels, often called 'pointing.' Each vowel letter already in place was given a sign to indicate which of the possible vowels it represented, and other vowels were indicated by adding a sign to the preceding consonant. The most important vowel signs are:

Sign	Sound	Pronunciation	Example with consonant		Example with vowel letter	
ַ	a	As in 'pat'	har	הַר	—	
ָ	a	As in 'part'	yad	יָד	ma	מָה
ֶ	e	As in 'pet'	ben	בֶּן	—	
ֵ	e	As in 'café'	ben	בֵּן	me	מֵי
ִ	i	As in 'pit'	min	מִן	—	
ִ	i	As in 'peat'	–		mi	מִי
ָ	o	As in 'pot'	kol	כָּל	—	
ֹ	o	As in 'pole'	kol	כֹּל	mo	מוֹ
ֻ	u	As in 'put'	mut	מֻת	—	
וּ	u	As in 'pool'	–		mu	מוּ

b. There are ten vowels, in pairs, roughly equivalent to the five English vowels *a, e, i, o,* and *u*. In each pair, the first is a short vowel and the second a long vowel. Sometimes these are distinguished in transliteration by marking the long vowel with a line (e.g. *ā*). Vowel signs with vowel letters may be marked with a circumflex (e.g. *â*) and these are mostly long vowels. For now, it is enough to recognize which of the five vowels *a, e, i, o,* and *u* is represented by each vowel sign.

c. Vowels are almost always pronounced after the consonant to which they are attached. For example, הַ is pronounced *ha* not *ah*. Most words end with a consonant or vowel letter, so there is no vowel sign on that final letter. However, the short *a* vowel sign (ַ) is sometimes attached to a final guttural and pronounced *before* the letter. For example, רוּחַ is pronounced *ruakh*, not *rukha*. The vowel sign is positioned to the right of the normal position to make this clear. The original pronunciation was probably without an *a* (רוּחַ = *rukh*), but later speakers found it difficult to pronounce a guttural after a vowel other than *a*, so this vowel was added to aid pronunciation. It makes a diphthong, not a separate syllable, with the first vowel prominent: *ua* (not *u'a*).

d. All vowel signs are written below the consonant they follow, except for the dot. The dot represents three different vowels that are distinguished depending on their position:

- above a consonant (ׂ = *o*) or vowel letter waw (וֹ = *o*)
- below a consonant (ִ = *i*)
- in vowel letter waw (וּ = *u*).

Note that vowel signs with the letter י are placed below the line, not immediately below the letter. For example: דְי (not דְי). The dot above a consonant is positioned at the left side (e.g. כֹ and לֹ), except for narrow letters when it is central (e.g. נֹ).

e. The cross (ָ) can represent long *a* or short *o*, but long *a* is most common. Each new Hebrew word in this book is transliterated to show the correct pronunciation.

f. Letters that represent both consonants and vowels can be confusing. The following rules will help to work out whether a letter ו or י is a consonant or vowel:

- If the letter is a vowel, the linked vowel sign is present and there is no other vowel:
  - For ו, the sign is placed over or in the letter, for example מוֹ (*mo*) and מוּ (*mu*).
  - For י, the sign is placed under the previous letter, for example מִי (*mi*) and מֵי (*me*).

- If the letter is a consonant, there is no linked vowel sign and it usually has a vowel of its own:
  - At the beginning and in the middle of a word, the vowel is marked with a sign on ו or י, for example וָרַע (*wara*), יָד (*yad*), and חַיִל (*khayil*).
  - At the end of a word there is no vowel on ו or י, for example עֵשָׂו (*esaw*) and חַי (*khay*).

The way to work out whether ה is a consonant or vowel will be explained below (4.4).

Tip: *When writing words in Hebrew, it is best to write all the consonants first, then to add the vowel signs.*

3.3 Shewa

a. Some Hebrew vowels are pronounced very quickly so they are hardly distinguishable from each other. The most common is a very short *e*, marked with two dots below the consonant, called shewa (שְׁוָא). The word שְׁוָא itself has this very short *e* in the first syllable and the stress is on the second syllable, so it is pronounced *sh^ewa̱*.

b. Shewa can also be combined with three other vowels to make a compound shewa, in each case making a shorter version of the standard vowel. Generally compound shewas are used with gutturals and a simple shewa with other letters. The four kinds of shewa are:

Sign	Sound	Pronunciation	Example	
ְ	*e*	short *e* as in 'token'	*w^e*	וְ
ֲ	*a*	short *a* as in 'alone'	*^adona̱y*	אֲדֹנָי
ֱ	*e*	short *e* as in 'token'	*^eloh̲im*	אֱלֹהִים
ֳ	*o*	short *o* as in 'obey'	*kh^ol̲i*	חֳלִי

c. The shewas are transliterated as superscript letters (*^e*, *^a*, *^e*, *^o*) in this book to indicate that they are very short vowels. Some books mark them with a breve above the letter (ĕ, ă, ĕ, ŏ) for the same purpose. In the International Phonetic Alphabet, shewa is indicated with the sign ə. Another use of the shewa will be explained below (4.1).

3.4 Syllables and Stress

a. Consonants and vowels do not exist on their own but are combined to form syllables and words. Syllables are the building blocks with which words are constructed, as in 'croc-o-dile,' 'el-eph-ant,' and 'hip-po-pot-a-mus.' In Hebrew, there are two kinds of syllable:

- Open syllables consist of a consonant followed by a vowel, for example מִי (*mi*).
- Closed syllables consist of a consonant followed by a vowel and another consonant, for example מִן (*min*).

It follows that Hebrew syllables never begin with a vowel.[1] However, they may begin with the letters א or ע, which represent a glottal stop (see 2.4.b), for example אִם (im) and עַל (al). In English transliteration, it appears that these syllables begin with a vowel, because the letters א and ע are silent; but in Hebrew understanding, they are consonants.

b. Most words have one or two syllables that are stressed more than the others, and in English it is often the first syllable. Generally, the stress in Hebrew is on the last syllable, for example *elohim*, *ne'um*, and *shalom*. Some words have the stress on the penultimate syllable, for example *erets* and *khayil*. The shewas are never stressed. In this book, it may be assumed that the last syllable is stressed unless otherwise marked (with an underline in the transliteration).

c. The use of short and long vowels is related to syllables and stress. It is not normally necessary to think about this, but sometimes the distinction is helpful, especially for the cross sign (ָ):

- In a closed unstressed syllable, it is short *o* (e.g. כָּל = *kol*).
- In other syllables, it is long *a* (e.g. שָׁלוֹם = *sha-lom*).

Vocabulary (3)

Memorize the writing, pronunciation, and meaning of these words:

'Lord'	*ªdonay*	אֲדֹנָי	1
'land, earth'	*erets*	אֶרֶץ	2
'son, child, person'	*ben*	בֵּן/בֶּן־	3
'covenant'	*berit*	בְּרִית	4
'this'	*ze*	זֶה	5
'hand'	*yad*	יָד	6
'no, not'	*lo*	לֹא	7
'what? how?'	*ma*	מָה	8
'who?'	*mi*	מִי	9

---

1. There is one exception to this rule. The waw conjunction (to be explained in lesson 6) is sometimes pronounced וּ (*u*).

'declaration'	n^{e}um	נְאֻם	10
'spirit, wind, breath'	r$\underline{u}$akh	רוּחַ	11
'peace, prosperity, wholeness'	shalom	שָׁלוֹם	12

Exercise (3)

1. For each letter וֹ and יֹ in the following words, state whether they are functioning as consonants or vowels:

יָם d	מָוֶת c	בֵּית b	בַּיִת a
וְרוּחַ h	רָאוּ g	הָאִישׁ f	הָיָה e

2. Copy these sentences three times in Hebrew script. Remember to write all the consonants for each word first, then add the vowel signs.

וַיֵּדְעוּ כִּי נָבִיא הָיָה בָּעִיר a

וְהָאָרֶץ הָיְתָה תֹהוּ וָבֹהוּ b

לֹא בְחַיִל וְלֹא בְכֹחַ אָמַר אֲדֹנָי צְבָאוֹת c

לָקְחוּ אֶת הָאִישׁ וְהָיָה לְכֹהֵן d

בָּרָא אֱלֹהִים אֶת הָאָרֶץ e

לֹא יִירְאוּ עוֹד נְאֻם אֲדֹנָי f

3. Transliterate the sentences above into Roman script to show their pronunciation. In this exercise, the sign ָ always represents an *a* and a final ה is always a vowel letter. Use only lower-case letters (no capitals) because there is no difference between capitals and lower-case letters in Hebrew. <u>Underline</u> if writing by hand or use *italics* if typing.

4. Practise reading the sentences above *without* looking at your transliteration.

Signs

As well as the vowels, several other signs are added to Hebrew letters to help in reading, especially silent shewa, weak dagesh, strong dagesh, mappiq, hyphen, and punctuation marks.

4.1 Silent Shewa

a. In contrast to the old system with no vowel signs at all, the Jewish scholars who perfected the Hebrew writing system insisted that *every* consonant must have a vowel sign, even those where no vowel was pronounced, except at the end of a word. Consonants without a vowel were given a simple shewa (̣). This is called 'silent shewa' to distinguish it from the shewa used to indicate very short vowels (see 3.3), which is therefore called 'vocal shewa.' There is no need to transliterate silent shewa when writing Hebrew in Roman script, because it is not pronounced. For example:

yisra'el (not *yis^era'el*)	יִשְׂרָאֵל
malka (not *mal^eka*)	מַלְכָּה

b. There are two main exceptions to the rule that every consonant must have a vowel sign except at the end of a word:

- כ usually has silent shewa at the end of a word, e.g. מֶלֶךְ (*mₑlekh*).
- א is silent in the middle of a word if it has no vowel of its own, e.g. רֹאשׁ (*rosh*). It has no vowel sign (the dot at the top right of א is the vowel belonging to ר) and it is not marked in transliteration (*rosh*, not *ro'sh*).

c. Sometimes it can be difficult to distinguish the two kinds of shewa. The basic principle is that shewa is *vocal in an open syllable* and *silent at the end of a closed syllable*. If you are not sure whether the syllable is open or closed, these rules should help:

- At the beginning of a word, shewa is vocal, e.g. בְּרִית (*b^e-rit*).
- At the end of a word, shewa is silent, e.g. מֶלֶךְ (*me-lekh*).
- In the middle of a word, when two shewas occur next to each other, the first is silent and the second vocal, e.g. יִמְלְכוּ (*yim-l^e-khu*).
- Between two identical consonants, shewa is vocal, e.g. הִנְנִי (*hi-n^e-ni*).
- On a double letter, shewa is vocal (see 4.3.d).
- In other circumstances, shewa is usually vocal after a long vowel (e.g. שִׂימְךָ= *si-m^e-kha*) and silent after a short vowel (e.g. שִׂמְךָ = *shim-kha*).

d. The last rule can be unclear when shewa follows the cross sign (ָ), which may represent long *a* or short *o*. In this case, a short vertical line with the vowel sign indicates long *a*. It is called מֶתֶג (*meteg*). For example, compare חָכְמָה (*kha-kh^e-ma*) and חָכְמָה (*khokh-ma*).

4.2 Weak Dagesh

a. We have already learnt that the letters בּ, כּ, and פּ have two pronunciations (see 2.2.b). The hard pronunciation of these three letters (*b, k, p*) is indicated with a dot in the middle of the letter, whereas a letter without the dot has a soft pronunciation (*v, kh, f*). The Hebrew word for this dot is דָּגֵשׁ (*dagesh*) and it is called a 'weak dagesh' to distinguish it from another kind of dagesh to be explained later ('strong dagesh'). Originally, six Hebrew letters had a hard and soft pronunciation, depending on their position in a word:

ת	פ	כ	ד	ג	ב

As time passed, the soft pronunciation of three letters (ג ד ת) was lost and only three letters maintain the distinction in Modern Hebrew (ב כ פ). The other three letters are still written with or without the dagesh, according to the former custom, but the pronunciation is not differentiated.

b. The hard pronunciation of these letters was probably original, and later the pronunciation was softened after vowels. It follows that the pronunciation is usually hard at the beginning of a word, indicated by a weak dagesh. For example:

bara	בָּרָא
tora	תּוֹרָה

The same applies in the middle of a word if the letter follows a consonant without a vowel (with a silent shewa). For example:

mizbeakh	מִזְבֵּחַ
mishpat	מִשְׁפָּט

c. If one of these letters follows a vowel or vocal shewa, however, the pronunciation is soft and there is no dagesh. For example:

av	אָב
bᵉvayit	בְּבַיִת

Occasionally, this happens after a silent shewa too. For example:

malkhe	מַלְכֵי

d. If a word ends with a vowel, that vowel sometimes affects the first letter of the next word so that the dagesh is omitted. For example:

bᵉkhayil	בְּחַיִל
lo vᵉkhayil	לֹא בְחַיִל

Tip: *The six letters that are written with or without a weak dagesh can be memorized with the formula 'beged kefet.'*

4.3 Strong Dagesh

a. Double letters are not written twice in Hebrew, as in Roman script, but are marked with a dot in the letter. It is called 'strong dagesh.' For example:

limmad	לִמַּד	*lamad*	לָמַד

All Hebrew letters can be doubled, except for gutturals and ר.

b. It is rare for ו to be doubled, so a dot in this letter usually indicates a long *u* vowel (וּ). There is no other vowel sign above or below the letter. But if it is a strong dagesh, indicating a double consonant, there will also be a vowel sign, for example חַוָּה (*khawwa* – see 3.2.f).

c. The six *beged kefet* letters may have either a weak or strong dagesh. The two kinds of dagesh look the same but can be distinguished as follows. A weak dagesh (= hard pronunciation) *never* follows a vowel whereas a strong dagesh (= double letter) *always* follows a vowel. For example:

- בְּרָא has no vowel before בְּ, so the dot is a weak dagesh, and the word is pronounced *bara* (not *bbara*).
- אַתָּה has a vowel before תָּ, so the dot is a strong dagesh, and the word is pronounced *atta* (not *ata*).

When any of these six letters is doubled, it always has the hard pronunciation. For example, בּ may represent *b* or *bb*, but never *vv*.

d. If a double letter has a shewa, it is always vocal, for example יְדַבְּרוּ (*yᵉdabbᵉru*).

e. In traditional grammars, the two kinds of dagesh are called dagesh *lene* (Latin for 'weak') and dagesh *forte* ('strong').

Tip: *To work out whether a dagesh is strong or weak, check whether the letter follows a vowel.*

4.4 Mappiq

As we have seen (3.1), the letter ה can be either a consonant or vowel:

- At the beginning and in the middle of a word, ה is always a consonant.
- A final ה is usually a vowel.

Occasionally, however, a final ה is a consonant. This is marked by a dot in the letter, called מַפִּיק (*mappiq*). For example:

| *malka* | vowel | מַלְכָּה |
| *malkah* | consonant | מַלְכָּהּ |

4.5 Hyphen

As in English, two Hebrew words can be linked with a hyphen and are then treated almost as one word. The hyphen in biblical Hebrew is written level with the top of the line of letters, not in the middle as in Roman script. The Hebrew name is מַקֵּף (*maqqef*). For example:

| *ruakh-ᵉlohim* | רוּחַ־אֱלֹהִים |

Modern Hebrew has been influenced by European languages, and the hyphen is often printed in the middle (e.g. רוּחַ-אֱלֹהִים). Unlike Roman script, the Hebrew hyphen is not used to divide long words between two lines, so each whole word should be written on one line.

4.6 Punctuation

a. Early Hebrew had no punctuation, so the Jewish scholars who invented the vowel signs added accents to mark stress and punctuation. About fifty different accents were used. Three are particularly important for punctuation:

׀ with ׃	end-of-sentence pause	*silluq + sof pasuq*
֑	mid-sentence pause	*atnakh*
֔	short pause	*zaqef qaton*

The *silluq* looks the same as *meteg* (4.1.d) but is only found on the stressed syllable at the end of a sentence.

b. The function of these three accents is similar to the full stop (.), semicolon (;), and comma (,) in English. Unlike English, however, they are placed on the stressed syllable rather than after the word (except for ׃). All three can be seen in Genesis 1:1–2:

בְּרֵאשִׁית בָּרָא אֱלֹהִים אֵת הַשָּׁמַיִם וְאֵת הָאָרֶץ׃

וְהָאָרֶץ הָיְתָה תֹהוּ וָבֹהוּ וְחֹשֶׁךְ עַל־פְּנֵי תְהוֹם

וְרוּחַ אֱלֹהִים מְרַחֶפֶת עַל־פְּנֵי הַמָּיִם׃

The pronunciation is given below for reference. The stress is always on the last syllable unless otherwise marked.

bᵉreshit bara ᵉlohim; et hashshamayim wᵉᵉt haarets.
wᵉhaarets hayᵉta tohu wavohu, wᵉkhoshekh al-pᵉne tᵉhom;
wᵉruakh ᵉlohim, mᵉrakhefet al-pᵉne hammayim.

c. Sometimes there is a change in the vowel or stress of a word with an end-of-sentence or mid-sentence pause. For example, אֶרֶץ (*erets*) becomes אָרֶץ (*arets*). This is called a 'pausal form.'

d. In Modern Hebrew, these ancient punctuation marks have been replaced with modern ones (comma, full stop, etc.).

Vocabulary (4)

'father, ancestor'	*av/ᵃvi*	אָב/אָבִי	13
'God, gods'	*ᵉlohim*	אֱלֹהִים	14
'you'	*atta*	אַתָּה	15
'create'	*bara*	בָּרָא	16
'mountain'	*har*	הַר	17
'power, wealth, army'	*khayil*	חַיִל	18
'good'	*tov*	טוֹב	19
'Israel'	*yisraʾel*	יִשְׂרָאֵל	20
'all, every, the whole'	*kol*	כֹּל/כָּל-	21
'water'	*mayim*	מַיִם	22
'prophet'	*navi*	נָבִיא	23
'head'	*rosh*	רֹאשׁ	24

Exercise (4)

1. Explain the use of shewa ( ) – simple and compound, vocal and silent. What is the function of the other double dots (and :)?

2. Explain the various uses of the single dot in Hebrew writing.

3. What are the three important accents that serve as punctuation marks in Hebrew? Give an example of each as used with a Hebrew word.

4. Copy Genesis 1:1–2 in Hebrew script three times.

5. Practise reading Genesis 1:1–2 until you can read it fluently, without looking at the transliteration.

6. Transliterate these words into Roman script. Be careful to distinguish between weak and strong dagesh, and between vocal and silent shewa.

a כִּי	b הַמֶּלֶךְ	c הַבְּרִית	d הִנֵּה
e תּוֹרָה	f בְּרִית	g הַמַּלְכָּה	h גְּדוֹלָה
i הַגָּדוֹל	j וַיַּעַל	k שִׁטִּים	l וַיִּבְדֵּל
m רֹאשָׁה	n פְּנֵי	o כֻּפַּר	p אֱלוֹהַּ
q יִשְׂרָאֵל	r בֵּרַכְנוּ	s חַסְדּוֹ	t הִנְנִי
u תִּשְׁמְרוּ	v שִׁימְךָ	w שְׁמֶךָ	x חָכְמָה

Figure 4. The Great Isaiah Scroll (showing Isa 5–6). Oldest complete manuscript of an Old Testament book, written about 100 BC, one of the Dead Sea Scrolls (1QIsaᵃ).[1]

1. Photo 'The Great Isaiah Scrolls MS A (1QIsa)' by Ardon Bar-Hama. Public Domain. https://commons.wikimedia.org/wiki/File:Great_Isaiah_Scroll.jpg.

Words

There are three main classes of words in Hebrew:

- nouns and adjectives (including nouns, proper nouns, pronouns, adjectives, and numbers)
- verbs
- particles (including adverbs, prepositions, conjunctions, and interjections).

5.1 Nouns and Adjectives

The most basic kind of word in Hebrew is the noun (*shem* שֵׁם), that provides a way of referring to a person, place, thing, or idea. Proper nouns are used to give a name to a specific person or place (e.g. 'girl' is a noun; 'Esther' is a proper noun). Pronouns replace a noun or proper noun when desired to avoid repetition (e.g. 'Esther' may be replaced by 'I', 'you', 'she', or 'her', depending on who is speaking and whether Esther is the subject or object of the sentence). The subject and object of a sentence is normally expressed with a noun, proper noun, or pronoun.

Adjectives qualify nouns to describe their characteristics (e.g. 'pretty girl'), and numbers indicate how many there are (e.g. 'seven girls'). Adjectives and numbers in Hebrew have similar forms to nouns, so they may be considered part of the same class of words. Hebrew examples of each kind of word are given in the tables.

a. Nouns

'God'	*ᵉlohim*	אֱלֹהִים
'hand'	*yad*	יָד
'day'	*yom*	יוֹם

'night'	layla	לַיְלָה
'king'	melekh	מֶלֶךְ

b. Proper Nouns

'Israel'	yisra'el	יִשְׂרָאֵל
'Moses'	moshe	מֹשֶׁה
'Ruth'	rut	רוּת

c. Pronouns

'you'	atta	אַתָּה
'who?'	mi	מִי
'this'	ze	זֶה

d. Adjectives

'good'	tov	טוֹב
'wise'	khakham	חָכָם
'holy'	qadosh	קָדוֹשׁ

Adjectives sometimes function as nouns in Hebrew. For example, the word טוֹב means 'good,' and can also denote 'goodness' or 'good things'; חָכָם means both 'wise' and 'wise person.'

e. Numbers

'one'	ekhad	אֶחָד
'two'	sheₙayim	שְׁנַיִם
'hundred'	me'a	מֵאָה

5.2 Verbs

a. The key characteristic of a Hebrew verb (*po'al* פֹּעַל) is that it has a root with three letters. For example:

'create'	b-r-'	ברא
'be'	h-y-h	היה
'say'	'-m-r	אמר
'keep'	sh-m-r	שמר

In its simplest form, a verb has these three letters with vowels to make it pronounceable. For example:

'create'	bara	בָּרָא
'be'	haya	הָיָה
'say'	amar	אָמַר
'keep'	shamar	שָׁמַר

Verbs are best learnt with these vowels because it is easier to memorize than without the vowels. The examples above have *a* vowels, which are very common, but we will learn others later.

b. Active verbs generally express an action by the subject of the sentence, whereas passive verbs express something that is done to or experienced by the subject. The examples above are all active verbs. Hebrew also has stative verbs that describe a state, functioning rather like an adjective in English, for example the verb קָדֵשׁ ('be holy').

5.3 Particles

The third word class is the particle (*milla* מִלָּה). There are various kinds of particles, each functioning to explain or connect nouns and verbs within a sentence. For example:

adverb	'no, not'	lo	לֹא
preposition	'on, over, against, about'	al	עַל
conjunction	'because, that, when'	ki	כִּי
interjection	'behold! look!'	hinne	הִנֵּה

Most Hebrew particles are short, and some are so short that they do not stand alone but are combined with the following word as a prefix, as explained below (6.5; 7.2; 8.1).

5.4 The Name of God

The most important proper noun in Hebrew is יהוה (*yhwh*), the name of the God of Israel, that is found 6,800 times in the Old Testament. It may once have been pronounced *yahwe* but – according to Jewish tradition – this holy name is no longer pronounced. This may be to avoid the risk of breaking the third commandment: 'You shall not misuse the name of יהוה your God' (Exod 20:7). So, when Jews read the Bible in Hebrew, they replace the name יהוה with the word אֲדֹנָי (*ᵃdonay*) 'Lord.' As a result, when Jewish scholars added vowels to the consonants of the Hebrew Bible, יהוה was given the vowels of אֲדֹנָי because that was its conventional pronunciation and it was written יֲהֹוָה. Compound shewas are never used with the letter י, so (ֲ) is replaced with a simple shewa (ְ). The *o* vowel is usually not written, so יְהֹוָה becomes יְהוָה.

If יְהוָה is transliterated into Roman script, the result is *yᵉhowa*, which is the origin of the English name *Jehovah*. This was a mistake made by Christian students of Hebrew in the Middle Ages who did not realize that the correct pronunciation was *ᵃdonay*, so it should not be perpetuated today. Some academic books today use the name Yahweh, following what is supposed to have been its original pronunciation. But almost all modern Bible translations follow the Jewish convention, also followed by Christians since New Testament times, in translating the name יהוה as 'Lord' (= Hebrew *ᵃdonay* and Greek *kurios*). Small capitals are commonly used to distinguish the translation of יהוה (= 'Lᴏʀᴅ') from the word אֲדֹנָי itself (= 'Lord').

So, יהוה should be pronounced *ᵃdonay*. If transliterated into Roman script, it is better to do so without vowels: *yhwh* (or *YHWH*). If translated into English, it should be written 'Lᴏʀᴅ' or 'the Lᴏʀᴅ,' depending on the sentence.

The name יהוה is sometimes linked with other words, especially in the expression יְהוָה צְבָאוֹת (*ᵃdonay tsᵉvaʾot*). This expression means literally 'Lᴏʀᴅ of armies,' perhaps alluding to the armies of heaven (angels) or the armies of Israel (whose leader is God). It is traditionally translated 'Lᴏʀᴅ of hosts' (NRSV; ESV; NJPS), while modern translations include 'Lᴏʀᴅ Almighty' (NIV; GNT), 'Lᴏʀᴅ of Heaven's Armies' (NLT), and 'Lᴏʀᴅ who rules over all' (NET).

There are also two short forms of the name: יָהּ (*yah*) and יָהוּ (*yahu*). The former is common in the Psalms, notably in the phrase הַלְלוּ־יָהּ (*halᵉlu-yah* = 'Praise the Lᴏʀᴅ!'). The latter is found as part of many personal names, such as יְשַׁעְיָהוּ (*yᵉshaʾyahu* = 'Isaiah').

To sum up, we may distinguish three important ways of referring to God in the Old Testament:

- יהוה is the name of the God of Israel, translated 'Lord' or 'the Lord' in English.
- אֲדֹנָי is a title appropriate for addressing God, translated 'Lord' in English.
- אֱלֹהִים is a noun referring to a divine being, making clear that he is a god rather than a human being, angel, or anything else. It is translated 'God' in English.

5.5 Hebrew Song 2 (Lo Vᵉkhayil)

(x2) לֹא בְחַיִל וְלֹא בְכֹחַ כִּי אִם־בְּרוּחִי

(x2) :אָמַר יְהוָה צְבָאוֹת אָמַר יְהוָה צְבָאוֹת

See mini songbook for music

'Not by power and not by strength, but by my Spirit;'
says the Lord Almighty, says the Lord Almighty. (Zech 4:6)

Vocabulary (5)

'one'	ekhad	אֶחָד	25
'say'	amar	אָמַר¹	26
'be, become, happen'	haya	הָיָה	27
'Lord, the Lord	ᵃdonay	יְהוָה	28
'strength, power'	koakh	כֹּחַ	29
'because, that, when, truly'	ki	כִּי	30
'but, unless, nevertheless'	ki im	כִּי אִם	31
'Moses'	moshe	מֹשֶׁה	32
'on, over, against, about'	al	עַל	33
'Almighty' (lit. 'armies')	tsᵉva'ot	צְבָאוֹת	34
'heaven, heavens, sky'	shamayim	שָׁמַיִם	35
'keep, guard, watch'	shamar	שָׁמַר	36

---

1. The root verb that means 'say' is really the three letters אמר, but it is easier to memorize the form with vowels because it is pronounceable, so verbs in the vocabularies are printed with vowels.

Exercise (5)

1. Practise writing and saying the Hebrew alphabet from memory in the correct order. Repeat the exercise until you can do it without error.

2. Name the three main classes of word in Hebrew. Arrange the thirty-six Hebrew words in vocabularies (3), (4), and (5) into these three classes, writing them with Hebrew letters.

3. Explain the difference in meaning between the words 'LORD,' 'Lord,' and 'God' in English Bibles.

4. Copy these Hebrew sentences three times:

קָרָא זֶה אֶל־זֶה וְאָמַר

קָדוֹשׁ קָדוֹשׁ קָדוֹשׁ יְהוָה צְבָאוֹת:

זֶה דְּבַר־יְהוָה אֶל־זְרֻבָּבֶל לֹא בְחַיִל וְלֹא בְכֹחַ

כִּי אִם־בְּרוּחִי אָמַר יְהוָה צְבָאוֹת:

5. Transliterate them into Roman script to show the pronunciation.

6. Practise reading them until you can do so fluently, without looking at your transliteration.

7. Can you guess where these sentences are found in the Bible?

8. Practise the Hebrew song *Lo V^{e}khayil*.

Sentences 1

In this lesson, we move from words to sentences. The basic structure of a Hebrew sentence will be explained, plus four aspects of the grammar that help to understand simple sentences: adjectives, gender, personal pronouns, and the waw conjunction.

6.1 Nominal Sentences

a. As in English, two or more Hebrew words can be arranged in sequence to form a sentence, usually expressing a statement, question, or command. Each word has a role to play in the sentence, for example as subject, predicate, or object. Simple sentences consist of a subject and predicate. The subject is a noun, proper noun, or pronoun, while the predicate may belong to any of the three classes of word. If the predicate is a verb, it is called a *verbal* sentence; if the predicate is from one of the other classes, it is a *nominal* sentence.

b. This lesson focuses on nominal sentences, beginning with those that consist of two words from the noun and adjective class, one functioning as subject and the other as predicate. The word 'is' or another form of the verb 'to be' may be added to make the sense clear when translating into English. An indefinite article ('a') may be needed too. For example:

Subject	Predicate	Nominal sentence	
proper noun	noun	'Moses is a prophet'	מֹשֶׁה נָבִיא
pronoun	noun	'Who is a prophet?'	מִי נָבִיא
proper noun	number	'The LORD is one'	יְהוָה אֶחָד

c. Nominal sentences may also be formed with particles as predicate or part of the predicate. For example:

Subject	Predicate	Nominal sentence	
proper noun	adverb	'Moses is there'	מֹשֶׁה שָׁם
noun	preposition + proper noun	'Peace on Israel'	שָׁלוֹם עַל־יִשְׂרָאֵל

6.2 Adjectives

Adjectives are used in two main ways: as the predicate in a nominal sentence and as part of an adjective-noun phrase.

a. First, when an adjective is a predicate, it usually comes before the subject, the opposite order from English. A form of the verb 'to be' is usually added in translation. For example:

Subject	Predicate	Nominal sentence	
proper noun	adjective	'Moses is good'	טוֹב מֹשֶׁה
pronoun	adverb + adjective	'You are not good'	לֹא־טוֹב אַתָּה

b. Second, when an adjective is linked with a noun to form a phrase, it follows the noun, again the opposite order from English. For example:

'holy prophet'	נָבִיא קָדוֹשׁ
'good father'	אָב טוֹב

c. This phrase can then function as the subject or predicate in a nominal sentence. For example:

Subject	Predicate	Nominal sentence	
noun + adjective	adverb	'A holy prophet is there'	נָבִיא קָדוֹשׁ שָׁם
pronoun	noun + adjective	'You are a good father'	אַתָּה אָב טוֹב

6.3 Gender

As in many languages, nouns and adjectives in Hebrew have gender (*min* מִין). In English, it is mostly people and animals that are regarded as having gender, but all Hebrew nouns can be classified as either masculine or feminine. For example:

Masculine		Feminine	
'father, ancestor'	אָב	'land, earth'	אֶרֶץ
'day'	יוֹם	'year'	שָׁנָה
'house, household'	בַּיִת	'city, town'	עִיר
'people'	עַם	'teaching, law'	תּוֹרָה

6.4 Personal Pronouns

a. Pronouns may replace nouns and proper nouns in sentences. In the following example, the pronoun הוּא ('he') in the second sentence replaces the proper noun מֹשֶׁה in the first sentence:

'Moses is good'	טוֹב מֹשֶׁה
'He is good'	טוֹב הוּא

b. The most common kind of pronoun is the personal pronoun, used to replace nouns and proper nouns that refer to people (and sometimes things). It has various forms, distinguished by three aspects:

- person – first (1), second (2), or third (3)
- gender – masculine (m.) or feminine (f.)
- number – singular (sg.) or plural (pl.)

First-person pronouns have the same form for both masculine and feminine, so their gender is regarded as 'common' (c.). The main forms are set out in the following table:

Singular				
1	c.	'I'	*ªni/anokhi*	אֲנִי/אָנֹכִי
2	m.	'you'	*atta*	אַתָּה
	f.	'you'	*att*	אַתְּ[1]
3	m.	'he, it'	*hu*	הוּא
	f.	'she, it'	*hi*	הִיא
Plural				
1	c.	'we'	*ªnakhnu*	אֲנַחְנוּ
2	m.	'you'	*attem*	אַתֶּם
	f.	'you'	*atten*	אַתֶּן
3	m.	'they'	*hem/hemma*	הֵם/הֵמָּה
	f.	'they'	*henna*	הֵנָּה

c. The subject of a sentence is often a personal pronoun. For example:

'I am the LORD'	אֲנִי יְהוָה
'You are a prophet'	אַתָּה נָבִיא
'He is there'	הוּא שָׁם

d. Pronouns agree with the noun or proper noun that they replace in gender and number. With mixed gender, as in a law applying to everyone or in speaking to a group of men and women, masculine forms are used.

6.5 Waw Conjunction

Some Hebrew conjunctions are independent words, as already mentioned (5.3), but the waw conjunction is so short that it is combined with the following word as a prefix: וְ (*wᵉ*). The usual English translation is 'and,' though alternatives such as 'but,' 'also,' 'or,' and 'then'

---

1. The form אַתְּ (*att*) is strange. It was originally written אַתִּי (*atti*), then in the course of time the *i* vowel dropped out but the strong dagesh (doubling dot) remained. The shewa is silent because it occurs at the end of the word.

are sometimes better. At the beginning of a sentence, it may be preferable not to translate it at all. The waw conjunction can have various vowels. There are five main possibilities.

a. The waw conjunction often has a simple shewa. For example:

'and Israel'	wᵉyisra'el	וְיִשְׂרָאֵל	←	וְ + יִשְׂרָאֵל
'and a man'	wᵉ'ish	וְאִישׁ	←	וְ + אִישׁ

b. It has a long *a* vowel before words with the stress on the first syllable, including words with only one syllable. For example:

'and day'	wayom	וְיוֹם	←	וְ + יוֹם
'and night'	walayla	וָלַיְלָה	←	וְ + לַיְלָה

Occasionally, the first vowel of the word changes. For example:

'and earth'	wa'arets	וָאָרֶץ	←	וְ + אֶרֶץ

c. The waw conjunction usually has a short *a*, *e*, or *o* vowel before words that begin with a compound shewa, matching the very short vowel represented by the shewa. For example:

'and I'	waᵃni	וַאֲנִי	←	וְ + אֲנִי
'and truth'	weᵉmet	וֶאֱמֶת	←	וְ + אֱמֶת

An exception to this rule is the word אֱלֹהִים, where the waw conjunction has a long *e* vowel and the א is silent: וֵאלֹהִים (welohim).

d. It becomes a vowel letter (long *u*) before words that begin with a 'bump' letter (במפ) and most letters with a simple shewa. For example:

'and a house'	uvayit	וּבַיִת	←	וְ + בַּיִת
'and Moses'	umoshe	וּמֹשֶׁה	←	וְ + מֹשֶׁה
'and Pharaoh'	ufar'o	וּפַרְעֹה	←	וְ + פַּרְעֹה
'and Samuel'	ushᵉmu'el	וּשְׁמוּאֵל	←	וְ + שְׁמוּאֵל

e. It has a long *i* vowel before words that begin with בְּ, and the consonant י becomes a vowel letter. For example:

'and Judah'	wihuda	וִיהוּדָה	←	וְ + יְהוּדָה

Tip: *It is easy to recognize the waw conjunction, because it is very rare for Hebrew words to begin with the letter ו. So, when a word begins with ו, it may be assumed that it is the waw conjunction.*

Vocabulary (6)

'man, husband, person'	ish	אִישׁ	37
'I'	ᵃni/anokhi	אֲנִי/אָנֹכִי	38
'great'	gadol	גָּדוֹל/גְּדֹל	39
'David'	dawid	דָּוִד	40
'he, it, that'	hu	הוּא	41
'and, but, or, then' (waw conjunction)	wᵉ	וְ	42
'wise, wise person'	khakham	חָכָם	43
'day'	yom	יוֹם	44
'night'	layla	לַיְלָה	45
'king'	melekh	מֶלֶךְ	46
'holy'	qadosh	קָדוֹשׁ	47
'there'	sham	שָׁם	48

Exercise (6)

1. Memorize the Hebrew personal pronouns (highlighted table above).

2. For each of the following sentences:
- Copy in Hebrew script.
- Transliterate into Roman script.
- Translate into English.
- Practise reading aloud until you can do so fluently.

a   מִי מֶלֶךְ: דָּוִד מֶלֶךְ:

b   מִי נָבִיא: מֹשֶׁה נָבִיא:

c   מִי שָׁם: מֹשֶׁה וְדָוִד שָׁם:

d   שָׁלוֹם עַל־יִשְׂרָאֵל:

e   יְהוָה מֶלֶךְ: יְהוָה אֶחָד:

f   מִי זֶה: זֶה דָּוִד:

g   טוֹב אַתָּה: לֹא־טוֹב אַתָּה:

h   לֹא־טוֹב הוּא:

i   אַתָּה אִישׁ חָכָם:

j   זֶה אִישׁ־טוֹב:

k   מִי הוּא: הוּא נָבִיא קָדוֹשׁ:

l   גָּדוֹל יְהוָה: אֲנִי יְהוָה:

m   קָדוֹשׁ קָדוֹשׁ קָדוֹשׁ יְהוָה צְבָאוֹת:

3. Copy this text in Hebrew script and practise reading it:

בָּרוּךְ הַבָּא בְּשֵׁם יְהוָה   בֵּרַכְנוּכֶם מִבֵּית יְהוָה:

הוֹדוּ לַיהוָה[2] כִּי־טוֹב   כִּי לְעוֹלָם חַסְדּוֹ:

---

2. The י is silent here and the word is pronounced *ladonay*.

Sentences 2

7.1 Verbal Sentences

Although the main components of a Hebrew sentence are similar to those in English, the word order is often different. In verbal sentences, verbs generally come before their subjects, so the order has to be reversed when translating. For example:

'God created'	bara ᵉlohim	בָּרָא אֱלֹהִים
'Moses said'	amar moshe	אָמַר מֹשֶׁה
'The LORD gave'	natan ᵃdonay	נָתַן יְהוָה

This verb form with *a* vowels usually refers to an action in the past, as in the translations above. This will be explained further in Lesson 9.

Tip: *There are two main ways that Hebrew word order differs from English order: adjectives follow the nouns they qualify, and verbs come before their subjects.*

7.2 Definite Article

a. English distinguishes nouns that are definite and indefinite, marking definite nouns with a definite article ('the') and indefinite nouns with an indefinite article ('a' or 'an'). Hebrew has a similar distinction, and there is a definite article that may be attached to the noun as a prefix: הַ (ha). The first letter of the noun is usually doubled as well, marked with a strong dagesh. For example:

'king' or 'a king'	melekh	מֶלֶךְ		
'the king'	hammelekh	הַמֶּלֶךְ	←	הַ + מֶלֶךְ

There is no indefinite article in Hebrew, so nouns are assumed to be indefinite unless marked otherwise. The word מֶלֶךְ may be translated 'king' or 'a king,' depending on the context.

b. Gutturals and ר cannot be doubled, as already explained, so when a definite article is prefixed to a word that begins with one of these letters the vowel on the prefix usually changes instead. For example:

| 'the head' | harosh | הָרֹאשׁ | ← | הַ + רֹאשׁ |
| 'the wise person' | hekhakham | הֶחָכָם | ← | הַ + חָכָם |

The first vowel of the noun sometimes changes too when a definite article is prefixed. For example:

| 'the mountain' | hahar | הָהָר | ← | הַ + הַר |
| 'the land' | ha'arets | הָאָרֶץ | ← | הַ + אֶרֶץ |

c. When a noun with a definite article is qualified by an adjective, the adjective is also prefixed with a definite article. For example:

| indefinite | 'a good king' | מֶלֶךְ טוֹב |
| definite | 'the good king' | הַמֶּלֶךְ הַטּוֹב |

The adjective follows the noun, as already learnt. It is unnecessary to translate the second definite article.

d. When an adjective is used with a definite noun to form a nominal sentence, it does *not* have a definite article. A form of the verb 'to be' may be added when translating. For example:

| definite | 'the king is good' | טוֹב הַמֶּלֶךְ |

e. The definite article may be omitted in translation if the English word is implicitly definite because it functions like a proper noun. For example:

| 'God' or 'the gods' (not 'the God') | ha'elohim | הָאֱלֹהִים |
| 'heaven' or 'the heavens' (not 'the heaven') | hashshamayim | הַשָּׁמַיִם |

7.3 Object Marker

a. The verb usually comes before both subject and object in Hebrew sentences. To prevent misunderstanding, the object is often marked by a particle that distinguishes it from the subject, especially in prose. The object marker has two spellings:

אֵת	standing alone, directly before the object
אֶת־	connected to the object with a hyphen

b. The function of this particle is simply to identify the object of the verb. There is no need to translate it because the object is normally clear from the English word order (subject, verb, object). For example:

'God created the heavens'	בָּרָא אֱלֹהִים אֵת הַשָּׁמַיִם
'God kept the covenant'	שָׁמַר אֱלֹהִים אֶת־הַבְּרִית

c. The object marker is only used with definite objects, such as a noun with a definite article or a proper noun. Indefinite objects are not marked in this way. For example:

'God gave wisdom'	נָתַן אֱלֹהִים חָכְמָה (khokhma)

7.4 Questions

a. Many questions in Hebrew are formed with interrogative pronouns like מִי ('who?') and מָה ('what?'). For example:

'Who are you?'	מִי אַתָּה
'Who is this man?'	מִי־הָאִישׁ הַזֶּה
'What did Elisha say?'	מָה אָמַר אֱלִישָׁע

These short pronouns are sometimes connected to the following word with a hyphen, as in the second example above. The pronoun מָה is also found with two other vowels (מַה, מֶה).

b. There is also an interrogative marker that changes a statement into a question: הֲ (h^a). It looks similar to the definite article (הַ), but the vowel is shorter and the first letter of the word to which it is prefixed is *not* doubled. For example:

| 'Is it peace?' | הֲשָׁלוֹם |
| 'Are you not a man?' | הֲלֹא־אִישׁ אַתָּה |

Before a guttural, or any consonant with shewa, the vowel of the interrogative marker usually changes so that it is pronounced הַ or הֶ, like the definite article. In this case, the two prefixes may usually be distinguished as follows:

- The interrogative marker is not followed by a double letter (strong dagesh).
- The definite article is only used with nouns and adjectives; the interrogative marker is used with verbs and particles too.

Tip: *The interrogative marker is quite rare, but the definite article is common, so if unsure it is safer to guess the latter.*

7.5 Demonstratives

Demonstrative pronouns and adjectives specify a noun more precisely than the definite article. The main demonstratives in English are 'this/these' and 'that/those', specifying things that are near or far away respectively.

a. The Hebrew demonstrative equivalent to English 'this' has two forms, depending on whether the noun it specifies is masculine or feminine: זֶה (*ze*, m.) and זֹאת (*zot*, f.). There is also a plural form equivalent to 'these', used with nouns of both genders: אֵלֶּה (*elle*).

b. Demonstratives may function as *adjectives*. For example:

'this day'	*hayyom hazze*	הַיּוֹם הַזֶּה
'this covenant'	*habb^erit hazzot*	הַבְּרִית הַזֹּאת
'these words'	*hadd^evarim ha'elle*	הַדְּבָרִים[1] הָאֵלֶּה

The definite article is prefixed to both the noun and its demonstrative adjective in Hebrew, whereas neither is necessary in English because the demonstrative itself shows that the noun is definite.

---

1. The word הַדְּבָרִים is plural. Plural nouns will be studied in Lesson 12.

c. Demonstratives may also function as *pronouns*, becoming the subject of a nominal sentence. For example:

'this is the day'	*ze hayyom*	זֶה הַיּוֹם
'this is the covenant'	*zot habbᵉrit*	זֹאת הַבְּרִית
'these are the words'	*elle haddᵉvarim*	אֵלֶּה הַדְּבָרִים

d. There is no Hebrew demonstrative equivalent to 'that' or 'those,' so third-person personal pronouns are used instead. The pronouns הוּא (m.) and הִיא (f.) specify 'that,' while הֵמָּה/הֵם (m.) and הֵנָּה (f.) specify 'those.' Like the demonstratives equivalent to 'this' and 'these,' they may function as adjectives or pronouns. For example:

| adjective | 'that man' | *ha'ish hahu* | הָאִישׁ הַהוּא |
| pronoun | 'that is the man' | *hu ha'ish* | הוּא הָאִישׁ |

In the first example, הוּא is a demonstrative adjective and has a definite article like the noun it qualifies. In the second, it is a demonstrative pronoun and does not need an article. When it functions as a demonstrative pronoun, the form and sentence structure is the same as for a personal pronoun, so the second sentence could alternatively be translated 'he is the man.' Hebrew does not distinguish these two meanings, so the best translation into English depends on the context.

Vocabulary (7)

'man, mankind, Adam'	*adam*	אָדָם	49
object marker	*et*	אֶת/אֶת־	50
'house, household'	*bayit/bet*	בַּיִת/בֵּית	51
'word, thing'	*davar*	דָּבָר	52
'the' (definite article)	*ha*	הַ	53
interrogative marker	*hᵃ*	הֲ	54
'behold! look!'	*hinne*	הִנֵּה	55
'give, set'	*natan*	נָתַן	56

'people'	*am*	עַם	57
'do, make'	*asa*	עָשָׂה	58
'righteous, just'	*tsaddiq*	צַדִּיק	59
'bad, evil, disaster'	*ra/ra'a*	רַע/רָעָה	60

Exercise (7)

1. Copy, transliterate, translate, and practise reading the following sentences. Verbs should be translated as simple past ('created,' etc.)

a   בָּרָא אֱלֹהִים אָדָם עַל־הָאָרֶץ:

b   צַדִּיק אַתָּה יְהוָה:

c   מִי עָשָׂה אֶת־הַדָּבָר הַזֶּה:

d   מִי־הָאִישׁ הֶחָכָם:

e   הִנֵּה נָתַן יְהוָה עַל־יִשְׂרָאֵל מֶלֶךְ:

f   אַתָּה הָאִישׁ:

g   טוֹב הַדָּבָר: לֹא־טוֹב הַדָּבָר:

h   אָמַר הַמֶּלֶךְ הֲשָׁלוֹם:

i   לֹא הָיָה דְּבַר רָע שָׁם:

j   הֲלֹא אֲנִי יְהוָה:

k   שָׁמַר יְהוָה אֶת־הַבְּרִית:

l   זֶה־הַיּוֹם עָשָׂה יְהוָה:

m   הוּא הַיּוֹם הַגָּדוֹל: גָּדוֹל הַיּוֹם הַהוּא:

n   אָמַר יְהוָה צְבָאוֹת:

o   לֹא עָשָׂה יִשְׂרָאֵל הַדָּבָר הָרָע הַזֶּה:

p   בָּרָא אֱלֹהִים אֵת הַשָּׁמַיִם וְאֵת הָאָרֶץ :

2. Read these sentences aloud:

q   דּוּ יוּ לַיְךְ תּוּ סְטֶדִי הִיבְּרוּ?

r   הִיא עִיץ רֶד מִית אַנְד שִׁיא עִיץ וַיְת פַּשׁ.

s   שֶׁל וִי הַב קְפָאִי אוֹר קוֹקָה קוֹלָה?

t   שִׁיא סֶלְס סִי שֶׁלְס אֹן אֶסִי שׁוֹר.

Figure 5. Printed Hebrew Bible (BHS).[2]

---

2. Photo by FotoRieth, pixabay. Used by Permission

Prepositions

There are four very common prepositions in Hebrew:

'in, at, with, by'	b^e	בְּ
'as, like, according to'	k^e	כְּ
'to, for'	l^e	לְ
'from'	min	מִן

8.1 Prefix Prepositions

a. The three prepositions בְּ (b^e), כְּ (k^e), and לְ (l^e) are prefixed to the following word in a similar way to the waw conjunction וְ (w^e). They are usually pronounced with a shewa. For example:

'in Israel'	b^eyisraʾel	בְּיִשְׂרָאֵל	←	בְּ + יִשְׂרָאֵל
'in peace'	b^eshalom	בְּשָׁלוֹם	←	בְּ + שָׁלוֹם

b. Sometimes, different vowels are used, depending on the opening sound of the following word. For example:

'in Jerusalem'	birushalaim	בִּירוּשָׁלַם	←	בְּ + יְרוּשָׁלַם
'like God'	kelohim	כֵּאלֹהִים	←	כְּ + אֱלֹהִים
'for what?' (= 'why?')	lamma/lama	לָמָּה/לָמָה	←	לְ + מָה

In the first two examples, the two shewas combine to become a full vowel. In the first, the initial י becomes a vowel letter; in the second, the initial א becomes silent.

c. If the first letter of a word has a weak dagesh, the dagesh is omitted when prefixed with one of these prepositions. For example:

'with strength'	b^ekhoakh	בְּכֹחַ	←	בְּ + כֹּחַ
'like David'	k^edawid	כְּדָוִד	←	כְּ + דָּוִד

8.2 Prefix Prepositions with Definite Article

a. When a prefix preposition is used before a word with a definite article, the two prefixes merge to become one. The weaker consonant (ה) and shorter vowel (shewa) are dropped, leaving a new prefix consisting of the stronger consonant (from the preposition) and longer vowel (from the definite article). For example:

'to the king'	lammelekh	לַמֶּלֶךְ	←	לְ + הַמֶּלֶךְ
'like the man'	ka'ish	כָּאִישׁ	←	כְּ + הָאִישׁ
'for the wise person'	lekhakham	לֶחָכָם	←	לְ + הֶחָכָם

b. If the first letter of the word with the definite article is doubled, as in the first example, this is not affected by the dropping of the letter ה and the strong dagesh indicates that the noun is definite. The vowel on the prefix preposition (la rather than l^e, etc.) indicates the same. Compare:

'in a house'	b^evayit	בְּבַיִת
'in the house'	babbayit	בַּבַּיִת

8.3 The Preposition מִן

a. The preposition מִן (min 'from') is also linked to the following word, but in a different way from the prefix prepositions. Sometimes, it is joined to the word with a hyphen. For example:

'from the man'	min-ha'ish	מִן־הָאִישׁ
'from the water'	min-hammayim	מִן־הַמַּיִם

b. More often, it is shortened to become מִ and prefixed to the word, in a similar way to the definite article (see 7.2.a). The final ן of מִן merges with the first letter of the following word, resulting in doubling of that first letter (marked with a strong dagesh). For example:

'from a king'	*mimmelekh*	מִמֶּלֶךְ	←	מִן + מֶלֶךְ

c. If the following word begins with a guttural or ר, that letter cannot be doubled, so מִן usually becomes מֵ. This is also similar to the way the definite article is prefixed (7.2.b). For example:

'from a man'	*me'ish*	מֵאִישׁ	←	מִן + אִישׁ
'from a mountain'	*mehar*	מֵהַר	←	מִן + הַר
'from a city'	*me'ir*	מֵעִיר	←	מִן + עִיר

8.4 Hebrew Song 3 (*Hinne Mattov*)

הִנֵּה מַה־טּוֹב[1] וּמַה־נָּעִים שֶׁבֶת אַחִים גַּם־יָחַד: (x2)
הִנֵּה מַה־טּוֹב שֶׁבֶת אַחִים גַּם־יָחַד: (x2)

See mini songbook for music

Look how good and how pleasant; [is the]
  dwelling of brothers [and sisters] in unity!
Look how good; [is the]
  dwelling of brothers [and sisters] in unity! *(Ps 133:1)*

Vocabulary (8)

'in, at, with, by'	*be*	בְּ	61
'blessed'	*barukh*	בָּרוּךְ	62
'go out'	*yatsa*	יָצָא	63
'Jerusalem'	*yerushalaim*	יְרוּשָׁלַם[2]	64

---

1. The double letter ט and shortening of vowel from long *a* (מָה) to short *a* (מַה), plus the hyphen, mark a close relationship between the two words, so they are pronounced as one: *mattov*. The same applies to the following word: *manna'im*.

2. This form is usual in the Hebrew Bible, but there is also a fuller form and it has become standard in Modern Hebrew: יְרוּשָׁלַיִם (*yerushalayim*).

'as, like, according to'	kᵉ	כְּ	65
'to, for'	lᵉ	לְ	66
'kingdom'	mamlakha	מַמְלָכָה	67
'from'	min	מִן	68
'Egypt'	mitsrₐyim	מִצְרַיִם	69
'pleasant, lovely'	na'im	נָעִים	70
'long time, eternity'[3]	olam	עוֹלָם	71
'Solomon'	shᵉlomo	שְׁלֹמֹה	72

Exercise (8)

1. Copy, transliterate, translate, and practise reading:

a הִנֵּה מַה־טּוֹב[4] וּמַה־נָּעִים:

b בְּלַיְלָה אֶחָד[5]:

c לֹא בְחַיִל וְלֹא בְכֹחַ:

d מִי גָדוֹל כֵּאלֹהִים:

e הַמֶּלֶךְ שְׁלֹמֹה בָּרוּךְ:

f יְהוָה מֶלֶךְ לְעוֹלָם:

g עַם קָדוֹשׁ אַתָּה לַיהוָה:

h בָּרוּךְ יְהוָה לְעוֹלָם:

i אֲנִי יְהוָה קָדוֹשׁ בְּיִשְׂרָאֵל:

j יָצָא[6] הָעָם מִמִּצְרָיִם:

k הִנֵּה יָצָא עַם מִמִּצְרָיִם:

---

3. The form לְעוֹלָם is very common, meaning 'forever' (lit. 'for eternity').

4. See footnote 1.

5. The number אֶחָד follows the noun it qualifies, like an adjective.

6. This verb form should be translated as simple past ('went out').

l   הָאִישׁ נָבִיא לֵאלֹהִים:

m   יָצָא הַמֶּלֶךְ מִשָּׁם בְּשָׁלוֹם:

n   יָצָא הָאִישׁ מִן־הַבַּיִת:

o   הָאֱלֹהִים בַּשָּׁמַיִם וְאַתָּה עַל־הָאָרֶץ:

p   נָתַן יְהוָה מַמְלָכָה לְדָוִד עַל־יִשְׂרָאֵל לְעוֹלָם:

q   בַּיּוֹם⁷ הַהוּא יָצָא הַמֶּלֶךְ מִירוּשָׁלַם:⁸

2. Practise the Hebrew song *Hinne Mattov*.

Figure 6. Road Signs in Hebrew, Arabic, and English.⁹

7. The preposition בְּ is best translated 'on' with the noun יוֹם.

8. When מִן is prefixed to a word that begins with יְ, it becomes מִ and the shewa drops out.

9. Photo 'Hebrew Arabic English road signs' by Justin McIntosh / CC BY 2.0.

Verbs 1

As we have seen (7.1), the subject of a Hebrew verb is often indicated by placing a noun after it. Another way of indicating the subject is by adding suffixes. The resulting forms are called 'perfect' (pf.), for reasons that will be explained below, and often refer to an action in the past. For example:

'I kept'	shamarti	שָׁמַרְתִּי	←	שָׁמַר + תִּי
'you said'	amarta	אָמַרְתָּ	←	אָמַר + תָּ

9.1 Perfect – Forms

a. The third-person masculine singular form has no suffixes and is simply the three root letters with vowels. This simple form is convenient for memorization, so it is used in vocabularies to represent the basic meaning of a verb (e.g. שָׁמַר 'keep'). In sentences, however, it may be translated with the pronoun and past tense (e.g. 'he kept').

b. There are eight more perfect forms, each with a suffix to indicate the subject. For example, these are the forms of שָׁמַר:

		Singular		
1	c.	'I kept'	shamarti	שָׁמַר תִּי
2	m.	'you kept'	shamarta	שָׁמַר תָּ
	f.	'you kept'	shamart	שָׁמַר תְּ
3	m.	'he/it kept'	shamar	שָׁמַר
	f.	'she/it kept'	shamᵉra	שָׁמְר ה

Plural					
1	c.	'we kept'	*shamarnu*	נוּ	שָׁמַר
2	m.	'you kept'	*sheᵉmartem*	תֶּם	שְׁמַר
	f.	'you kept'	*sheᵉmarten*	תֶּן	שְׁמַר
3	c.	'they kept'	*shameᵉru*	וּ	שָׁמְר

c. The second-person suffixes and first-person plural suffix are abbreviated forms of personal pronouns (cf. 6.4):

			Singular	Pronoun	Suffix
2	m.	'you'		אַתָּה	תָּ
	f.	'you'		אַתְּ	תְּ
Plural					
1	c.	'we'		אֲנַחְנוּ	נוּ
2	m.	'you'		אַתֶּם	תֶּם
	f.	'you'		אַתֵּן	תֶּן

d. Three things should be noted about pronunciation:

- Four suffixes are unstressed, so the pronunciation of the root verb is not affected: first-person (sg. and pl.) and second-person singular (m. and f.).
- Four suffixes are stressed, so one vowel in the root verb is shortened to vocal shewa: third-person singular (f.), second-person plural (m. and f.), and third-person plural.
- There is a *meteg* (short vertical line) next to the first vowel sign in two forms (3 f. sg. and 3 c. pl.) to indicate a long *a* followed by vocal shewa.

9.2 Perfect – Meaning

a. Biblical Hebrew does not have tenses that indicate past, present, and future as in English. However, verbs have 'conjugations' that distinguish between different kinds of action. The conjugation studied in this lesson is commonly called 'perfect,' because the action described is complete ('perfect'). Some scholars prefer the term 'suffix conjugation' because the subject is indicated by adding suffixes to the root.

b. The perfect conjugation often refers to something that happened in the past. For example, the form אָמַרְתִּי may be translated 'I said' or 'I have said' or 'I had said.' The context of a sentence determines which translation is best.

c. The perfect may also be used to describe a state of being (e.g. זָקַנְתִּי 'I am old,' lit. 'I have become old') and with verbs signifying perception or attitude (e.g. יָדַעְתָּ 'you know'; אָהֵב 'he loves').

d. Sometimes, the perfect is used in prophecy, to describe a future action that is considered complete because it is already part of God's plan and therefore quite certain ('prophetic perfect').

e. Finally, a distinctive feature of Hebrew grammar must be noted. When a waw conjunction is prefixed to a perfect verb, it usually changes the meaning to an action that is *not yet* complete.[1] For example:

'he kept' *or* 'he has kept'	שָׁמַר
'and he will keep' *or* 'and he may keep'	וְשָׁמַר

9.3 Subjects

a. Perfect verbs in Hebrew have implied subjects, indicated by their suffixes, so they may stand alone in a sentence without a separate subject. However, nouns and proper nouns are often used too, especially for third-person forms, in which case the implied subject in the verb does not need to be translated as well. For example:

'he gave'	נָתַן
'God gave' (not 'God he gave')	נָתַן אֱלֹהִים

---

1. The perfect with waw conjunction occasionally indicates a complete action, in a series of perfect verbs, but this is rare.

b. The gender and number of the verb match the gender and number of the subject. For example:

'David said'	אָמַר דָּוִד
'Esther said'	אָמְרָה אֶסְתֵּר
'Dan and Asher said'	אָמְרוּ דָּן וְאָשֵׁר

9.4 Strong and Weak Verbs

a. Verbs that follow the regular pattern like שָׁמַר are called 'strong' and those with variations are 'weak.'

b. One common kind of weak verb has ה as the final root letter. The ה changes or is omitted when perfect suffixes are added, and there are vowel changes too, as in the verb רָאָה ('see'):

		Singular			
1	c.	'I saw'	ra'iti	תִי	רָאִי
2	m.	'you saw'	ra'ita	תָ	רָאִי
	f.	'you saw'	ra'it	ת	רָאִי
3	m.	'he/it saw'	ra'a		רָאָה
	f.	'she/it saw'	ra'ata	ה	רָאֲתָ
		Plural			
1	c.	'we saw'	ra'inu	נוּ	רָאִי
2	m.	'you saw'	re'item	תֶם	רָאִי
	f.	'you saw'	re'iten	תֶן	רָאִי
3	c.	'they saw'	ra'u	וּ	רָא

c. The main changes from the regular verb pattern are:

- In first- and second-person forms, final ה becomes י and the vowel changes from *a* to *i*.
- In the third-person feminine singular, final ה becomes ת.
- In the third-person plural, final ה drops out.
- Where there is ת in the suffix, it loses the dagesh because of the vowel before it.

Vocabulary (9)

'brother'	akh/ᵃkhi	אָח/אֲחִי	73
'to, toward'	el-	אֶל-	74
'know'	yada	יָדַע	75
'sit, dwell, live'	yashav	יָשַׁב	76
'priest'	kohen	כֹּהֵן	77
'take'	laqakh	לָקַח	78
'serve, work, worship'	avad	עָבַד	79
'town, city'	ir	עִיר	80
'call, proclaim, read'	qara	קָרָא	81
'see'	ra'a	רָאָה	82
'beginning'	reshit²	רֵאשִׁית	83
'hear, listen to'	shama	שָׁמַע	84

Exercise (9)

1. Memorize the perfect forms of שָׁמַר and רָאָה (highlighted tables).

2. Copy, transliterate, translate, and practise reading:

a   יָדַע: יְדַעְתֶּן: יָצְאוּ:

b   יָצָאתָ³: קָרָאת: יָשַׁבְנוּ:

c   אָמַרְתָּ: אָמַרְתִּי: אֲמַרְתֶּם:

d   נָתְנָה: נָתְנוּ: נָתַנּוּ:

e   לֹא יָשַׁבְתִּי בְּבֵיִת:

f   רָאִינוּ אֶת־הָאָרֶץ:

g   לֹא יָדַעְתִּי: הֲלֹא יָדַעְתָּ:

---

2. The א is silent, as for רֹאשׁ (vocabulary item 24), so not marked in transliteration. See 4.1.b.

3. The א is silent in this and the following form, so the preceding vowel softens the ת in the suffix to ת.

h יְהוָה נָתַן וַיהוָה לָקֶח:[4]

i שָׁמַע הַנָּבִיא: שָׁמַע אֶת־הַנָּבִיא:

j רָאוּ אֶת־הַבַּיִת הַגָּדוֹל:

k וְלָקְחוּ אֶת־הָאִישׁ מִשָּׁם:

l וְיָדְעוּ כִּי הָיָה נָבִיא שָׁם:

m עֲבַדְתֶּם אֵת יְהוָה אֱלֹהִים:

n לֹא שָׁמַעְנוּ אֶל־יְהוָה אֱלֹהִים:

o יֵשְׁבוּ בְמִצְרַיִם: יְצָאתֶם מִמִּצְרַיִם:

p וְהָיָה יְהוָה לְמֶלֶךְ עַל־כָּל־הָאָרֶץ:

Figure 7. Ketef Hinnom Amulet (KH2). One of two tiny seventh-century BC silver scrolls, the oldest known texts from the Hebrew Bible, quoting Numbers 6:24-26.[5]

---

4. The unusual word order in this sentence (noun-verb instead of verb-noun), repeated twice, places extra emphasis on the noun.

5. Scan of the KH2 Ketef Hinnom Silver Scroll, the oldest artifact containing text from the Hebrew Bible. Public Domain. https://commons.wikimedia.org/wiki/File:Ketef_Hinnom_KH2_Scroll.jpg.

Reading 1
Genesis 1:1–2

It is time to begin reading the Old Testament in Hebrew, beginning at the beginning! You should be able to read this text directly from the Hebrew script by now, but there is a transliteration above if required (see 4.6.b).

10.1 The Beginning (Gen 1:1a)

בְּרֵאשִׁית בָּרָא אֱלֹהִים

The first word of the Bible is formed from the noun רֵאשִׁית and preposition בְּ, commonly translated 'In the beginning.' There is no definite article with רֵאשִׁית, but it is definite in meaning (there is only one beginning). The definite article should therefore be used in English translation. This opening may be compared with the opening of John's Gospel, which has several allusions to the Genesis passage (see John 1:1; cf. Ps 111:10; Isa 46:10).

It is followed by a distinctive Hebrew verb: בָּרָא ('create'). This verb is used forty-eight times in the Old Testament, always to describe the work of God, distinguishing his creation from human achievements. In contrast, the verb עָשָׂה ('do, make') is much broader in meaning and used for both human and divine work (over 2,600 times in the Old Testament). God can create (בָּרָא) something new, whereas human beings can only make (עָשָׂה) something from material that has already been created by God. For example:

בָּרָא אֱלֹהִים אָדָם עַל־הָאָרֶץ

'God created mankind on the earth' (Deut 4:32)

עָשָׂה בְצַלְאֵל אֶת־הָאָרוֹן עֲצֵי שִׁטִּים

'Bezalel made the ark [of] acacia wood' (Exod 37:1)

The word אֱלֹהִים ('God') appears 2,600 times in the Old Testament. Note the mid-sentence pause here: אֱלֹהִים. There are also two shorter forms of this important word:

אֱלוֹהַ	*eloah*	57 times in the Old Testament, mostly in Job
אֵל	*el*	240 times in the Old Testament

There is little difference in meaning between the three, and all are used for the God of Israel and also the gods of other nations. The word-group is related to the Arabic words for God ('ilah' and 'Allah'):

Hebrew	*e*	*l*	
	e	*l*	*oah*
	e	*l*	*ohim*
Arabic	*i*	*l*	*ah*
	Al	*l*	*ah*

The oldest form (אֵל) is found in most Semitic languages and was the name of the Canaanite high god in Ugaritic texts. It is found in many Hebrew personal names, for example Bezal*el*, Ezeki*el*, Jo*el*, *El*ijah, and *El*isha. Other words are linked with it to make divine titles, especially in Genesis, for example אֵל עֶלְיוֹן ('God Most High'), אֵל עוֹלָם ('the Eternal God'), and אֵל שַׁדַּי ('God Almighty').

It is no accident that אֱלֹהִים is the subject of the first sentence in the Bible. The word appears thirty-two times in Genesis 1 alone, and it may be said that God is the prime subject of the whole Old Testament.

10.2 The Universe (Gen 1:1b)

אֵת הַשָּׁמַיִם וְאֵת הָאָרֶץ:

The object marker is used before both nouns, and both are prefixed with the definite article. There is no need to translate the object marker, but the definite article should be translated so the phrase becomes 'the heavens and the earth.' Note the end-of-sentence pause on הָאָרֶץ: – the short *e* in the first syllable of אֶרֶץ has already been changed to a long *a* because of the presence of the definite article, so there is no further change in pronunciation or stress for the pausal form.

The phrase 'the heavens and the earth' is a Hebraic way of saying 'the universe' (so GNT). Biblical Hebrew does not have a single word that means 'universe,' so this meaning is conveyed by stating two key parts of the whole. The technical term for this is 'merism.' It may be compared with the phrase מִטּוֹב עַד־רָע (Gen 31:24; cf. 2 Sam 13:22) that means literally 'from good until bad.' In context, God's warning to Laban, 'Be careful not to say anything to Jacob, either good or bad' (NIV) means not to say anything at all (so NJB: 'On no account say anything whatever to Jacob'). Similarly, the phrase 'when I sit and when I rise' (Ps 139:2) means 'everything I do' (GNT).

Some translators take Genesis 1:1 to be a subordinate clause: 'In the beginning *when* God created the heavens and the earth, …' The main clause is then in verse 2 (NRSV) or 3 (CEB). This translation is possible grammatically; but I believe the traditional translation more likely to be correct, understanding verse 1 as an independent sentence: 'In the beginning God created the heavens and the earth.' (so NIV; ESV; NET; NLT; cf. NJB).[1]

10.3 Darkness (Gen 1:2a)

וְהָאָרֶץ הָיְתָה תֹהוּ וָבֹהוּ וְחֹשֶׁךְ עַל־פְּנֵי תְהוֹם

הָיְתָה is a perfect form of the verb הָיָה (3 f. sg.) The feminine form is used because the earth is considered feminine in Hebrew thought. Even in English, where nouns do not normally have gender, the idea of 'mother earth' is familiar. So it is not surprising that the Hebrew noun אֶרֶץ is feminine rather than masculine.

The phrase תֹהוּ וָבֹהוּ consists of two nouns, תֹהוּ (*tohu*) 'formlessness' and בֹהוּ (*bohu*) 'emptiness,' joined with the waw conjunction. The two words are used together to mean one thing, like 'nice and warm' in English. The technical term for this is 'hendiadys.' 'Formlessness' and 'emptiness' are not two separate things but different ways of describing the same thing, so the phrase may be translated 'a formless void' (NRSV). NIV translates the phrase with two adjectives, so the clause becomes 'the earth was formless and empty.' This expresses the meaning with a dynamic equivalent translation and is perhaps more easily understood than the formal equivalent of NRSV.

חֹשֶׁךְ (*khoshekh*) means 'darkness.' It is followed by two linked nouns. פְּנֵי is a short form of פָּנִים ('face'). תְהוֹם ('the deep') has no weak dagesh because the word before it ends with a vowel. These two nouns have a genitive relationship and may be translated 'the face of the deep.' This relationship is called 'construct' in Hebrew and will be explained further in the next lesson (11.3). People in the ancient Near East were afraid of the ocean, so תְהוֹם adds to the ominous feeling already implied by תֹהוּ וָבֹהוּ and חֹשֶׁךְ. Note the short pause in וָבֹהוּ and mid-sentence pause in תְהוֹם.

---

1. See the major commentaries for further discussion of this issue.

10.4 The Spirit (Gen 1:2b)

וְרוּחַ אֱלֹהִים מְרַחֶפֶת עַל־פְּנֵי הַמָּיִם:

The word רוּחַ may be translated 'Spirit' (NIV; ESV; NET) or 'wind' (NRSV; NJB; NJPS). Either is possible, and both may convey part of the meaning. These two aspects of the Hebrew word could be combined if the Spirit of God is envisaged as a great wind blowing over the primeval ocean. It is linked with the word אֱלֹהִים in a genitive relationship, so the phrase should be translated 'Spirit of God.'

מְרַחֶפֶת (m^erakhefet) is a participle of the verb רָחַף and means 'hovering' (see 23.4.d). The first part of the sentence has a perfect verb (הָיְתָה), referring to something that happened in the past, so it may be assumed that the hovering also happened in the past and the word 'was' should be supplied in English translation to make the sentence flow smoothly. The same verb is used in Deuteronomy 32:11 for an eagle hovering over its nest. Perhaps the Spirit of God is pictured as a mother bird hovering over its nest (primeval ocean), waiting for its young to hatch (creation).

The phrase עַל־פְּנֵי הַמָּיִם at the end of the sentence is parallel to the ending of the first part of the sentence (עַל־פְּנֵי תְהוֹם), also indicating a genitive relationship. Parallelism is characteristic of Hebrew thought and is frequently used in poetry. For example:

'He makes me lie down in green pastures,
    he leads me beside quiet waters' (Ps 23:2, NIV).

Genesis 1:2 is quite poetic in form, though not strictly a poem:

'The earth was a formless void,
    and darkness was over the face of the deep;
but the Spirit of God
    was hovering over the face of the water.'

Note the punctuation in אֱלֹהִים and הַמָּיִם:.

Vocabulary (10)

'light'	or	אוֹר	85
'God, god'	el	אֵל	86
'who, which, what, that'	^asher	אֲשֶׁר	87
'build'	bana	בָּנָה	88

'loyalty, steadfast love'	khesed	חֶסֶד	89
'darkness'	khoshekh	חֹשֶׁךְ	90
'very'	me'od	מְאֹד	91
'hovering'	merakhefet	מְרַחֶפֶת	92
'go up'	ala	עָלָה	93
'face'[2]	panim/pene	פָּנִים/פְּנֵי	94
'formless void'	tohu wavohu	תֹהוּ וָבֹהוּ	95
'the deep'	tehom	תְהוֹם	96

Exercise (10)

1. Memorize Genesis 1:1–2 in Hebrew so you can recite it and write it in Hebrew script from memory.

2. Copy, transliterate, translate, and practise reading:

a יָדְעָה: יָדְעוּ: בָּנִיתִי: בָּנוּ:

b בָּנִינוּ: וּבָנִיתָ: לֹא־בְּנִיתֶם:

c עָבַדְתִּי: עָבְדוּ: לֹא־עָלָה:

d וְעָלִיתָ: עָלְתָה: עָלֵינוּ:

e עָלָה מֹשֶׁה אֶל־הָאֱלֹהִים:

f מִי־אֵל בַּשָּׁמַיִם וּבָאָרֶץ:

g קָרָא יְהוָה אֶל־מֹשֶׁה מִן־הָהָר:

h רָאִיתִי אֶת־הָאָרֶץ וְהִנֵּה־תֹהוּ וָבֹהוּ:

i הוּא כֹהֵן בַּבַּיִת אֲשֶׁר־בָּנָה שְׁלֹמֹה בִּירוּשָׁלַיִם:

j הָאִישׁ מֹשֶׁה גָּדוֹל מְאֹד בְּמִצְרַיִם:

---

2. לִפְנֵי (short form with prefix לְ) = 'before.'

k עָשָׂה הַמֶּלֶךְ אֶת־הַטּוֹב לִפְנֵי יְהוָה אֱלֹהִים׃

l רָאָה אֱלֹהִים אֶת־כָּל־אֲשֶׁר עָשָׂה וְהִנֵּה־טוֹב מְאֹד׃

m הָיִיתִי מֶלֶךְ עַל־יִשְׂרָאֵל בִּירוּשָׁלָ͏ִם׃

> בְּרֵאשִׁית הָיָה הַדָּבָר
> וְהַדָּבָר הָיָה עִם הָאֱלֹהִים
> וֵאלֹהִים הָיָה הַדָּבָר

John 1:1 in Hebrew (MHT)

**Figure 8. The Ancient of Days. A famous design by William Blake
(1794), depicting God setting a compass to the earth.[3]**

Nouns

In this lesson we study two important ways in which nouns are formed, with the suffix הָ
and prefix מ, and a distinctive Hebrew way of linking two nouns to give a more complex
meaning ('construct').

11.1 The Suffix הָ

a. Feminine nouns in Hebrew often end with הָ (*a*), for example שָׁנָה ('year') and תּוֹרָה
('teaching, law'). Sometimes this ending takes other forms like ת, as in בַּת ('daughter').
Unfortunately, this usage is not consistent, and some feminine nouns have different endings
while a few masculine nouns end with הָ.

b. The suffix הָ is added to some masculine nouns to give a feminine meaning. It is
comparable to the suffix 'ess' in English, which denotes a female (actress, goddess, lioness,
etc.). For example:

| 'mare' | susa | סוּסָה | ← | 'horse' | סוּס |

Often the noun is shortened when the suffix is added. For example:

'prophetess'	n°via	נְבִיאָה	←	'prophet'	נָבִיא
'woman, wife'	ishsha	אִשָּׁה	←	'man, husband'	אִישׁ
'queen'	malka	מַלְכָּה	←	'king'	מֶלֶךְ

c. When an adjective qualifies a feminine singular noun, the suffix הָ is added so that its
gender matches that of the noun. For example:

| m. | 'great day' | yom gadol | יוֹם גָּדוֹל |
| f. | 'great city' | ir g°dola | עִיר גְּדוֹלָה |

d. The suffix הָ is always stressed, following the rule that the stress is on the final syllable in Hebrew.

11.2 The Prefix מ

a. Nouns in Hebrew are often formed by adding מ as a prefix to a root. The prefix is usually pronounced *ma* or *mi*, but occasionally becomes *me*, *mo*, or *mu*, depending on the first syllable of the following word. For example:

Noun				Root	
'custody, guard'	*mishmar*	מִשְׁמָר	←	'keep, guard'	שׁמר
'deed, product'	*ma'ªse*	מַעֲשֶׂה	←	'do, make'	עשׂה
'holy place'	*miqdash*	מִקְדָּשׁ	←	'be holy'	קדשׁ
'altar'	*mizbeakh*	מִזְבֵּחַ	←	'offer [sacrifice]'	זבח
'number'	*mispar*	מִסְפָּר	←	'count'	ספר
'judgement, justice'	*mishpat*	מִשְׁפָּט	←	'judge'	שׁפט
'psalm'	*mizmor*	מִזְמוֹר	←	'sing, praise'	זמר
'commandment'	*mitswa*	מִצְוָה	←	'command'	צוה

b. Some nouns with the prefix מ also have a feminine suffix (הָ, ‑ת, or ‑ת). For example:

Noun				Root	
'kingdom'	*mamlakha*	מַמְלָכָה	←	'reign'	מלך
'deputation, mission'	*mishlakhat*	מִשְׁלַחַת	←	'send'	שׁלח
'birthplace, relatives'	*moledet*	מוֹלֶדֶת	←	'give birth'	ילד

c. The prefix מ is superficially like the short form of the preposition מִן, which often becomes מִ or מֵ when combined with the following word (see 8.3). However, the two may be distinguished as follows:

- מִ followed by a double letter is a short form of מִן.
- מֵ followed by a guttural or ר is usually a short form of מִן.
- מ followed by any other letter or with any other vowel is probably the noun prefix מ.

11.3 The Construct (Genitive)

a. Two or more Hebrew nouns may be linked to indicate a genitive relationship, as mentioned above (10.3). The word 'of' or an apostrophe is added in English translation to make the meaning clear. For example:

רוּחַ אֱלֹהִים	←	אֱלֹהִים	+	רוּחַ
'Spirit of God' *or* 'God's Spirit'	←	'God'	+	'Spirit'

The first noun is always unstressed, so it is pronounced as one word with the following noun and the stress occurs at the end. Sometimes, the two nouns are joined with a hyphen.

b. The first noun is often shortened. For example:

בֵּית אֱלֹהִים	←	אֱלֹהִים	+	בַּיִת
'house of God' *or* 'God's house'	←	'God'	+	'house'

The standard form of the noun (בַּיִת) is called 'absolute' and that used before another noun (בֵּית) is called 'construct.' Where the two forms are significantly different, both are listed in the vocabulary, separated by /. Here are some more examples:

Construct			Absolute	
'word of the LORD	דְּבַר־יְהוָה	←	'word'	דָּבָר
'death of Moses'	מוֹת מֹשֶׁה	←	'death'	מָוֶת
'army of Pharaoh'	חֵיל פַּרְעֹה	←	'army'	חַיִל
'face of the deep'	פְּנֵי תְהוֹם	←	'face'	פָּנִים

c. Usually, only the vowels change in the construct form, not the consonants. But the feminine suffix ה‎ָ becomes ת‎ַ (or ת‎ֶ). For example:

Construct			Absolute	
'law of God'	תּוֹרַת הָאֱלֹהִים	←	'law'	תּוֹרָה
'year of jubilee'	שְׁנַת הַיּוֹבֵל	←	'year'	שָׁנָה
'wisdom of Solomon'	חָכְמַת שְׁלֹמֹה	←	'wisdom'	חָכְמָה
'wife of Abraham'	אֵשֶׁת אַבְרָהָם	←	'wife'	אִשָּׁה

d. The construct form never has a definite article, even though it is often definite. Its meaning matches that of the absolute noun with which it is linked, so both are either definite or indefinite. For example:

'a king of a land'	מֶלֶךְ אֶרֶץ
'the king of the land'	מֶלֶךְ הָאָרֶץ
'the king of Israel'	מֶלֶךְ יִשְׂרָאֵל

'Israel' is definite in the last example because it is a name.

e. When an adjective qualifies two or more nouns in a genitive relationship, it follows the last noun, even if it qualifies the first noun. Sometimes, it may be unclear which of the nouns is qualified by the adjective. For example:

'the good king of the land'	מֶלֶךְ הָאָרֶץ הַטּוֹב
'the king of the good land'	מֶלֶךְ הָאָרֶץ הַטּוֹבָה

In this example, it is possible to work out which noun is qualified by the adjective because מֶלֶךְ is masculine and אֶרֶץ is feminine, so the gender of the adjectives makes it clear. In other cases, it may be less clear, and the sense will need to be worked out from the context. Adjectives do not have a construct form, except on rare occasions when used as nouns.

Vocabulary (11)

'woman, wife'	ishsha	אִשָּׁה	97
'she, it, that'	hi	הִיא	98
'psalm'	mizmor	מִזְמוֹר	99
'queen'	malka	מַלְכָּה	100
'judgement, justice'	mishpat	מִשְׁפָּט	101
'horse'	sus	סוּס	102
'Philistine'	p^elishti	פְּלִשְׁתִּי	103
'holiness'	qodesh	קֹדֶשׁ	104
'voice, sound'	qol	קוֹל/קֹל	105
'name'	shem	שֵׁם	106

| 'year' | shana | שָׁנָה | 107 |
| 'teaching, law' | tora | תּוֹרָה | 108 |

Exercise (11)

1. Work out the roots of these nouns:

מִשְׁפָּט: מִקְרָא: מִסְפָּר: מִלְחָמָה: מִשְׁמֶרֶת: מַעֲשֶׂה

2. Work out whether the initial מ in the following words is a noun prefix or a short form of the preposition מִן:

מִבַּיִת: מֵעִיר: מִזְמוֹר: מַחֲנֶה: מִשָּׁם: מֵאָב: מַרְאֶה:

3. Copy, transliterate, translate, and practise reading:

a טוֹבָה הָאָרֶץ מְאֹד מְאֹד:

b הִיא הָעִיר הַגְּדֹלָה:

c יָשְׁבָה אִשָּׁה גְדוֹלָה שָׁם:

d הָיָה¹ דְּבַר יְהוָה אֶל־שְׁלֹמֹה:

e נָתַן הַמֶּלֶךְ לַמַּלְכָּה אֶת־הַבָּיִת:

f רָאִינוּ אֶת־הָאָרֶץ וְהִנֵּה טוֹבָה מְאֹד:

g שָׁמְעוּ קוֹל סוּס² קוֹל חַיִל גָּדוֹל:

h יָשְׁבוּ בִּירוּשָׁלַם עִיר הַקֹּדֶשׁ:

i בָּנָה שְׁלֹמֹה אֶת־בֵּית־יְהוָה וְאֶת־בֵּית הַמֶּלֶךְ:

j שָׁמַרְתָּ אֶת־תּוֹרַת הָאֱלֹהִים אֲשֶׁר נָתַן בְּיַד מֹשֶׁה:

k נָתַן יְהוָה אֶת־עַם יִשְׂרָאֵל בְּיַד הַפְּלִשְׁתִּי:

l לָקַח דָּוִד אֶת־רֹאשׁ הַפְּלִשְׁתִּי:

m לֹא־נָבִיא אָנֹכִי וְלֹא בֶן־נָבִיא אָנֹכִי:

n הָיָה דְּבַר־יְהוָה בְּיַד־הַנָּבִיא:

---

1. Lit. 'was' but better translated 'came' in this context.
2. The form is singular, but the meaning in this context is plural or collective: 'horses' or 'cavalry'.

Figure 9. Tel Dan Inscription. This ninth-century Aramaic inscription has the earliest known mention of David as king of Israel, in the phrase בית דוד ('house of David').[3]

---

3.   Top image: photo 'Tel Dan Stele' by Oren Rozen / CC BY-SA 4.0. Bottom image: drawing 'Tel Dan inscription' by Schrieber / CC BY-SA 3.0.

Plurals and Numbers

Most nouns and adjectives in Hebrew have singular and plural forms. Both kinds of words are usually stated and memorized in the singular form. Plurals are formed by adding suffixes to the singular.

12.1 Masculine Plurals

a. Two common suffixes are used to form the plural of masculine nouns:

- יִם (*im*) when the noun stands alone (absolute form).
- ֵי (*e*) when the noun is followed by another noun in a genitive relationship (construct form).

For example:

Plural construct		Plural absolute		Singular
סוּסֵי אֵשׁ 'horses of fire'	←	סוּסִים 'horses'	←	סוּס 'horse'

b. The suffix יִם is always stressed. This often leads to a vowel change in the word to which it is added:

- The first vowel may be shortened to a shewa (e.g. the plural of דָּבָר is דְּבָרִים).
- The first vowel may be replaced with a different vowel (e.g. the plural of בֵּן is בָּנִים).

c. In the construct form, the stress moves to the following word, and this often leads to a further shortening or replacement of vowels in the first word. For example, דְּבָרִים becomes דִּבְרֵי and בָּנִים becomes בְּנֵי. The following should make this clearer:

Plural construct		Plural absolute		Singular
דִּבְרֵי שָׁלוֹם 'words of peace'	←	דְּבָרִים 'words'	←	דָּבָר 'word'
בְּנֵי הַמֶּלֶךְ 'sons of the king'	←	בָּנִים 'sons'	←	בֵּן 'son'
מַלְכֵי יִשְׂרָאֵל 'kings of Israel'	←	מְלָכִים 'kings'	←	מֶלֶךְ 'king'

12.2 Feminine Plurals

a. The feminine plural is usually indicated with the suffix וֹת (ot). The same suffix is used for both absolute and construct forms. As with the masculine plural suffixes, this may lead to shortening or replacement of vowels in the word to which it is added.

Plural construct			Plural absolute			Singular	
'hands of'	יְדוֹת	←	'hands'	יָדוֹת	←	'hand'	יָד
'lands of'	אַרְצוֹת	←	'lands'	אֲרָצוֹת	←	'land'	אֶרֶץ

b. If a singular noun ends with הָ, this ending is omitted and replaced by וֹת. For example:

'laws of'	תּוֹרוֹת	←	'laws'	תּוֹרוֹת	←	'law'	תּוֹרָה

12.3 Irregular Plurals

The plurals of some words do not follow the rules above.

a. A few masculine nouns have the suffix וֹת in the plural. For example:

Plural construct			Plural absolute			Singular	
'fathers of'	אֲבוֹת	←	'fathers'	אָבוֹת	←	'father'	אָב
'names of'	שְׁמוֹת	←	'names'	שֵׁמוֹת	←	'name'	שֵׁם

b. A few feminine nouns have the suffix יִם in the plural. For example:

'years of'	שְׁנֵי	←	'years'	שָׁנִים	←	'year'	שָׁנָה
'cities of'	עָרֵי	←	'cities'	עָרִים	←	'city'	עִיר

c. A few words have a change of consonants in the plural. For example:

'men of'	אַנְשֵׁי	←	'men'	אֲנָשִׁים	←	'man'	אִישׁ
'women of'	נְשֵׁי	←	'women'	נָשִׁים	←	'woman'	אִשָּׁה
'peoples of'	עַמֵּי	←	'peoples'	עַמִּים	←	'people'	עַם
'daughters of'	בְּנוֹת	←	'daughters'	בָּנוֹת	←	'daughter'	בַּת

The plural of יָם ('sea') is יַמִּים (*yammim*), similar to that of עַם. It should be distinguished carefully from the plural of יוֹם ('day'), which is יָמִים (*yamim*).

d. Now that we have studied plurals, it becomes clear that אֱלֹהִים is the plural form of אֱלוֹהַּ ('God, god'). It is used with a plural meaning for the gods of the nations and a singular meaning for the God of Israel. Perhaps this is because Israel believed in only one God who includes all the deity worth worshipping, so they used the plural form when referring to him. It is like the convention in many languages that a plural is appropriate when referring to someone who deserves respect (e.g. French 'vous' rather than 'tu,' and the royal 'we' in English). When אֱלֹהִים means 'God,' it usually has a singular verb, even though its grammatical form is plural; but when it means 'gods,' the verb is plural.

12.4 Duals

a. As well as the singular and plural, a few nouns have dual forms, especially words for parts of the body that occur in pairs and for time. They are formed with suffixes, which are the same for both masculine and feminine nouns:

- יִם (*ayim*) when the noun stands alone (absolute form)
- ֵי (*e*) when the noun is followed by another noun in a genitive relationship (construct form)

For example:

	Plural		**Dual**		**Singular**
m.	יָמִים '[three or more] days'	←	יוֹמַיִם '[two] days'	←	יוֹם '[one] day'
f.	יָדוֹת '[three or more] hands'	←	יָדַיִם '[two] hands'	←	יָד '[one] hand'

b. The above examples are in the absolute form. In the construct form, the dual is the same as the masculine plural. For example:

singular	'the hand of Esau'	יַד עֵשָׂו
dual	'the hands of Esau'	יְדֵי עֵשָׂו
plural	'the hands of the people'	יְדֵי הָעָם

c. A few nouns are always dual in form, for example מַיִם and שָׁמַיִם. They have no singular or plural form. The name מִצְרַיִם is also dual, in accordance with the Egyptian understanding of their country as the 'Two Lands' (Upper and Lower Egypt).

d. The plural and dual suffixes may now be summarized:

	Masculine		**Feminine**	
Plural absolute	*im*	◌ִים	*ot*	וֹת
Plural construct	*e*	◌ֵי	*ot*	וֹת
Dual absolute	*ayim*	◌ַיִם	*ayim*	◌ַיִם
Dual construct	*e*	◌ֵי	*e*	◌ֵי

12.5 Plurals of Adjectives

Adjectives match the form of the nouns they qualify, both in gender (see 11.1.c) and in number. They have the same suffixes as nouns:

m. sg.	'a good day'	יוֹם טוֹב
f. sg.	'a good year'	שָׁנָה טוֹבָה

| m. pl. | 'good words' | דְּבָרִים טוֹבִים |
| f. pl. | 'good laws' | תּוֹרוֹת טוֹבוֹת |

There are no dual forms for adjectives, so an adjective with a dual noun has the plural form.

12.6 Numbers

a. As in many languages, numbers are used to specify a more precise quantity than simply singular, dual, or plural. Numbers are always *singular* in form, even when the noun they qualify is plural.

b. The suffix הָ may be added to numbers from three to ten, but the result is opposite to when it is added to nouns and adjectives:

- The basic form of the number is used with *feminine* nouns.
- The form with suffix הָ is used with *masculine* nouns.

For example:

| feminine noun | 'five hands' | חָמֵשׁ יָדוֹת |
| masculine noun | 'five days' | חֲמִשָּׁה יָמִים |

c. If a plural suffix is added to numbers three to nine, it multiplies the number by ten, like the suffix 'ty' in English. For example, חָמֵשׁ ('five') becomes חֲמִשִּׁים ('fifty'). The same form is used with both masculine and feminine nouns:

| masculine noun | 'fifty men' | חֲמִשִּׁים אִישׁ |
| feminine noun | 'fifty years' | חֲמִשִּׁים שָׁנָה |

The noun is singular in both these examples, but it may also be plural.

d. The Hebrew number system is complicated, but there is no need to learn all the rules to understand texts. More information about numbers and their forms is given below (25.3).

Vocabulary (12)

| 'last, latter, behind' | akhᵃron | אַחֲרוֹן | 109 |
| 'these' (pl.) | elle | אֵלֶּה | 110 |

'they' (m.)	hem/hemma	הֵם/הֵמָּה	111
'five' (pl. 'fifty')	khamesh	חָמֵשׁ	112
'Jacob'	ya'aqov	יַעֲקֹב	113
'death'	mawet/mot	מָוֶת/מוֹת	114
'number' (noun)	mispar	מִסְפָּר	115
'prophetess'	nᵉvi'a	נְבִיאָה	116
'fall' (verb)	nafal	נָפַל	117
'until, as far as'	ad	עַד	118
'Esau'	esaw	עֵשָׂו	119
'send'	shalakh	שָׁלַח	120

Exercise (12)

1. Memorize the plural and dual suffixes, and irregular plurals.

2. Copy, transliterate, translate, and practise reading:

חָמֵשׁ שָׁנִים: חֲמִשִּׁים אֲנָשִׁים: a

אֵלֶּה דִּבְרֵי דָוִד הָאַחֲרֹנִים: b

לֹא שְׁמַעְתֶּם בְּקוֹל¹ יְהוָה: c

נָתַן יְהוָה אֶת־בְּנֵי יִשְׂרָאֵל בְּיַד־פְּלִשְׁתִּים²: d

וַיֵּשֶׁב שָׁם עַד־מוֹת הַכֹּהֵן הַגָּדוֹל³: e

בִּשְׁנַת־מוֹת הַמֶּלֶךְ עֻזִּיָּהוּ⁴ רָאִיתִי אֶת־אֲדֹנָי: f

אָמַר יְהוָה צְבָאוֹת עַל־הַנְּבִיאִים לֹא־שָׁלַחְתִּי אֶת־הַנְּבִיאִים הָהֵם: g

---

1. The preposition בְּ does not need to be translated into English here.
2. Although there is no definite article with this noun, it functions here as the name of a people and is therefore definite, so the article may be added in English translation: 'the Philistines.'
3. Lit. 'the great priest,' usually called 'the high priest.'
4. עֻזִּיָּהוּ (uzziyy_ahu) is a personal name: 'Uzziah.'

h וְנָתַן יְהֹוָה לְיִשְׂרָאֵל עָרִים גְּדוֹלוֹת וְטוֹבוֹת אֲשֶׁר לֹא־בָנָה:[5]

i הַקֹּל קוֹל יַעֲקֹב וְהַיָּדַיִם יְדֵי עֵשָׂו:

j אֵלֶּה שְׁמוֹת הָאֲנָשִׁים אֲשֶׁר־שָׁלַח מֹשֶׁה:

k הִנֵּה שָׁמַעְנוּ כִּי מַלְכֵי בֵּית יִשְׂרָאֵל כִּי־מַלְכֵי חֶסֶד[6] הֵם:

l שָׁמַעְתָּ אֵת כָּל־הַדְּבָרִים הָאֵלֶּה:

m לֹא יוֹם אֶחָד וְלֹא יוֹמָיִם וְלֹא חֲמִשָּׁה יָמִים:

Figure 10. Traditional Jew Reading Hebrew Book in Jerusalem.[7]

---

5. The implied subject ('Israel') is singular and takes a singular verb in Hebrew, but it is better to use 'they' rather than 'he' when translating into English.

6. חֶסֶד ('loyalty, steadfast love') includes the idea of 'mercy,' so this genitive expresssion means 'kings of mercy,' i.e. 'merciful kings.'

7. Photo by Tom Gordon, pixabay. Used by Permission.

Verbs 2

In Lesson 9 we studied the perfect conjugation of the verb. A complementary conjugation is called 'imperfect' (impf.) because it generally describes an incomplete action. Some scholars prefer the term 'prefix conjugation' because the subject is indicated by adding prefixes to the root.

13.1 Imperfect – Forms

a. There are ten imperfect forms, each with a prefix to indicate its subject. Some have suffixes too. The forms of the verb שָׁמַר are:

Singular					
1	c.	'I will keep'	eshmor	אֶ שְׁמֹר	
2	m.	'you will keep'	tishmor	תִּ שְׁמֹר	
	f.	'you will keep'	tishm^eri	תִּ שְׁמְר י	
3	m.	'he/it will keep'	yishmor	יִ שְׁמֹר	
	f.	'she/it will keep'	tishmor	תִּ שְׁמֹר	
Plural					
1	c.	'we will keep'	nishmor	נִ שְׁמֹר	
2	m.	'you will keep'	tishm^eru	תִּ שְׁמְר וּ	
	f.	'you will keep'	tishmorna	תִּ שְׁמֹר נָה	
3	m.	'they will keep'	yishm^eru	יִ שְׁמְר וּ	
	f.	'they will keep'	tishmorna	תִּ שְׁמֹר נָה	

b. Sometimes the suffixes יָ and וּ have an extra ן. For example, תִּשְׁמְרוּ can also be תִּשְׁמְרוּן (tishmᵉrun). This is purely aesthetic and does not affect the meaning, like the forms 'a' and 'an' in English.

13.2 Imperfect – Meaning

a. The function of the two verb conjugations we have studied may be summarized as follows:

- The perfect is used for complete actions, mostly in the past, but sometimes for a state of being or an attitude, or a future action that is sure to be completed.
- The imperfect is used for incomplete actions, mostly in the future, especially actions that are planned or desired, but sometimes for actions that are in process or done repeatedly.

b. Imperfect verbs are often translated by adding words like 'will', 'shall', 'should', or 'may' to the basic meaning. The best translation depends on the context. For example, 'will' indicates a simple future, whereas 'shall' or 'must' is better for a command, and 'may' or 'might' for a possible outcome.

c. The function of the two conjugations is often switched when the verb is prefixed with a waw (וֹ). As explained above (9.2.e), the perfect with a waw conjunction usually indicates an incomplete action. In a similar way, the imperfect with a waw prefix indicates a complete action. When the waw is used for this purpose, it is prefixed to the imperfect like the definite article, taking a short *a* vowel (וַ) and doubling the first letter of the following word. It is called *waw consecutive*,[1] because this form often follows a previous verb and is common in Hebrew narrative. It is equivalent to a simple past tense in English. For example:

| imperfect | 'he will keep' | יִשְׁמֹר |
| imperfect with waw consecutive | 'and he kept' | וַיִּשְׁמֹר |

d. There is no doubling after waw consecutive in two cases:

- The first-person singular imperfect begins with a guttural (א), which cannot be doubled, so the vowel on the waw is lengthened instead to long *a* (וָ). For example: וָאֶשְׁמַע ('and I heard').

---

1. Some scholars call this verb form 'waw conversive', 'preterite', or *wayyiqtol* (וַיִּקְטֹל, from the relevant form of קטל). The root קטל is rare in the Bible but is used as an example of a regular verb in some textbooks.

- In some imperfect forms (to be learnt later), if the third-person prefix has a shewa (יְ), the י is not doubled after waw consecutive. For example: וַיְדַבֵּר ('and he spoke').

e. The ordinary waw conjunction (וְ) is occasionally used with the imperfect, *without* doubling the following letter. In this case, it usually refers to an incomplete action and may be a way of expressing purpose ('so that'). For example:

imperfect with waw conjunction	'and he will keep'	וְיִשְׁמֹר

f. To summarise, the five main uses of perfect and imperfect with a waw prefix are:

complete	perfect	'he kept' or 'he has kept'	שָׁמַר
incomplete	perfect + waw conjunction	'and he will keep'	וְשָׁמַר
incomplete	imperfect	'he will keep'	יִשְׁמֹר
simple past	imperfect + waw consecutive	'and he kept'	וַיִּשְׁמֹר
incomplete	imperfect + waw conjunction	'and he will keep	וְיִשְׁמֹר

13.3 Weak Verbs

The precise forms of the imperfect conjugation vary depending on the three root letters. The forms of the strong verb are given in the table above. Four variations should be noted in weak verbs.

a. Weak verbs often have an *a* or *e* vowel in the stressed syllable (e.g. אָבְנֶה, אֶשְׁלַח) instead of the *o* vowel that is usual in strong verbs (e.g. אֶשְׁמֹר).

b. The verb אָמַר has an *o* vowel on the imperfect prefix and a silent א (e.g. יֹאמַר).

c. If the initial root letter is ה, ח, or ע, the prefix vowel is often *a* (e.g. יַעֲשֶׂה). This is different from strong verbs, where the prefix vowel is *i* (e.g. יִשְׁמֹר), except for the first-person singular (e.g. אֶשְׁמֹר).

d. If the final root letter is ה, the ה is usually omitted when waw consecutive is prefixed. For example:

Imperfect with waw consecutive				Imperfect		Root
'and he did'	wayyaʿas	וַיַּעַשׂ	←	יַעֲשֶׂה	←	עשׂה
'and he went up'	wayyaʿal	וַיַּעַל	←	יַעֲלֶה	←	עלה
'and he built'	wayyiven	וַיִּבֶן	←	יִבְנֶה	←	בנה
'and he saw'	wayyar	וַיַּרְא	←	יִרְאֶה	←	ראה

In the fourth example, the א becomes silent. Further irregular forms of the imperfect are explained below (15.1).

13.4 Analysis

To properly understand the Hebrew verb system, it is important to clearly distinguish the different verb forms. The following method of analysis is helpful for this purpose:

- root (written without vowels)
- conjugation (pf., impf., etc.)
- person (1, 2, or 3)
- gender (m. or f.)
- number (sg. or pl.)
- any extra items (prefix, suffix, etc.).

Example:

- שְׁמַרְתֶּם: root שׁמר, pf., 2 m. pl.
- וַיִּשְׁמֹר: root שׁמר, impf., 3 m. sg., waw consecutive.

Vocabulary (13)

'we'	ᵃnakhnu	אֲנַחְנוּ	121
'way, road'	derekh	דֶּרֶךְ	122

'walk, go'	halakh	הָלַךְ 123
'Isaac'	yitskhaq	יִצְחָק 124
'glory, honour'	kavod	כָּבוֹד 125
'cut'[2]	karat	כָּרַת 126
'desert, wilderness'	midbar	מִדְבָּר 127
'become king, reign'	malakh	מָלַךְ 128
'Noah'	noakh	נֹחַ 129
'stand'	amad	עָמַד 130
'now'	atta	עַתָּה 131
'Pharaoh' (title)	par'o	פַּרְעֹה 132

Exercise (13)

1. Memorize the imperfect forms of שָׁמַר (highlighted table above).

2. Analyse these verb forms, following the examples:

Form	Root	Conjugation	PGN	Extras
אָמַר	אמר	pf.	3 m. sg.	—
וְלָקַחְתָּ	לקח	pf.	2 m. sg.	waw conjunction
תִּרְאֶה	ראה	impf.	2 m. sg.	or 3 f. sg.
וַיֹּאמֶר				
שָׁמַעְתָּ				
רָאִיתִי				
יִמְלֹךְ				
אֶהְיֶה				
אֶעֱשֶׂה				

---

2. כָּרַת בְּרִית = 'make a covenant.'

וַיִּ֫בֶן				
וַיַּ֫עַשׂ				
תִּכְרְתוּ				
תַּעֲשׂוּ				

3. Copy, transliterate, translate, and practise reading:

a   יְהוָה יִמְלֹךְ[3] לְעוֹלָם:

b   וַיִּ֫בֶן שְׁלֹמֹה אֶת־הַבָּֽיִת:

c   מָה תִּרְאֶה בִּירוּשָׁלָ֑ם: בִּירוּשָׁלַ֫ם תִּרְאֶה אֵת הַכֹּל:

d   וַיֹּ֫אמֶר יְהוָה אֶל־מֹשֶׁה עַתָּה תִרְאֶה אֲשֶׁר אֶעֱשֶׂה לְפַרְעֹה:

e   וַיֹּ֫אמֶר אֱלֹהִים אֶל־מֹשֶׁה אֶהְיֶה[4] אֲשֶׁר אֶהְיֶה:

f   וְלָקַחְתָּ אִשָּׁה לְיִצְחָק מִשָּֽׁם:

g   וַיַּ֫עַשׂ נֹחַ אֶת־כָּל־אֲשֶׁר אָמַר אֱלֹהִים:

h   וַיַּ֫עַל מֹשֶׁה אֶל־הַר הָאֱלֹהִים:

i   וַיַּ֫עַל כְּבוֹד יְהוָה מִן־הָעִיר וַיַּעֲמֹד עַל־הָהָר:

j   אֵ֫לֶּה הַדְּבָרִים אֲשֶׁר תַּעֲשֽׂוּ:

k   קְדוֹשִׁים תִּהְיוּ כִּי קָדוֹשׁ אֲנִי יְהוָה אֱלֹהִים:

l   וַיִּכְרֹת הַמֶּ֫לֶךְ אֶת־הַבְּרִית לִפְנֵי יְהוָה:

m   לֹא־תִכְרְתוּ בְרִית לְאַנְשֵׁי[5] הָאָֽרֶץ:[6]

---

3. The unusual word order places extra emphasis on the noun.

4. This imperfect form may be translated 'I am' or 'I will be.'

5. לְ may be translated 'with' in this sentence.

6. אֶ֫רֶץ means 'land' rather than 'earth' here.

Reading 2
Genesis 1:3–5

First, try to recite Genesis 1:1–2 from memory. For the reading in this lesson, read directly from the Hebrew script if you can, and only refer to the transliteration if you need to check the pronunciation.

14.1 Light (Gen 1:3)

וַיֹּאמֶר אֱלֹהִים יְהִי אוֹר וַיְהִי־אוֹר:

wayyomer ᵉlohim yᵉhi or; wayhi-or.

וַיֹּאמֶר: The verb אמר is very common in the Old Testament (5,300 times), but its meaning here is profound because the subject is God. By his word, God creates light then divides it from darkness. Ten key stages in the process of creation begin with the same expression: וַיֹּאמֶר אֱלֹהִים (see also Gen 1:6, 9, 11, 14, 20, 24, 26, 28, 29). God's word is his primary tool, so powerful that simply to speak a word is enough to bring something into existence (cf. Ps 33:6, 9; Lam 3:37). This expression also shows that God is personal: he does not exercise his power mechanically but develops a relationship with the world he has created by speaking to it. The opening of John's gospel alludes to creation by word, as it explains about the 'Word' (*logos*) that was present at the beginning and involved in the work of creation.

יְהִי: root היה, impf., 3 m. sg. The usual imperfect form of this verb is יִהְיֶה, and this shortened form is called *jussive*. It refers to an incomplete action, like all imperfects, specifically something that *should* be done. So, it is like a third-person imperative (expressing a command, request, or wish). In this sentence it is commonly translated, 'Let there be …'

וַיְהִי: root היה, impf., 3 m. sg., waw consecutive. This is an example of the rule that the י of the third-person prefix is not doubled after waw consecutive if it has a shewa (13.2.d). The shewa becomes silent because it now follows a short vowel, so the word is pronounced *wayhi*. The final ה drops out because it is a weak letter (13.3.d). With the waw consecutive, the meaning changes to the past tense, stating that what was commanded in the previous clause has now taken place. The expression וַיְהִי is very common in the Old Testament (about 800 times). It means literally 'and it was' and may be translated 'and there was' (Gen 1:3), 'and [he] became' (Gen 2:7), or 'and [he] was' (Gen 4:2). Often it is used to introduce narratives (e.g. Gen 4:3; 6:1; Josh 1:1; Judg 1:1) and to join sections of narrative (e.g. Gen 15:17; 27:1; Exod 1:21). In this sense, it was translated 'And it came to pass' in the KJV; while modern translations have various alternatives (e.g. 'After this') and sometimes simply omit it.

14.2 Goodness (Gen 1:4)

וַיַּרְא אֱלֹהִים אֶת־הָאוֹר כִּי־טוֹב וַיַּבְדֵּל אֱלֹהִים
בֵּין הָאוֹר וּבֵין הַחֹשֶׁךְ:

wayyar ᵉlohim et-haʾor ki-ṭov; wayyavdel ᵉlohim,
ben haʾor uven hakhoshekh.

וַיַּרְא: root ראה, impf., 3 m. sg., waw consecutive. The final ה is omitted because of the waw consecutive, and the א is silent (see 13.3.d). There are two nouns with the verb: the first (אֱלֹהִים) is its subject and the second (הָאוֹר) its object, as indicated by the object marker.

כִּי־טוֹב: a conjunction (כִּי) is used with an adjective (טוֹב) to clarify what God saw. There is an element of evaluation here, as God examines what he has created and determines that it is 'good,' according to plan (cf. Ps 104:31).

וַיַּבְדֵּל: verb הִבְדִּיל ('separate'), impf., 3 m. sg., waw consecutive. This complex verb is formed from root בדל with ה prefix and י infix. Verbs like this are called 'hiphil' and are explained in Lesson 21.

בֵּין: preposition meaning 'between.' It is used twice in Hebrew, before each noun, literally: 'between the light and between the darkness.' The second 'between' may be omitted when translating into English. The pronunciation is the same as the noun בֵּן ('son, child, person') but the spelling is different.

14.3 Day and Night (Gen 1:5)

וַיִּקְרָא אֱלֹהִים לָאוֹר יוֹם וְלַחֹשֶׁךְ קָרָא לָיְלָה
וַיְהִי־עֶרֶב וַיְהִי־בֹקֶר יוֹם אֶחָד:

wayyiqra ᵉlohim la'or y<u>o</u>m, wᵉlakh<u>o</u>shekh qara l<u>a</u>yla;

wayhi-<u>e</u>rev wayhi-v<u>o</u>qer, yom ekh<u>a</u>d.

וַיִּקְרָא: root קרא, impf., 3 m. sg., waw consecutive. When the verb קָרָא is followed by the preposition לְ (lit. 'called to'), the preposition should not be translated because the meaning is simply 'call' or 'name.' Name-giving indicates authority over the person or thing that is named (e.g. Gen 2:19–20; 2 Sam 12:28; Isa 4:1; 48:13). So, by naming light 'day' and darkness 'night,' God asserts his authority over them. People in the ancient world thought of light and darkness as supernatural powers in conflict with each other; whereas people today are inclined to think of them as effects of the earth's rotation. According to the Old Testament, however, light and darkness were created by God. He evaluated them and fixed their places (v. 4) and named them (v. 5).

לָאוֹר: this word has three elements: noun + article + preposition.

לָיְלָה: the mid-sentence pause results in a change of vowel from לַיְלָה to לָיְלָה. The first syllable remains closed (*lay*) so the shewa is silent (see 4.1.c).

עֶרֶב (*erev* 'evening') and בֹקֶר (*boqer* 'morning'): two parts of one יוֹם ('day'). These words are still common in Modern Hebrew, for example in the greeting בֹּקֶר טוֹב ('good morning').

Days were reckoned from morning to evening in ancient Egypt, and it seems this reckoning was followed by the Israelites in Canaan (e.g. Gen 19:34; Judg 6:38; 1 Sam 19:11; 30:12; Isa 28:19; Jer 33:20). But in Mesopotamia, days were reckoned from sunset to the following afternoon, and this reckoning is implied in several Old Testament texts from the exile or later (e.g. Esth 4:16; Dan 8:14). In New Testament times, Jews followed the second method and it is still used today, so a new day begins at sunset. It seems that Genesis 1 follows the first method (morning till evening), though some interpreters argue for the second. Assuming the first, God's creative work took place during the day, while the time between one day and the next is described with the refrain: וַיְהִי־עֶרֶב וַיְהִי־בֹקֶר יוֹם אֶחָד (vv. 5, 8, 13, 19, 23, 31).

Vocabulary (14)

'ark [of covenant], chest'	ᵃron	אֲרוֹן	133
'between'	ben	בֵּין	134
'morning'	boqer	בֹּקֶר	135
'separate' (verb)	hivdil	הִבְדִּיל	136
'thus, so'[1]	ken	כֵּן	137
'find'	matsa	מָצָא	138
'evening'	erev	עֶרֶב	139
'many, much, great'	rav	רַב	140
'dome, expanse'	raqia	רָקִיעַ	141
'second'	sheni	שֵׁנִי	142
'middle, midst'	tawekh/tokh	תָּוֶךְ/תּוֹךְ	143
'under, instead of'	takhat	תַּחַת	144

Exercise (14)

1. Memorize Genesis 1:3–5 in Hebrew so you can recite and write it.

2. Analyse these verb forms:

Form	Root	Conjugation	PGN	Extras
יְהִי				
וַיַּרְא				
לְקָחוּ				
יִמְצָא				
אֶמְצָא				
יִבְנֶה				

---

1. In Modern Hebrew, כֵּן also means 'yes.'

תִּמְלֹךְ				
וַיִּכְרְתוּ				
תִּרְאֶה				
וּלְקַחְתֶּם				

3. Copy, transliterate, translate, and practise reading:

a   וַיַּעַשׂ אֶת־הָאָרֹן׃

b   וּלְקַחְתֶּם אֶת־אֲרוֹן יְהוָה׃

c   הֵמָּה יָדְעוּ דֶּרֶךְ יְהוָה׃

d   הוּא־יִבְנֶה בַיִת לְשֵׁם־יְהוָה׃

e   וַיֹּאמֶר אֱלֹהִים יְהִי רָקִיעַ בְּתוֹךְ הַמָּיִם׃

f   וַיַּעַשׂ אֱלֹהִים אֶת־הָרָקִיעַ וַיַּבְדֵּל בֵּין הַמַּיִם אֲשֶׁר מִתַּחַת לָרָקִיעַ[2]
וּבֵין הַמַּיִם אֲשֶׁר מֵעַל לָרָקִיעַ וַיְהִי־כֵן׃

g   וַיִּקְרָא אֱלֹהִים לָרָקִיעַ שָׁמָיִם וַיְהִי־עֶרֶב וַיְהִי־בֹקֶר יוֹם שֵׁנִי׃

h   לָקְחוּ פְלִשְׁתִּים אֵת אֲרוֹן הָאֱלֹהִים׃

i   וַיֹּאמֶר יְהוָה הַאֶמְצָא חֲמִשִּׁים צַדִּיקִים בְּתוֹךְ הָעִיר׃

j   וַיֹּאמֶר אֶל־דָּוִד אַתָּה תִמְלֹךְ עַל־יִשְׂרָאֵל וַיִּכְרְתוּ בְּרִית לִפְנֵי יְהוָה׃

k   וַיֹּאמֶר יַעֲקֹב הֲשָׁלוֹם וַיֹּאמְרוּ שָׁלוֹם׃

l   בָּרוּךְ־יְהוָה אֱלֹהֵי יִשְׂרָאֵל מִן־הָעוֹלָם וְעַד הָעוֹלָם׃

---

2. The prepositions מִן ('from') and לְ ('to') here, and later in the sentence, seem strange to an English reader, but this usage is quite common in Hebrew. They can be omitted when translating the sentence into English.

Roots

As explained in Lesson 5, Hebrew verbs usually have three-letter roots. Prefixes and suffixes are added to these roots to modify the meaning, as seen in the tables of perfect and imperfect forms above (9.1 and 13.1). Most verbs studied so far have 'strong' roots, which follow regular patterns. We have also learnt that 'weak' verbs may have different forms, specifically:

- Verbs with final ה have distinctive perfect forms (9.4.b).
- There are four important variations of the imperfect in weak verbs (13.3).

In this lesson, we study verbs with weak initial letters and 'hollow' verbs, before summarizing the twelve kinds of Hebrew root.

15.1 Weak Initial Letters

a. If the initial root letter is א, it usually has a compound shewa in the imperfect, instead of the silent shewa for a strong verb. For example:

Imperfect				Root	
'he will keep'	yishmor	יִשְׁמֹר	←	'keep'	שמר
'he will love'	ye'ᵉhav	יֶאֱהַב	←	'love'	אהב
'he will gather'	ye'ᵉsof	יֶאֱסֹף	←	'gather'	אסף

But there are a few verbs where the initial א is silent in the imperfect and there is no shewa at all. For example:

'he will say'	yomar	יֹאמַר	←	'say'	אמר
'he will eat'	yokhal	יֹאכַל	←	'eat'	אכל

In the first-person singular imperfect, the א of the prefix merges with the initial א to become one letter. For example:

'I will say'	omar	אֹמַר	←	[אאֹמַר]	←	'say'	אמר

b. If the initial root letter is י, this weak letter drops out or becomes a vowel letter in the imperfect. For example:

'he will go out'	yetse	יֵצֵא	←	[יִיְצֵא]	←	'go out'	יצא
'he will know'	yeda	יֵדַע	←	[יִיְדַע]	←	'know'	ידע
'he will inherit'	yirash	יִירַשׁ	←	[יִיְרַשׁ]	←	'inherit'	ירשׁ

If the י drops out (as in the first two examples), the vowel on the prefix lengthens from short *i* to long *e*. If the י becomes a vowel letter (third example), the vowel on the prefix lengthens from short *i* to long *i*. Note the difference between יָצָא (perfect) and יֵצֵא (imperfect), also יָדַע and יֵדַע. The perfect can be recognized from the two *a* vowels.

c. If the initial root letter is נ, this weak letter usually merges with the following letter in the imperfect, making a double letter, and occasionally drops out completely. The second vowel may be *o* (as in the strong verb), *a*, or occasionally *e*. For example:

'he will fall'	yippol	יִפֹּל	←	[יִנְפֹּל]	←	'fall'	נפל
'he will lift'	yissa	יִשָּׂא	←	[יִנְשָׂא]	←	'lift'	נשׂא
'he will give'	yitten	יִתֵּן	←	[יִנְתֵּן]	←	'give'	נתן

d. There are two roots that do not have initial י or נ but behave in a similar way. הלך is similar to a root with initial י, and לקח is similar to a root with initial נ. For example:

'he will go'	yelekh	יֵלֵךְ	←	[יִהְלֵךְ]	←	'go'	הלך
'he will take'	yiqqakh	יִקַּח	←	[יִלְקַח]	←	'take'	לקח

15.2 Hollow Verbs

a. Most verbs have three consonants and two syllables in their root form, for example אָמַר (*a-mar*). But 'hollow' verbs have a vowel letter in the middle and are pronounced as one syllable in their root form, for example בּוֹא (bo, 'come, go in'). They are sometimes called 'biconsonantal' because only two root letters are consonants.

b. The vowel letter always drops out in the perfect and often in the imperfect as well. For example:

Imperfect			Perfect		Root form
'he will come'	יָבֹא	or	יָבוֹא	'he came'	בָּא	בּוֹא
'you will come'	תָּבֹא	or	תָּבוֹא	'you came'	בָּאתָ	בּוֹא
'they will come'	יָבֹאוּ	or	יָבוֹאוּ	'they came'	בָּאוּ	בּוֹא
'he will rise'	יָקֵם	or	יָקוּם	'he rose'	קָם	קוּם
'he will put'	יָשֵׂם	or	יָשִׂים	'he put'	שָׂם	שִׂים

c. Two forms of these verbs should be memorized: the three-letter root form and the third-person masculine singular perfect, for example בּוֹא and בָּא (bo/ba).

15.3 Key Characteristics

There are twelve kinds of root in Hebrew, many of which have now been studied in outline. Key characteristics are summarized in the table below. Fuller details are given in some larger Hebrew introductions (e.g. Kelley; Pratico and van Pelt).

Name	Example	Characteristics
Strong	שמר	Vowels in imperfect are *i* and *o* (e.g. יִשְׁמֹר)
Stative	קדש	Second vowel in imperfect is *a* (e.g. יִקְדַּשׁ)
Initial א	אהב	Compound shewa in imperfect (e.g. יֶאֱהַב) unless א is silent
Initial ה, ח, or ע	עבד	First vowel in imperfect is *a* or *e* (e.g. יַעֲבֹד)
Initial י	ישׁב	י drops out or becomes vowel letter in imperfect (e.g. יֵשֵׁב)
Initial נ	נפל	נ usually merges with following letter in imperfect (e.g. יִפֹּל)

Middle guttural or ר	בחר	Second vowel in imperfect is *a* (e.g. יִבְחַר)
Middle vowel ('Hollow')	קום	First vowel in perfect is *a* or *e*, unlike the root form (e.g. קָם)
Final א	מצא	Second vowel in imperfect is *a* or *e* (e.g. יִמְצָא)
Final ה	ראה	ה often becomes י or ת or drops out in perfect (e.g. רָאִיתִי)
Final ח or ע	שלח	Second vowel in imperfect is *a* (e.g. יִשְׁלַח)
Geminate (middle letter = final letter)	סבב	Final letter often drops out or merges with middle letter (e.g. יְסֹב, יִסֹבּוּ)

15.4 Hebrew Song 4 (*Barukh Habba*)

בָּרוּךְ הַבָּא בְּשֵׁם יְהוָה בֵּרַכְנוּכֶם מִבֵּית יְהוָה: (x2)
הוֹדוּ לַיהוָה כִּי־טוֹב כִּי לְעוֹלָם חַסְדּוֹ: (x2)

> See mini songbook for music

Blessed [is] the one who comes in the name of the LORD;
> we bless you from the house of the LORD.
Give thanks to the LORD because [he is] good;
> because his steadfast love [is] forever. (*Ps 118:26, 29*)

Vocabulary (15)

'after, behind'	*akhar/akh^are*	אַחַר/אַחֲרֵי	145
'with'	*et*	אֶת/אֶת־[1]	146
'come, go in'	*bo/ba*	בּוֹא/בָּא	147
'this' (f. sg.)	*zot*	זֹאת	148
'companion, partner'	*khaver*	חָבֵר	149

---

1. This preposition has the same spelling and pronunciation as the object marker (vocabulary item 50), so the two can only be distinguished by their context in a sentence.

'new'	khadash	חָדָשׁ 150
'wisdom'	khokhma	חָכְמָה 151
'Judah'	yᵉhuda	יְהוּדָה 152
'die'	mut/met	מוּת/מֵת 153
'servant, slave'	eved	עֶבֶד 154
'rise, stand'	qum/qam	קוּם/קָם 155
'turn, return'	shuv/shav	שׁוּב/שָׁב 156

Exercise (15)

1. Memorize the names of the twelve main kinds of root with one example of each (first two columns of highlighted table above).

2. Analyse these verb forms:

Form	Root	Conjugation	PGN	Extras
יֶאֱהַב				
אֹמַר				
תֵּצְאוּ				
יֵדְעוּ				
אֶשָּׂא				
נֵלֵךְ				
וַיֵּלֶךְ				
אֶקַּח				
בָּאָה				
יָקוּם				
וַיָּבֹא				
וְקַמְתָּ				

3. Copy, translate, and practise reading (transliteration not required):

a   מַה־זֹּאת עֲשִׂיתֶם:

b   וַיֵּלֶךְ בְּדֶרֶךְ מַלְכֵי יִשְׂרָאֵל:

c   שָׁלוֹם חֲבֵרִים:

d   זֹאת הַבְּרִית אֲשֶׁר תִּשְׁמֹרוּ:

e   וְקַמְתָּ וְעָלִיתָ אֶל־הָעִיר:

f   דְּבַר אֱלֹהִים יָקוּם לְעוֹלָם:

g   אֲנַחְנוּ נֵלֵךְ בְּשֵׁם־יְהוָה אֱלֹהֵים:

h   וַיָּבֹא שְׁלֹמֹה לִירוּשָׁלַם וַיִּמְלֹךְ עַל־יִשְׂרָאֵל:

i   בָּאוּ אֶל־בֵּית הַנָּבִיא אֲשֶׁר בָּעִיר:

j   הִנֵּה בָּאָה רוּחַ גְּדוֹלָה מִן־הַמִּדְבָּר:

k   לֹא־קָם נָבִיא בְיִשְׂרָאֵל כְּמֹשֶׁה:

l   וַיָּקָם וַיֵּצֵא מִשָּׁם וַיָּבֹא אֶל־הָאִישׁ וַיֹּאמֶר הַאַתָּה הָאִישׁ וַיֹּאמֶר אָנִי[2]:

m   עַתָּה תָּשׁוּב הַמַּמְלָכָה[3] לְבֵית דָּוִד:

n   יֵדְעוּ כָּל־עַמֵּי הָאָרֶץ אֶת־שֵׁם יְהוָה:

o   אַחֲרֵי שָׁנִים רַבּוֹת תֵּצְאוּ מִמִּצְרַיִם וּמִבֵּית עֲבָדִים:

p   וַיְהִי בַּיּוֹם הַהוּא[4] וַיָּבֹאוּ עַבְדֵי יִצְחָק וַיֹּאמְרוּ מָצָאנוּ מָיִם:

q   זֹאת הַבְּרִית אֲשֶׁר אֶכְרֹת אֶת־בֵּית יִשְׂרָאֵל אַחֲרֵי הַיָּמִים הָהֵם נְאֻם־יְהוָה:

4. Practise the Hebrew song *Barukh Habba*.

---

2. The pronoun may be translated here 'I am.'

3. The noun has no object marker, so it is the subject of the verb, not its object.

4. הוּא is used here as a demonstrative adjective (see 7.5.d).

Suffix Pronouns

The personal pronouns studied above (6.4) usually function as the subject of a sentence or clause (e.g. I, you, he, she). There are two other uses for pronouns, to indicate:

- the object of a sentence or clause (e.g. me, you, him, her)
- a possessive relationship (e.g. my, your, his, her).

When used in either of these ways, Hebrew pronouns are attached as suffixes to other words:

- With nouns, they indicate possession (e.g. *my* book).
- With verbs and most other words, they indicate the object (e.g. kept *me*, sent *him*, for *her*, over *it*).

Suffix pronouns should be distinguished carefully from the suffixes that indicate the subject in perfect forms of the verb (see 9.1).

16.1 Forms

Many suffix pronouns are shortened forms of independent personal pronouns. For example, the pronoun אֲנִי ('I') is shortened to יִ or נִ when it becomes a suffix. In the table below, the most common suffixes are listed on the right and should be memorized. Several suffixes have alternative forms, listed in the centre, and these are for reference only. Sometimes extra vowels or consonants are inserted to link suffixes with the word to which they are attached.

Singular					
			Alternative		**Common**
1	c.	'me, my'	-ni/-enni	נִי/נִֶּ	-i	יִ
2	m.	'you, your'	-ekka	כָּה/ךְָ	-kha	ךָ
	f.	'you, your'			-kh	ךְ

3	m.	'him, his, its'	-w/-hu/-ennu	וֹ/הוּ/נּוּ	-o	וֹ
	f.	'her, its'	-ha/-enna	הָ/נָּה	-ah	הָ
Plural						
			Alternative		**Common**	
1	c.	'us, our'			-nu	נוּ
2	m.	'you, your'			-khem	כֶם
	f.	'you, your'			-khen	כֶן
3	m.	'them, their'	-m/-mo	ם/מוֹ	-hem	הֶם
	f.	'them, their'	-n	ן	-hen	הֶן

One of the third-person masculine singular forms (נּוּ) is similar to the first-person plural form (נוּ). The two can be distinguished by the double letter in the first form.

16.2 Possessive Suffixes

a. Suffix pronouns with *nouns* are possessive. They may indicate relationship (e.g. my husband), ownership (e.g. my horse), authorship (e.g. my covenant), or experience (e.g. my suffering). The suffix is usually attached to the construct form of the noun. For example:

				Construct	**Absolute**
'your house'	bet^{e}kha	בֵּיתְךָ ←	ךָ +	בֵּית	בַּיִת
'my law'	torati	תּוֹרָתִי ←	ִי +	תּוֹרַת	תּוֹרָה
'his eye'	eno	עֵינוֹ ←	וֹ +	עֵין	עַיִן
'our God'	^{e}lohenu	אֱלֹהֵינוּ ←	נוּ +	אֱלֹהֵי	אֱלֹהִים
'his wife'	ishto	אִשְׁתּוֹ ←	וֹ +	אֵשֶׁת	אִשָּׁה

b. Nouns that do not have a distinct construct form (e.g. מֶלֶךְ) may also be shortened when suffix pronouns are attached. For example:

'my king'	malki	מַלְכִּי ←	ִי +	מֶלֶךְ
'your servant'	avd^{e}kha	עַבְדְּךָ ←	ךָ +	עֶבֶד

c. With plural and dual nouns, the suffix יְ (-*i*) merges with the letter י in the construct form of these nouns to become יַ (-*ay*). In a similar way, the suffix וֹ (-*w*) merges with the letter י to become יוָ (pronounced -*aw*, not -*ayw*). For example:

				Construct	Absolute
'my brothers'	*akhay*	אַחַי ←	+ יְ	אֲחֵי	אַחִים
'his eyes'	*enaw*	עֵינָיו ←	+ וֹ	עֵינֵי	עֵינַיִם

16.3 Objective Suffixes

a. Suffix pronouns with *verbs* indicate the object. The verbs are often shortened when these suffixes are attached. For example:

'he cut it'	*k^erato*	כְּרָתוֹ ←	וֹ +	כָּרַת
'he sent me'	*sh^elakhani*	שְׁלָחַנִי ←	נִי +	שָׁלַח

With perfect forms of verbs (except 3 m. sg.), suffix pronouns merge with the perfect suffix to create a compound suffix. The first part indicates the subject, and the second indicates the object. For example:

'we blessed you'	*berakhnukhem*	בֵּרַכְנוּכֶם ←	כֶם +	בֵּרַכְנוּ
'you knew me'	*y^eda'tani*	יְדַעְתָּנִי ←	נִי +	יָדַעְתָּ
'she found us'	*m^etsa'atnu*	מְצָאַתְנוּ ←	נוּ +	מָצְאָה
'she gave birth to me'	*y^eladatni*	יְלָדַתְנִי ←	נִי +	יָלְדָה

b. Suffix pronouns with *prepositions* and *interjections* also indicate their object. For example:

'in them'	*bam*	בָּם ←	ם +	בְּ
'to/for you'	*l^ekha*	לְךָ ←	ךָ +	לְ

Sometimes, extra letters are added. For example, י is usually added when אֶל־ ('to, toward') has a suffix pronoun:

'to/toward you'	*elekha*	אֵלֶיךָ ←	ךָ +	אֶל־

The letter מ may be added with מִן and כְּ. For example:

'from me'	*mimmenni*	מִמֶּנִּי ←	מִן + נִי
'like you'	*kamokha*	כָּמוֹךָ ←	כְּ + ךָ

Occasionally, a letter is omitted. For example:

'here I am' (lit. 'behold me!')	*hineni*	הִנְנִי ←	הִנֵּה + נִי

16.4 Suffix Pronouns with אֵל and אֵת

There are two pairs of similar words that are pronounced the same but have different meanings. They need special attention because suffix pronouns are attached to them in distinctive ways.

a. The noun אֵל ('God, god') and preposition אֶל־ ('to, toward'):

- With a first-person singular suffix pronoun, they have different forms: אֵלִי (*eli* 'my God') and אֵלַי (*elay* 'to me').
- With any other suffix pronoun, אֵל means 'to' because the noun אֵל ('God') never has a suffix pronoun except י.

b. The object marker (אֵת) and preposition אֵת ('with'):

- A suffix pronoun with the *preposition* indicates its object. The pronunciation usually changes in two ways: the vowel becomes *i* and the *t* is doubled. For example:

'with you'	*ittekhem*	אִתְּכֶם ←	כֶם +	אֵת

- A suffix pronoun with the *object marker* becomes an independent object pronoun. Sometimes it retains the *e* vowel, but more often it has an *o* vowel. For example:

'you'	*etkhem*	אֶתְכֶם ←	כֶם +	אֵת
'me'	*oti*	אֹתִי/אוֹתִי ←	י +	אֵת
'him'	*oto*	אֹתוֹ/אוֹתוֹ ←	וֹ +	אֵת

c. These independent object pronouns are comparable to the pronouns used for subjects (אַתֶּם 'you'; אֲנִי 'I'; etc.). In both cases, the subject or object may be included in the verb form or indicated with a separate word. For example, 'you knew me' can be expressed in four ways in Hebrew, with or without independent pronouns:

pronoun + verb + pronoun	אַתָּה יָדַעְתָּ אֹתִי
verb + pronoun	יָדַעְתָּ אֹתִי
pronoun + verb + suffix pronoun	אַתָּה יְדַעְתַּנִי
verb + suffix pronoun	יְדַעְתַּנִי

Vocabulary (16)

'Abraham'	avraham	אַבְרָהָם	157
'bless'	berakh	בֵּרַךְ	158
'speak'	dibber	דִּבֶּר	159
'praise! give thanks!'[1]	hodu	הוֹדוּ	160
'Joseph'	yosef	יוֹסֵף	161
'there is' or 'there are'[2]	yesh	יֵשׁ/יֶשׁ	162
'thus, so'	ko	כֹּה	163
'lift, carry'[3]	nasa	נָשָׂא	164
'soul, life, person'	nefesh	נֶפֶשׁ	165
'eye, spring [of water]'	ayin/en	עַיִן/עֵין	166
'ten' (pl. 'twenty')	eser	עֶשֶׂר	167
'rejoice'	samakh	שָׂמַח	168

---

1. This is an imperative form, which is used to give instructions and commands. Imperatives are explained further below (18.1).

2. This particle has a similar meaning to the French phrase il y a.

3. נָשָׂא עֵינַיִם = 'look up'; נָשָׂא פָּנִים = 'be favourable, show partiality.'

Exercise (16)

1. Memorize the common suffix pronouns (highlighted table above).

2. Identify the suffix pronouns below, following the example:

Form	Suffix pronoun	Form	Suffix pronoun
לְךָ	2 m. sg.	לִי	
אֱלֹהֶיךָ		אֲלֵיכֶם	
יָדָם		אֵלַי	
נַפְשְׁךָ		עֵינָיו	
בֵּרַכְנוּכֶם		לְפָנֶיךָ	
חַסְדּוֹ		לָהֶם	
עֲבָדֶיךָ		שְׁמִי	
אֹתָנוּ		רוּחִי	
בֵּיתְךָ		בָּכֶם	
אֲבֹתֵיכֶם		שְׁלָחַנִי	

3. Translate and practise reading (copying not required):

a יָדַע כִּי יֵשׁ נָבִיא בְּיִשְׂרָאֵל׃

b מַה־תִּתֶּן־לִי׃

c וְשָׂמַחְתָּ בְכָל־הַטּוֹב אֲשֶׁר נָתַן־לְךָ יְהוָה אֱלֹהֶיךָ׃

d יְהוָה יִשְׁמָרְךָ מִכָּל־רָע יִשְׁמֹר אֶת־נַפְשֶׁךָ׃

e בָּרוּךְ הַבָּא⁴ בְּשֵׁם יְהוָה בֵּרַכְנוּכֶם⁵ מִבֵּית יְהוָה׃

f הוֹדוּ לַיהוָה כִּי־טוֹב כִּי לְעוֹלָם חַסְדּוֹ׃

g אֶקְרָא לֵאלֹהִים יִשְׁלַח מִשָּׁמַיִם יִשְׁלַח אֱלֹהִים חַסְדּוֹ׃

h תֹּאמְרוּ לְיוֹסֵף אֲנַחְנוּ עֲבָדֶיךָ תִּקַּח אֹתָנוּ אֶל־בֵּיתֶךָ׃

i וּשְׁלַחְתֶּם בְּיֶדְכֶם אֵלַי כָּל־דָּבָר אֲשֶׁר תִּשְׁמָעוּ׃

---

4. הַבָּא is a participle with definite article, meaning 'the one who comes.' Participles will be explained below (18.2).

5. This perfect form is best translated here as a present tense.

j וַיֹּאמֶר אֱלֹהִים אֶל־מֹשֶׁה כֹּה־תֹאמַר אֶל־בְּנֵי יִשְׂרָאֵל יְהוָה אֱלֹהֵי אֲבֹתֵיכֶם

אֱלֹהֵי אַבְרָהָם אֱלֹהֵי יִצְחָק וֵאלֹהֵי יַעֲקֹב שְׁלָחַנִי אֲלֵיכֶם זֶה־שְּׁמִי לְעֹלָם:

k וַיִּשָּׂא יַעֲקֹב עֵינָיו וַיַּרְא וְהִנֵּה עֵשָׂו בָּא:

l וַיֹּאמֶר אַבְרָהָם הֲלֹא כָל־הָאָרֶץ לְפָנֶיךָ:

m וְהָיִיתִי לָהֶם לֵאלֹהִים[6] וְהֵמָּה יִהְיוּ־לִי לְעָם:

n וַיֹּאמֶר אֵלֶיהָ מָה אֶעֱשֶׂה־לָּךְ מַה־יֶּשׁ־לָךְ בַּבָּיִת:

o וְנָתַתִּי[7] רוּחִי בָכֶם וִידַעְתֶּם כִּי־אֲנִי יְהוָה דִּבַּרְתִּי וְעָשִׂיתִי נְאֻם־יְהוָה[8]:

p וַיֹּאמֶר דָּוִד הֲלֹא־אִישׁ אַתָּה וּמִי כָמוֹךָ בְּיִשְׂרָאֵל:

Figure 11. Seal of Jaazaniah. This sixth-century seal has two lines of early Hebrew
script and an image of a fighting cock. In the script used in this book, it reads:

ליאזניהו עבד המלך
'[belonging] to Jaazaniah, servant of the king'
It probably belonged to the official mentioned in 2 Kings 25:23 and Jeremiah 40:8.[9]

---

6. Suffix pronouns with לְ may be possessive, so this phrase means 'their God' (lit. 'to them for God').

7. Root נתן: the final נ merges with ת in perfect suffixes.

8. Note that three verbs in this sentence have a waw conjunction, and one does not, and translate accordingly.

9. Photo from Nahman Avigad and Benjamin Sass, *Corpus of West Semitic Stamp Seals* (Jerusalem: Israel Academy of Sciences and Humanities, 1997), 52, seal #8. Used with permission from the Israel Antiquities Authority.

Reading 3
Exodus 20:1–3

There are two great works of God according to the Bible: creation and salvation. The first Hebrew readings in this course have been chosen because of their theological importance in relation to these two matters. We have already studied the first part of the primary text about creation (Gen 1) and we move on to one concerned with salvation: the opening of the 'Ten Words' (עֲשֶׂרֶת הַדְּבָרִים¹), commonly called the Decalogue or Ten Commandments. The people of Israel were at a turning-point in their history when they met with God at Mount Sinai. We read that God spoke to them (Exod 20:1), summing up the history of salvation to that point (v. 2), then setting out the principles that were to regulate Israel's life as the chosen people (v. 3 onwards). First, however, it will be helpful to learn a little more about accents.

17.1 Accents

Hebrew Bibles have many more accents than have been studied so far. Most words have one accent, usually on the stressed syllable. When two words are joined with a hyphen, only the second word has an accent. Some accents indicate a pause ('disjunctive'), while others link words together ('conjunctive'). The four accents already mentioned (4.1.d; 4.6.a) may now be supplemented with four more, all indicating short pauses:

׀	distinguishes long *a* from short *o*	*meteg*
׀ with ׃	end-of-sentence pause	*silluq + sof pasuq*
֑	mid-sentence pause	*atnakh*

---

1. עֲשֶׂרֶת is a construct form of עֶשֶׂר ('ten').

:	short pause	*zaqef qaton*
׀:	short pause	*zaqef gadol*
∴	short pause	*s^egolta*[2]
ֽ	short pause	*tifkha*
̇	short pause	*r^ev̱ia*

There is a *tifkha* in each verse of the reading in this lesson. Apart from these eight accents, most others can be ignored. Occasionally, accents are modified slightly in the texts and exercises in this book if sentences are shortened or an unfamiliar accent occurs in the original.

17.2 Introduction (Exod 20:1)

וַיְדַבֵּר אֱלֹהִים אֵת כָּל־הַדְּבָרִים הָאֵלֶּה לֵאמֹר: ס

וַיְדַבֵּר: verb דָּבַר ('speak'), impf., 3 m. sg., waw consecutive. The **י** of the third-person prefix is not doubled after waw consecutive because it has a shewa (13.2.d). This kind of verb with a double middle letter is called 'piel' and will be explained in Lesson 23.

אֱלֹהִים: The subject of this sentence is God, who is stated to be the source of the following commandments. In this way, it is affirmed that Old Testament law is not a set of rules designed by human beings but comes from God. This short sentence does not have a mid-sentence pause, but there are two short pauses on אֱלֹהִים and הָאֵלֶּה.

לֵאמֹר: root אמר, infinitive construct with preposition לְ. Infinitives will be explained in Lesson 19. The literal meaning of this form is 'to say' or 'saying', and its meaning is like the phrase 'as follows' or quotation marks in English. It is often used in the Old Testament to introduce direct speech because Hebrew does not have quotation marks.

ס: Abbreviation of סְתוּמָא (s^etuma), that often marks the space between paragraphs in Hebrew manuscripts. Alternatively, paragraphs may be marked by the letter **פ**, an abbreviation of פְּתוּחָא (p^etukha), as between verses 7 and 8.

---

2. This accent is always on the last letter of the word, irrespective of the stressed syllable.

17.3 Theology and History (Exod 20:2)

אָנֹכִי יְהוָה אֱלֹהֶיךָ אֲשֶׁר הוֹצֵאתִיךָ מֵאֶרֶץ מִצְרַיִם מִבֵּית עֲבָדִים:

יְהוָה is the name of Israel's God (see 5.4). It appears to have been known in early days (Gen 4:26) but not commonly used before the time of Moses. In the desert near Horeb (Sinai), Moses experienced a theophany (Exod 3). The speaker initially introduced himself as the God of Israel's ancestors (v. 6), then sent Moses to free Israel from their slavery in Egypt (vv. 7–10). Finally, God revealed his name to Moses, with its meaning: 'I am who I am' (vv. 13–15). Israel may have heard the divine name previously but only began to use it regularly after the exodus, the event with which it was closely connected in their memory (see also Exod 6:1–7). So, in the confirmation of the covenant between God and his people at Sinai, the four-letter name is here given as the legal name of the first party to the agreement (Exod 20:2).

אֱלֹהֶיךָ: In many Hebrew manuscripts, this word is printed אֱלֹהֶיךָ with two punctuation marks (mid-sentence pause and short pause). This is due to two different Jewish traditions for reading the Decalogue in worship that are preserved in the one text. The tradition that is assumed by the verse numbering in most Bibles has a mid-sentence pause here (אֱלֹהֶיךָ), followed by an end-of-sentence pause on עֲבָדִים, as printed above. According to the alternative tradition, however, there is a short pause here (אֱלֹהֶיךָ), then a mid-sentence pause on עֲבָדִים, and the sentence continues into verse 3.

הוֹצֵאתִיךָ: verb הוֹצִיא ('bring out'), pf., 1 c. sg., suffix pronoun (2 m. sg.). This is a hiphil verb (to be explained in Lesson 21). Note the singular pronoun here; elsewhere plural pronouns are used in a similar context (e.g. Exod 6:6). The exodus from Egypt was liberation both for individuals and for the nation.

מִבֵּית עֲבָדִים: The word בֵּית here is better translated 'place' rather than the literal 'house.' There is a poetic element in this clause, with the parallelism between מִבֵּית עֲבָדִים and מֵאֶרֶץ מִצְרַיִם.

This concise declaration sums up the narrative about God's revelation of himself and salvation of his people in the preceding chapters (Exod 3–19). The God of the ancestors has shown himself to Israel as the God who is (יְהוָה, v. 2a) and who acts (הוֹצֵאתִיךָ, v. 2b). This mini creed is the basis for the laws that follow.

17.4 First Commandment (Exod 20:3)

לֹא יִהְיֶה לְךָ אֱלֹהִים אֲחֵרִים עַל־פָּנָי:

לֹא יִהְיֶה: the imperfect form with negative here conveys the meaning 'there must not be.' Several Hebrew manuscripts have a hyphen between these two words; in others, the hyphen links יִהְיֶה with the following word. The hyphen does not affect the meaning, so is simply omitted here.

אֱלֹהִים: not 'God' in this sentence but 'gods' (plural of אֱלוֹהַ, see 12.3.d). Note the plural adjective (אֲחֵרִים 'other'), matching the meaning, though the verb is singular (יִהְיֶה). The singular form may be intended to disparage these worthless 'gods.' Plural nouns denoting animals or things sometimes have singular verbs, so perhaps the singular verb here implies that these gods are like animals or things.

פָּנָי: In many Hebrew manuscripts, this is written פָּנָ֑י, a strange form resulting from the combination of פָּנַי and פָּנֶי, because of the two traditions for reading the Decalogue mentioned above. The expression עַל־פָּנָי means literally 'over/against my face' and may be translated 'before me' (NIV, NRSV) or perhaps better 'besides me' (NJPS).

Vocabulary (17)

'other, another'	akher	אַחֵר	169
'there is/are not'[3]	ayin/en	אַיִן/אֵין	170
'if'	im	אִם	171
'you' (m. pl.)	attem	אַתֶּם	172
'nation, people'	goy	גּוֹי	173
'bring out'	hotsi	הוֹצִיא	174
'sin' (verb)	khata	חָטָא	175
'write'	katav	כָּתַב	176
'hundred'	me'a	מֵאָה	177
'personal property'	s^egulla	סְגֻלָּה	178

---

3. Opposite of יֵשׁ (vocabulary item 162).

'again, still, more'	*od*	עוֹד 179
'image'	*tselem*	צֶלֶם 180

Exercise (17)

1. Memorize Exodus 20:1–3 in Hebrew.

2. Analyse these verb forms, following the example.

Form	Root	Conjugation	PGN	Extras
שְׁלָחַנִי	שלח	pf.	3 m. sg.	suffix pronoun (1 c. sg.)
שְׁמַרְתִּיךָ				
אֶחֱטָא				
וָאֶשָּׂא				
יִשָּׂאֻהוּ				
וַיִּשָּׂאֶהָ				
יָשַׁבְתָּ				
יָשׁוּב				
וַיֵּשְׁבוּ				
וַיִּשְׁבּוּ				
וַיֵּשְׁבוּ				
תִּשְׂמַחְנָה				
יִכְתְּבֵם				

3. Translate and practise reading:

a לֹא־נָפַל דָּבָר מִכֹּל הַדָּבָר הַטּוֹב אֲשֶׁר־דִּבֶּר יְהוָה אֶל־בֵּית יִשְׂרָאֵל
הַכֹּל בָּא:

b הוֹדוּ לֵאלֹהֵי הָאֱלֹהִים   כִּי לְעוֹלָם חַסְדּוֹ:
הוֹדוּ לַאֲדֹנֵי הַשָּׁמָיִם   כִּי לְעוֹלָם חַסְדּוֹ:

c וַיֹּאמֶר אֱלֹהִים נַעֲשֶׂה⁴ אָדָם בְּצַלְמֵנוּ: וַיִּבְרָא אֱלֹהִים אֶת־הָאָדָם בְּצַלְמוֹ בְּצֶלֶם אֱלֹהִים בָּרָא אֹתוֹ:

d עָלָה מֹשֶׁה אֶל־הָאֱלֹהִים וַיִּקְרָא יְהוָה אֵלָיו⁵ מִן־הָהָר לֵאמֹר כֹּה תֹאמַר לְבֵית יַעֲקֹב: אַתֶּם רְאִיתֶם אֲשֶׁר עָשִׂיתִי לְמִצְרָיִם:

e וְעַתָּה אִם־תִּשְׁמְעוּ בְּקֹלִי וּשְׁמַרְתֶּם אֶת־בְּרִיתִי וִהְיִיתֶם⁶ לִי סְגֻלָּה מִכָּל־הָעַמִּים כִּי־לִי⁷ כָּל־הָאָרֶץ:

f וְאַתֶּם תִּהְיוּ־לִי מַמְלֶכֶת⁸ כֹּהֲנִים וְגוֹי קָדוֹשׁ אֵלֶּה הַדְּבָרִים אֲשֶׁר תְּדַבֵּר אֶל־בְּנֵי יִשְׂרָאֵל:

g וַיִּכְתֹּב מֹשֶׁה אֵת דִּבְרֵי הַבְּרִית עֲשֶׂרֶת הַדְּבָרִים:

h וַיֹּאמֶר מֹשֶׁה לְפַרְעֹה תֵּדַע כִּי־אֵין כַּיהוָה אֱלֹהֵינוּ:

i וְיָדַעְתָּ הַיּוֹם⁹ כִּי יְהוָה הוּא הָאֱלֹהִים בַּשָּׁמַיִם וְעַל־הָאָרֶץ אֵין עוֹד¹⁰:

j רָאִיתִי אֶת־הָאָרֶץ וְהִנֵּה־תֹהוּ וָבֹהוּ וְאֶל־הַשָּׁמַיִם וְאֵין אוֹרָם¹¹:

k וַיֹּאמְרוּ נִבְנֶה־לָּנוּ עִיר וְנַעֲשֶׂה¹²־לָּנוּ שֵׁם:

---

4. The first-person imperfect here is used for a plan: 'Let us …'. The form נִבְנֶה in sentence k is similar.

5. Preposition אֶל־ with suffix pronoun, not the noun אֵל (see 16.4.a).

6. The third waw conjunction in this sentence opens a subclause ('then').

7. לִי here means 'is mine' (lit. 'for me').

8. מַמְלֶכֶת (*mamlekhet*) is the construct form of מַמְלָכָה.

9. 'Today' (lit. 'the day').

10. 'There is no other' (lit. 'there is not more').

11. 'There was no light' (lit. 'there was not their light').

12. This is an example of the occasional use of imperfect with waw conjunction (not waw consecutive) to express purpose (see 13.2.e).

Verbs 3

The conjugations studied so far indicate the subject of the verb by means of suffixes (perfect, Lesson 9) and prefixes (imperfect, Lesson 13). However, Hebrew verbs are also found without either suffixes or prefixes that indicate their subject. In this lesson, we learn about the imperative (impv.) and participle (pt.).

18.1 Imperative

Imperatives express a command or request, generally addressed to another person (the second person in grammatical terms).

a. Hebrew imperatives are second-person imperfect forms without their prefixes. For example:

Imperative				Imperfect			Root
'hear!'	sh^{e}ma	שְׁמַע	←	'you hear'	tishma	תִּשְׁמַע	שמע
'take!'	qakh	קַח	←	'you take'	tiqqakh	תִּקַּח	לקח
'go!'	lekh	לֵךְ	←	'you go'	telekh	תֵּלֵךְ	הלך
'return!'	shuv	שׁוּב	←	'you return'	tashuv	תָּשׁוּב	שׁוּב

b. There are four imperative forms to match the gender and number of the person addressed. Here are the forms for שָׁמַר:

Imperative					Imperfect
2	m. sg.	'keep!'	sh^{e}mor	שְׁמֹר	←	תִּשְׁמֹר
	f. sg.	'keep!'	shimri	שִׁמְרִי	←	תִּשְׁמְרִי

2	m. pl.	'keep!'	*shimru*	שִׁמְרוּ	←	תִּשְׁמְרוּ
	f. pl.	'keep!'	*shemorna*	שְׁמֹרְנָה	←	תִּשְׁמֹרְנָה

In the first and last forms, the silent shewa on the first root letter becomes a vocal shewa. In the other two forms, it becomes an *i* vowel and the second (vocal) shewa becomes a silent shewa.

c. The masculine singular form sometimes has the suffix הָ. This often leads to a vowel change, as with other imperative suffixes. For example:

'keep!'	*shomra*	שָׁמְרָה	←	*shemor*	שְׁמֹר
'hear!'	*shim'a*	שִׁמְעָה	←	*shema*	שְׁמַע
'take!'	*qekha*	קְחָה	←	*qakh*	קַח

This suffix does not affect the meaning and may be ignored in translation.

d. Hebrew imperatives may be made more polite or emphatic by adding the word נָא (*na*, 'please'), often linked with a hyphen. For example:

'take!'	*qakh*	קַח
'please take'	*qakh-na*	קַח־נָא

e. Commands and requests refer to actions that are incomplete, so they may also be expressed in Hebrew by the imperfect, which is broad enough to include meanings like 'shall' and 'must'. For example:

'you shall say to Joseph'	תֹּאמְרוּ לְיוֹסֵף
'you must be holy'	קְדוֹשִׁים תִּהְיוּ

f. Hebrew imperatives are always positive, so prohibitions are expressed with the imperfect plus לֹא ('no, not') or אַל ('not'). For example:

'you shall not do' (= 'do not do')	לֹא תַעֲשֶׂה
'you must not say' (= 'do not say')	אַל־תֹּאמַר

g. The *jussive* is like a third-person imperative and expresses a command, request, or wish to a third party. It is often the same as the third-person imperfect, but sometimes has a shortened form (see 14.1). Jussive forms are explained as they occur in this book (see lesson 21 footnote 7; lesson 25 footnote 8; lesson 28.2; 29.4).

h. The *cohortative* is like a first-person imperative. It expresses a command, request, or wish to oneself or a group of people including the speaker. It is formed from the first-person imperfect by adding the suffix הָ. Cohortative forms are explained as they occur in this book (see 27.3; 28.3; lesson 30 footnotes 2 and 3).

18.2 Active Participle

Participles are verb forms that function as adjectives. They do not indicate tense, or whether an action is complete or incomplete, but describe a situation. In English, we are familiar with active participles like 'weeping' in 'a weeping child,' and passive participles like 'fortified' in 'a fortified city' and 'written' in 'a written account.'

a. Hebrew participles are formed from a root without prefixes or suffixes to indicate the subject. Active participles usually have an *o* vowel followed by an *e* vowel. For example:

Active participle				Root
'keeping'	*shomer*	שֹׁמֵר	←	שמר
'giving'	*noten*	נֹתֵן	←	נתן
'serving'	*oved*	עֹבֵד	←	עבד

Like adjectives, Hebrew participles sometimes function as nouns. So, in some contexts these participles could be translated 'keeper' (= 'one who keeps'), 'giver,' and 'servant' respectively.

b. The forms of active participles match their gender and number, with the same suffixes as for adjectives and nouns (see 11.1.c; 12.5). These are the forms for שָׁמַר:

Active participle			
m. sg.	'keeping, keeper'	*shomer*	שֹׁמֵר
f. sg.	'keeping, keeper'	*shomᵉra*	שֹׁמְרָה
m. pl.	'keeping, keepers'	*shomᵉrim*	שֹׁמְרִים
f. pl.	'keeping, keepers'	*shomᵉrot*	שֹׁמְרוֹת

It is enough to memorize these forms of the active participle, but three variations should be noted:

- The first vowel is often written with a vowel letter, for example שׁוֹמֵר (shomer, m. sg.).
- There is an alternative feminine singular form: שֹׁמֶרֶת (shomeret).
- The table gives the absolute forms. There are also construct forms, for example שֹׁמְרֵי (shomᵉre, m. pl.).

c. Active participles of hollow verbs (see 15.2) are the same as the simplest perfect form (3 m. sg.). For example:

Active participle				Perfect (3 m. sg.)		Root form
'coming'	ba	בָּא	←	'he came'	בָּא	בּוֹא
'dying, dead'	met	מֵת	←	'he died'	מֵת	מוּת

Suffixes are added to indicate gender and number, as above (18.2.b).

d. Participles may have a definite article, in which case the first letter is doubled as with adjectives and nouns. For example:

'the keeper'	hashshomer	הַשֹּׁמֵר	=	שֹׁמֵר	+	הַ
'the one who dies/is dead'	hammet	הַמֵּת	=	מֵת	+	הַ

e. Participles may also have suffix pronouns, and these are added to the construct or other short form as usual. For example:

'your keepers'	shomᵉrekha	שֹׁמְרֶיךָ	=	ךָ	+	שֹׁמְרִים
'his dying/dead'	meto	מֵתוֹ	=	וֹ	+	מֵת

18.3 Passive Participle

a. Hebrew participles also have passive forms, except for hollow verbs. Their distinctive vowels are *a* followed by *u*, and the *u* is usually written with a vowel letter. For example:

Passive participle				Root
'kept, guarded'	shamur	שָׁמוּר	←	שמר
'done, made'	asuy	עָשׂוּי	←	עשה
'blessed'	barukh	בָּרוּךְ	←	ברד

b. The forms of passive participles match their gender and number. These are the forms for שָׁמַר:

Passive participle			
m. sg.	'kept, guarded'	shamur	שָׁמוּר
f. sg.	'kept, guarded'	sheᵉmura	שְׁמוּרָה
m. pl.	'kept, guarded'	sheᵉmurim	שְׁמוּרִים
f. pl.	'kept, guarded'	sheᵉmurot	שְׁמוּרוֹת

There is one variation worth noting: the second vowel is often written without the vowel letter, for example שְׁמֻרָה (sheᵉmura, f. sg.).

Vocabulary (18)

'love' (verb)	ahav	אָהַב	181
'eat'	akhal	אָכַל	182
'daughter'	bat	בַּת[1]	183
'also, even'[2]	gam	גַּם	184
'living, alive' (adj.)[3]	khay	חַי	185
'give birth to, beget'	yalad	יָלַד	186
'sea'	yam	יָם	187

---

1. The plural is בָּנוֹת (banot). The a vowel becomes i with suffix pronouns: בִּתִּי etc.

2. Adds emphasis to the following word.

3. The singular form is used in the oath formula חַי־יְהוָה ('[as] the LORD is alive'). The plural חַיִּים (khayyim) can be a noun meaning 'life, lifetime.'

	'heart, mind'	lev/levav	לֵב/לֵבָב 188
	'please'	na	נָא 189
	'Nathan'	natan	נָתָן 190
	'midst, inward part'	qerev	קֶרֶב 191
	'put, place'	sim/sam	שִׂים/שָׂם 192

Exercise (18)

1. Memorize the imperative and participle forms of the verb שָׁמַר (see highlighted tables above).

2. Analyse the form of each imperative and participle:

Form	Root	Conjugation	PGN	Extras
שְׁמַע	שׁמע	impv.	2 m. sg.	—
שְׁמוּרָה	שׁמר	passive pt.	f. sg.	—
אֹהֲבָיו	אהב	active pt.	m. pl.	suffix pronoun (3 m. sg.)
שִׁמְרוּ				
קְחוּ				
לֵךְ				
שָׂא־נָא				
עֲשֵׂה				
נֹתֵן				
שֹׁמְעִים				
עֲשׂוֹת				
יָלוּד				
כְּתוּבוֹת				
שָׁמְעִי				
הָמֵת				

3. Translate and practise reading:

a   וַיֹּאמֶר יְהוָה שְׁמַע בְּקוֹל הָעָם לְכֹל אֲשֶׁר־יֹאמְרוּ אֵלֶיךָ:

b   וַיִּקְרָא הַמֶּלֶךְ אֶל־דָּוִד וַיֹּאמֶר אֵלָיו עַתָּה שׁוּב וְלֵךְ בְּשָׁלוֹם
וְלֹא־תַעֲשֶׂה רָע בְּעֵינֵי פְלִשְׁתִּים:

c   הָיָה דָבָר אֶל־הַנָּבִיא מֵאֵת⁴ יְהוָה לֵאמֹר: שִׁמְעוּ
אֶת־דִּבְרֵי הַבְּרִית הַזֹּאת:

d   שׁוֹמֵר יְהוָה אֶת־כָּל־אֹהֲבָיו: יְהוָה אֹהֵב צַדִּיקִים:

e   עֹשֶׂה שָׁלוֹם וּבֹרֵא רָע אֲנִי יְהוָה עֹשֶׂה כָל־אֵלֶּה:

f   בָּרֲכִי⁵ נַפְשִׁי אֶת־יְהוָה וְכָל־קְרָבַי אֶת־שֵׁם קָדְשׁוֹ⁶:

g   יְהוָה עָשָׂה שָׁמַיִם וָאָרֶץ אֶת־הַיָּם וְאֶת־כָּל־אֲשֶׁר־בָּם:

h   אָמַר־לָהּ הֲשָׁלוֹם לָךְ הֲשָׁלוֹם לְאִישֵׁךְ וַתֹּאמֶר שָׁלוֹם:

i   וַיֹּאמֶר שְׁלֹמֹה יְהוָה אֱלֹהֵי יִשְׂרָאֵל אֵין־כָּמוֹךָ⁷ אֱלֹהִים בַּשָּׁמַיִם וְעַל־
הָאָרֶץ שֹׁמֵר הַבְּרִית וְהַחֶסֶד לַעֲבָדֶיךָ הַהֹלְכִים לְפָנֶיךָ בְּכָל־לִבָּם⁸:

j   וְנָתַתִּי לָכֶם לֵב חָדָשׁ וְרוּחַ חֲדָשָׁה אֶתֵּן בְּקִרְבְּכֶם:

k   בַּגּוֹיִם⁹ הָרַבִּים לֹא־הָיָה מֶלֶךְ כִּשְׁלֹמֹה מֶלֶךְ יִשְׂרָאֵל
וְאָהוּב לֵאלֹהָיו¹⁰ הָיָה וַיִּתְּנֵהוּ אֱלֹהִים מֶלֶךְ עַל־כָּל־יִשְׂרָאֵל:

l   כַּאֲשֶׁר כָּתוּב בְּתוֹרַת מֹשֶׁה כָּל־הָרָעָה הַזֹּאת בָּאָה עָלֵינוּ:

m   וַיֹּאמֶר דָּוִד אֶל־נָתָן חַי־יְהוָה כִּי בֶן־מָוֶת¹¹ הָאִישׁ הָעֹשֶׂה זֹאת:
וַיֹּאמֶר נָתָן אֶל־דָּוִד אַתָּה הָאִישׁ:

---

4. Preposition מִן with preposition אֵת ('with'), not the word מֵאָה.

5. Imperative, 2 sg. f., addressed to the speaker's own נֶפֶשׁ.

6. The first vowel has no *meteg*, so it is pronounced *o*, not *a*.

7. Preposition כְּ with suffix pronoun (see 16.3.b).

8. Noun לֵב with suffix pronoun.

9. The preposition בְּ here may be translated 'among.'

10. The preposition לְ means 'by' in this sentence.

11. Literally, 'son of death.' It may be translated 'should die' in this context.

Verbs 4

There are two further conjugations of the verb in Hebrew that do not have prefixes or suffixes to indicate their subject. Both are called 'infinitive' because they are not limited to a specific subject:

- The infinitive absolute (inf. abs.) functions like an adverb, usually to add emphasis to a regular verb form.
- The infinitive construct (inf. cstr.) functions like an English infinitive or verbal noun (gerund).

Neither conjugation changes to match person, gender, or number, so they each have only one form. The forms for four key kinds of root are:

	Strong	**Final ה**	**Initial י**	**Hollow**
Infinitive absolute	שָׁמוֹר *shamor*	רָאֹה *ra'o*	יָשׁוֹב *yashov*	שׁוֹב *shov*
Infinitive construct	שְׁמֹר *sheᵉmor*	רְאוֹת *reᵉ'ot*	שֶׁבֶת *shevet*	שׁוּב *shuv*

These will now be explained in more detail.

19.1 Infinitive Absolute

a. The distinctive vowels of the infinitive absolute are *a* and *o*. Often the *o* is written with a vowel letter. For example:

Infinitive absolute			Root
akhol	אָכֹל	←	אכל
halokh	הָלוֹךְ	←	הלך
ra'o	רָאֹה	←	ראה
naton	נָתוֹן	←	נתן

Hollow verbs have only one syllable in the infinitive absolute, with an *o* vowel. For example:

shov	שׁוֹב	←	שׁוּב

b. The most common use of the infinitive absolute is together with another form of the same verb, functioning as an adverb to strengthen or add certainty. For example:

'you shall watch'	תִּשְׁמֹר
'you shall watch watchfully'	שָׁמוֹר תִּשְׁמֹר

The word 'watchfully' is an adverb formed from the verb 'watch,' so is an approximate equivalent in English. But this rarely works with English verbs, so it is usually best to add an alternative adverb that fits the context. For example:

'listen carefully!'	שִׁמְעוּ שָׁמוֹעַ	'listen!'	שִׁמְעוּ
'you may eat freely'	אָכֹל תֹּאכֵל	'you may eat'	תֹּאכֵל
'you will surely die'	מוֹת תָּמוּת	'you will die'	תָּמוּת

This makes more sense than to translate the expressions literally as 'listen listeningly' or 'eat eatingly.' As the examples show, the infinitive absolute may come before or after the verb with which it is linked.

c. Sometimes an infinitive absolute is used as an imperative. For example:

'keep the sabbath day'	שָׁמוֹר אֶת־יוֹם הַשַּׁבָּת

d. Occasionally a pair of infinitive absolutes is used as an adverbial phrase to describe two actions that occur at the same time. For example:

'and the water receded gradually'	וַיָּשֻׁבוּ הַמַּיִם הָלוֹךְ וָשׁוֹב
(lit. 'and the water returned goingly and returningly')	

19.2 Infinitive Construct – Forms

There are several ways in which the infinitive construct is formed.

a. For strong verbs, and some weak verbs, the infinitive construct is a shortened form of the infinitive absolute, usually with a shewa in the first syllable and *o* vowel in the second. For example:

Infinitive construct			Infinitive absolute		Root
sh^{e}mor	שְׁמֹר	←	שָׁמוֹר	←	שמר
^{e}mor	אֱמֹר	←	אָמוֹר	←	אמר

This form is usually identical to the imperative, 2 m. sg. (see 18.1), so the two can only be distinguished from their context in a sentence.

b. For roots with final ה, the infinitive construct is also a shortened form of the infinitive absolute. The letter ה usually becomes ת and the *o* vowel is written with a vowel letter. This is like the change of ה to ת in the construct form of feminine nouns (11.3.c). For example:

Infinitive construct			Infinitive absolute		Root
r^{e}ot	רְאוֹת	←	רָאֹה	←	ראה
^{a}sot	עֲשׂוֹת	←	עָשֹׂה	←	עשה

c. For roots with initial **י**, this weak letter is usually omitted in the infinitive construct and **ת** added at the end. The two syllables often have identical vowels. It is similar for the roots **הלך** and **לקח**. For example:

Infinitive construct			Root
da̲at	דַּעַת	←	ידע
she̲vet	שֶׁבֶת	←	ישׁב
le̲khet	לֶכֶת	←	הלך
qa̲khat	קַחַת	←	לקח

d. For roots where the initial and final letters are both weak, there may be further changes from the patterns explained above. For example:

Infinitive construct			Root
tset	צֵאת	←	יצא
te̲t	תֵּת	←	נתן

The root **יצא** loses the initial **י** and gains a **ת** in the infinitive construct, following the pattern in the previous paragraph. In addition, the final **א** of the root becomes silent, so the resulting form has just one syllable. The root **נתן** has a final **ן** as well as an initial **נ**. Both are omitted in the infinitive construct, so only the middle **ת** and added **ת** remain. The form **תֵּת** is very common so is worth memorizing.

e. For hollow verbs (see 15.2), the infinitive construct is the same as the root form. For example:

Infinitive construct			Root form
bo	בּוֹא/בֹּא	←	בּוֹא
shuv	שׁוּב	←	שׁוּב

19.3 Infinitive Construct – Meaning

The infinitive construct in Hebrew is similar to an English infinitive (e.g. 'to do') or verbal noun ending with 'ing' (gerund). For example, עֲשׂוֹת may be translated 'to do' or 'doing', depending on the context.

a. The infinitive construct is often prefixed with the preposition לְ ('to, for'). It functions like an English infinitive, expressing the purpose or result of an action. For example:

'I promised to keep your words' (lit. 'I said to keep your words')	אָמַרְתִּי לִשְׁמֹר דְּבָרֶיךָ
'Then they sat [down] to eat'	וַיֵּשְׁבוּ לֶאֱכֹל
'he came to see the house'	בָּא לִרְאוֹת אֶת־הַבַּיִת

b. The infinitive construct of אמר with preposition לְ is distinctive. The initial א becomes silent, so it is written לֵאמֹר (lemor). It introduces direct speech and is equivalent to quotation marks. For example:

'The LORD said, "…"' (lit. 'The LORD spoke, to say, "…"')	דִּבֶּר יְהוָה לֵאמֹר …

c. The infinitive construct may also be prefixed by other prepositions, especially בְּ and כְּ, with a temporal meaning. The preposition may be translated 'when' or 'while'. For example:

'when Nathan came to him' (lit. 'at the coming to him of Nathan')	בְּבוֹא־אֵלָיו נָתָן
'when Moses went out' (lit. 'as the going out of Moses')	כְּצֵאת מֹשֶׁה

d. The infinitive construct may be linked with a noun, with the noun functioning as its subject or object. For example:

'dwelling of brothers' (subject)	שֶׁבֶת אַחִים
'knowing good and evil' (object)	דַּעַת טוֹב וָרָע

Some of these infinitives function more like nouns than verbs and may be preceded by another noun in the construct form, for example עֵץ הַדַּעַת ('tree of knowing').

e. The infinitive construct may be used with suffix pronouns, with the pronoun functioning as the subject or object. For example:

'your going out and your coming in' (subject)	צֵאתְךָ וּבֹאֶךָ
'to keep you from an evil woman' (object)	לִשְׁמָרְךָ מֵאִשָּׁה רָעָה

In this case, the infinitive construct is often shortened, as when suffix pronouns are added to nouns (16.2) and verbs (16.3). For example, שֶׁבֶת with a suffix pronoun is shortened to שִׁבְתִּי etc.

'a house for me to dwell' (lit. 'a house for my dwelling')	בַּיִת לְשִׁבְתִּי
'when you are at home or away' (lit. 'in your sitting and in your going')	בְּשִׁבְתְּךָ וּבְלֶכְתְּךָ

Vocabulary (19)

'not'	al	אַל	193
'understand'	bin	בִּין[1]	194
'not, except'	bilti	בִּלְתִּי	195
'tell'	higgid	הִגִּיד	196
'dry land'	yabbasha	יַבָּשָׁה	197
'unity, together'	yakhad	יַחַד	198
'work, occupation'	melakha	מְלָאכָה	199
'Hebrew' (noun and adj.)[2]	ivri	עִבְרִי	200
'with'	im	עִם[3]	201

---

1. Although this is a hollow verb, the 3 m. sg. perfect form is usually the same as the root form.

2. This word denotes ethnicity. There is no word for the language in biblical Hebrew, but it is called עִבְרִית (ivrit) in Modern Hebrew.

3. The מ is doubled when עִם has suffix pronouns, e.g. עִמִּי (immi) 'with me'; עִמָּנוּ אֵל (immanu el) 'God with us' (Isa 7:14; cf. Matt 1:23). Often the letter ד is added too, e.g. עִמָּדִי (immadi) 'with me.'

'tree, wood'[4]	ets	עֵץ	202
'command' (verb)	tsiwwa	צִוָּה	203
'tend, graze'	ra'a	רָעָה	204

Exercise (19)

1. Memorize the infinitive absolute and construct forms of the four key roots in the highlighted table above.

2. Analyse the infinitive forms below:

Form	Root	Conjugation	PGN	Extras
וְשׁוֹב	שׁוֹב	inf. abs.	—	waw conjunction
לֶכֶת	הלך	inf. cstr.	—	—
הָלוֹךְ				
שָׁמוֹעַ				
רָאֹה				
רְאוֹת				
לַעֲשׂוֹת				
דַּעַת				
בְּבוֹא				
אֲכָלְךָ				
צֵאתְךָ				
שִׁבְתִּי				
בְּלֶכְתְּךָ				
בְּצֵאתוֹ				

4. The meaning 'wood' refers to timber, not a group of trees.

3. Translate and practise reading:

a וַיָּשֻׁבוּ הַמַּיִם מֵעַל הָאָרֶץ הָלוֹךְ וָשׁוֹב:

b וָאֶשְׁמַע אֶת־קוֹל אֲדֹנָי אֹמֵר אֶת־מִי אֶשְׁלַח וּמִי יֵלֶךְ־לָנוּ וָאֹמַר
הִנְנִי שְׁלָחֵנִי: וַיֹּאמֶר לֵךְ וְאָמַרְתָּ לָעָם הַזֶּה שִׁמְעוּ שָׁמוֹעַ וְאַל־תָּבִינוּ
וּרְאוּ רָאֹה וְאַל־תֵּדָעוּ:

c וְאַחַר כֵּן⁵ יָבֹא הַכֹּהֵן לִרְאוֹת אֶת־הַבָּיִת:

d הִנֵּה מַה־טּוֹב וּמַה־נָּעִים שֶׁבֶת אַחִים גַּם־יָחַד⁶:

e מִזְמוֹר לְדָוִד⁷ בְּבוֹא־אֵלָיו נָתָן הַנָּבִיא כַּאֲשֶׁר⁸־בָּא אֶל־בַּת־שָׁבַע⁹:

f וַיְצַו¹⁰ יְהוָה אֱלֹהִים עַל־הָאָדָם¹¹ לֵאמֹר מִכֹּל עֵץ אָכֹל תֹּאכֵל: וּמֵעֵץ הַדַּעַת
טוֹב וָרָע לֹא תֹאכַל מִמֶּנּוּ¹² כִּי בְּיוֹם אֲכָלְךָ¹³ מִמֶּנּוּ מוֹת תָּמוּת:

g וַתֵּרֶא הָאִשָּׁה כִּי טוֹב הָעֵץ וַתִּקַּח וַתֹּאכַל וַתִּתֵּן גַּם־לְאִישָׁהּ עִמָּהּ וַיֹּאכַל:

h וַיֹּאמֶר יְהוָה אֱלֹהִים הָאָדָם הָיָה כְּאַחַד מִמֶּנּוּ לָדַעַת טוֹב וָרָע:

i יְהוָה יִשְׁמָר צֵאתְךָ וּבוֹאֶךָ מֵעַתָּה וְעַד־עוֹלָם:

j אַתָּה יָדַעְתָּ¹⁴ שִׁבְתִּי וְקוּמִי:

k וַיִּשְׂאוּ אֶת־עֵינֵיהֶם וַיִּרְאוּ אֶת־הָאָרוֹן וַיִּשְׂמְחוּ לִרְאוֹת:

l וַיַּרְא מֹשֶׁה אֶת־כָּל־הַמְּלָאכָה וְהִנֵּה עָשׂוּ אֹתָהּ כַּאֲשֶׁר צִוָּה יְהוָה כֵּן עָשׂוּ
וַיְבָרֶךְ אֹתָם מֹשֶׁה:

---

5. כֵּן ('thus, so') means 'this' here.

6. This phrase may be translated 'in unity' or 'all together' (lit. 'even together').

7. The preposition לְ probably means 'of' in this context.

8. כַּאֲשֶׁר ('as that') means 'after' in this sentence.

9. בַּת־שָׁבַע (*bat-shẹva*) is a personal name: 'Bathsheba.'

10. וַיְצַו is from צָוָה (not יָצָא), impf., 3 m. sg., with waw consecutive. The third-person prefix י is not doubled because it has a shewa (13.2.d). The final ה has dropped out because of the waw consecutive (13.3.d).

11. אָדָם with the definite article means 'the man' or 'mankind'; without it, it is 'a man,' 'mankind,' or 'Adam.'

12. מִמֶּנּוּ is from מִן with a suffix pronoun, plus an extra מ between the preposition and suffix (cf. 16.3.b). The suffix appears to be 3 m. sg. (נוּ ָ), but with מִן the 1 c. pl. suffix also has a double letter (נּוּ ָ instead of נוּ). Both meanings are found in this exercise, and they can only be distinguished from the context.

13. The suffix pronoun makes the word definite, so when translating בְּיוֹם add a definite article (cf. 11.3.d).

14. The perfect with a verb of perception may be translated as present tense (see 9.2.c).

Conversation

We are studying biblical Hebrew as a written language, like other ancient languages that are studied through books and written exercises. However, languages are first spoken and later written. Although we only have access to the language of the Old Testament in its written form, Hebrew was a spoken language long before anyone wrote it down. We should also be aware that it is still used as an everyday language by several million people today.

This lesson aims to give some idea of what Hebrew conversation might have been like, making use of two short conversations recorded in the Old Testament. The modern Hebrew word for 'conversation' is שִׂיחָה (sikha), from the Old Testament verb שִׂיחַ ('meditate, talk').

20.1 Jacob and the Angel (Gen 32:28, 30)

שִׂיחָה א׳

ANGEL:	מַה־שְּׁמֶךָ׃
JACOB:	יַעֲקֹב הַגִּידָה־נָּא שְׁמֶךָ׃

The verse numbering here follows the Hebrew Bible. In English Bibles, this short conversation is found in Genesis 32:27, 29.

מַה־שְּׁמֶךָ 'What [is] your name?': the noun שֵׁם ('name') has a suffix pronoun (2 m. sg.). The double שׁ and shortened vowel from long *a* (מָה) to short *a* (מַה), plus the hyphen, mark a close relationship between the two words, so they are pronounced as one: *mashsh^emekha*.

יַעֲקֹב: Jacob replies by simply stating his name.

הַגִּידָה־נָּא: Then Jacob asks the angel's name, in different words. The first word is an imperative form of the hiphil verb הִגִּיד ('tell'). This is supplemented by the word נָא

('please'), linked to the verb with a hyphen and doubling of the נ. The accent in the second syllable of הַגִּידָה indicates that the pronunciation should be *haggida*, not *haggidā*.

20.2 Jonah and the Sailors (Jonah 1:8–9)

שִׂיחָה ב׳

SAILORS:	מַה־מְּלַאכְתְּךָ וּמֵאַיִן תָּבוֹא מָה אַרְצֶךָ וְאֵי־מִזֶּה עַם אָתָּה:
JONAH:	עִבְרִי אָנֹכִי וְאֶת־יְהוָה אֱלֹהֵי הַשָּׁמַיִם אֲנִי יָרֵא אֲשֶׁר־עָשָׂה אֶת־הַיָּם וְאֶת־הַיַּבָּשָׁה:

The sailors discover that Jonah is responsible for the terrible storm that is endangering their lives and ask him four questions.

a. מַה־מְּלַאכְתְּךָ 'What is your occupation?'
The noun מְלָאכָה ('work, occupation') has a suffix pronoun (2 m. sg.). Note the double מ, indicating that the two words should be pronounced as one: *mammᵉlakhtᵉkha*. Jonah does not answer the sailors' first question. He could have replied:

'I am a prophet'	נָבִיא אָנֹכִי

But he may be embarrassed to say this when he is running away from God's call to prophesy in Nineveh. Interestingly, Amos – who prophesies obediently in Israel when God calls him – denies he is a professional prophet and prefers to be known for his everyday occupation (7:14):

'I am not a prophet … I am a herdsman'	לֹא נָבִיא אָנֹכִי … בּוֹקֵר אָנֹכִי

Participles are often used to describe occupations. For example:

- רֹעֵה צֹאן 'one who tends sheep' = 'shepherd' (Gen 4:2);
- עֹבֵד אֲדָמָה 'one who works land' = 'farmer' (Gen 4:2);
- שֹׁפֵט 'judge, leader' (from verb שָׁפַט 'judge')
- כֹּהֵן 'priest' (from root כהן 'be a priest').

Other occupations mentioned in the Old Testament include:

מֶלֶךְ	'king'	2500 times
עֶבֶד	'servant'	800 times
חָכָם	'wise [person]'	Jer 18:18
גִּבּוֹר	'hero, warrior'	Gen 6:4; 10:8
מְלַמֵּד	'teacher'	Ps 119:99
לִמּוּד	'student, disciple'	Isa 8:16; 50:4
חָרָשׁ	'skilled worker'	2 Kgs 24:16

b. מֵאַיִן תָּבוֹא 'From where do you come?'

מֵאַיִן: particle אַי ('where?, which?'), not אַיִן ('there is not'), with short form of מִן. Compare the sailors' second question with Joshua's question to the Hivites (Josh 9:8): מִי אַתֶּם וּמֵאַיִן תָּבֹאוּ ('Who are you and from where do you come?'). The Hivites give a false answer (v. 9), but Jonah simply ignores the question. He could have replied:

'From Gath Hepher'	מִגַּת הַחֵפֶר

This was Jonah's hometown in northern Israel (2 Kgs 14:25).

c. מָה אַרְצֶךָ 'What is your land?'

מָה stands alone this time, so is not pronounced as one word with אַרְצֶךָ. The sailors' third question is also not answered by Jonah. His land was called אֶרֶץ כְּנַעַן (erets kᵉnaʿan) in Old Testament times, though Israelis now call it אֶרֶץ יִשְׂרָאֵל while Arabs and most other people prefer 'Palestine.'

Other important lands mentioned in the Old Testament are מִצְרַיִם ('Egypt'), אֲרָם ('Aram'), בָּבֶל ('Babylon'), and אַשּׁוּר ('Assyria'). Modern Hebrew has many new names, for example אַנְגְּלִיָּה ('England'), אַרְצוֹת הַבְּרִית ('United States'), and סִין ('China').

d. אֵי־מִזֶּה עַם אָתָּה 'From which people are you?'

אֵי־מִזֶּה means literally 'where (or which) from this?', but here can be translated simply 'from which.' Absalom's question to Israelites on their way to the royal court of appeal has the same form (2 Sam 15:2):

'From which town are you?'	אֵי־מִזֶּה עִיר אָתָּה

In modern terms, the sailors are asking, 'What is your nationality?' Only this last question is answered by Jonah, in just two words:

'I am a Hebrew'	עִבְרִי אָנֹכִי

Israelites usually identify themselves as עִבְרִי when speaking to foreigners (e.g. Gen 40:15; Exod 1:19). The term יִשְׂרְאֵלִי ('Israelite') is only found five times in the Old Testament. Much more common is the phrase בְּנֵי יִשְׂרָאֵל (lit. 'children of Israel'), which is usually translated 'Israelites' or 'people of Israel.' Other important peoples in Old Testament times were פְּלִשְׁתִּי ('Philistine'), כְּנַעֲנִי ('Canaanite'), מִצְרִי ('Egyptian'), and אֲרַמִּי ('Aramean').

e. Jonah answers just one of the sailors' four questions, then supplements his brief answer with a confession of faith: 'I am a worshipper of the LORD, God of heaven, who made the sea and dry land.' One detail may be noted about the language. יָרֵא is an active participle of the verb יָרֵא ('be afraid, fear') and means 'fearing' or 'one who fears' (cf. ESV). In this context the translation 'worship' is also appropriate (so NIV, NRSV).

The content of Jonah's confession is significant. He begins by stating the name of his God (יְהוָה), then mentions two key beliefs about him in language that is sufficiently general and simple to be understood by the pagan sailors: he is 'God of heaven' and he 'made the sea and dry land.' Abraham's description of the LORD is similar (Gen 24:3):

'God of heaven and God of earth'	אֱלֹהֵי הַשָּׁמַיִם וֵאלֹהֵי הָאָרֶץ

We may compare it with how Nehemiah addresses God when he prays (Neh 1:5):

'God of heaven, the great and awesome God; keeping the covenant and steadfast love, with those who love him and keep his commandments'	אֱלֹהֵי הַשָּׁמַיִם הָאֵל הַגָּדוֹל וְהַנּוֹרָא שֹׁמֵר הַבְּרִית וָחֶסֶד לְאֹהֲבָיו וּלְשֹׁמְרֵי מִצְוֹתָיו׃

Belief in the LORD as maker of sea and land is also expressed by a psalmist (Ps 95:5):

'The sea is his and he made it; and his hands formed dry land.'	לוֹ הַיָּם וְהוּא עָשָׂהוּ וְיַבֶּשֶׁת יָדָיו יָצָרוּ:

יַבֶּשֶׁת (yabbǝshet) is an alternative form of יַבָּשָׁה.

20.3 Hebrew Song 5 (*Adonay Yishmorkha*)

יְהוָה יִשְׁמָרְךָ מִכָּל־רָע יִשְׁמֹר אֶת־נַפְשֶׁךָ מִכָּל־רָע:
יְהוָה יִשְׁמָר צֵאתְךָ וּבוֹאֶךָ מֵעַתָּה וְעַד־עוֹלָם: (x2)

> See mini songbook for music

The LORD will keep you from all evil;
   he will keep your life from all evil.
The LORD will keep your going out and your coming in;
   from now and until eternity. *(Ps 121:7–8)*

Vocabulary (20)

'perish, be lost'	avad	אָבַד	205
'land, ground'[1]	ᵃdama	אֲדָמָה	206
'where? which?'[2]	e/ayye	אֵי/אַיֵּה	207
'mother'	em	אֵם[3]	208
'curse' (verb)	arar	אָרַר	209
'fire'	esh	אֵשׁ	210
'be afraid, fear'	yare	יָרֵא	211
'thing, vessel, utensil'	kᵉli	כְּלִי	212
'learn'	lamad	לָמַד	213
'naked'	erom	עֵירֹם	214
'sheep, goats, flock'	tson	צֹאן	215
'go near, approach'	qarav	קָרַב	216

---

1. See Gen 2:7 and 3:19 for the connection between אֲדָמָה ('land, ground') and אָדָם ('man, mankind').
2. With prefix preposition מִן, this word becomes מֵאַיִן ('from where?').
3. The plural is אִמּוֹת. With a suffix pronoun, it becomes אִמִּי etc.

Exercise (20)

1. Memorize the two conversations in this lesson so that you can take parts to act them out. There is no need to memorize the written form.

2. Translate and practise reading the following. There are three new personal names in this exercise that are not in the vocabularies: הֶבֶל (hevel) 'Abel'; חַוָּה (khawwa) 'Eve'; and קַיִן (qayin) 'Cain.'

a וַיִּקְרָא יְהוָה אֱלֹהִים אֶל־הָאָדָם וַיֹּאמֶר לוֹ אַיֶּכָּה:
וַיֹּאמֶר אֶת־קֹלְךָ שָׁמַעְתִּי וָאִירָא כִּי־עֵירֹם אָנֹכִי:

b וַיֹּאמֶר מִי הִגִּיד לְךָ כִּי עֵירֹם אָתָּה הֲמִן הָעֵץ אֲשֶׁר צִוִּיתִיךָ
לְבִלְתִּי אֲכָל־מִמֶּנּוּ אָכָלְתָּ:

c וַיֹּאמֶר הָאָדָם הָאִשָּׁה אֲשֶׁר נָתַתָּ עִמָּדִי⁴ הִיא נָתְנָה־לִי
מִן־הָעֵץ וָאֹכֵל⁵: וַיֹּאמֶר יְהוָה אֱלֹהִים לָאִשָּׁה מַה־זֹּאת עָשִׂית:

d וּלְאָדָם אָמַר כִּי שָׁמַעְתָּ לְקוֹל אִשְׁתֶּךָ וַתֹּאכַל מִן־הָעֵץ אֲשֶׁר צִוִּיתִיךָ לֵאמֹר
לֹא תֹאכַל מִמֶּנּוּ אֲרוּרָה הָאֲדָמָה כֹּל יְמֵי חַיֶּיךָ⁶:

e וַיִּקְרָא הָאָדָם שֵׁם אִשְׁתּוֹ חַוָּה כִּי הִיא הָיְתָה אֵם כָּל־חָי:

f יָדַע הָאָדָם אֶת־חַוָּה אִשְׁתּוֹ וַתֵּלֶד אֶת־קַיִן: וַיְהִי־הֶבֶל רֹעֵה צֹאן
וְקַיִן הָיָה עֹבֵד אֲדָמָה:

g וַיֹּאמֶר יְהוָה אֶל־קַיִן אֵי הֶבֶל אָחִיךָ וַיֹּאמֶר לֹא יָדַעְתִּי⁷ הֲשֹׁמֵר אָחִי אָנֹכִי:
וַיֹּאמֶר מֶה⁸ עָשִׂיתָ וְעַתָּה אָרוּר אַתָּה מִן־הָאֲדָמָה: וַיֵּצֵא קַיִן מִלִּפְנֵי יְהוָה:

h וַיִּקְרָא מֹשֶׁה אֶל־כָּל־יִשְׂרָאֵל וַיֹּאמֶר אֲלֵהֶם שְׁמַע יִשְׂרָאֵל אֶת־הַמִּשְׁפָּטִים
וּלְמַדְתֶּם אֹתָם וּשְׁמַרְתֶּם לַעֲשֹׂתָם:

i רְאוּ עַתָּה כִּי אֲנִי אֲנִי הוּא וְאֵין אֱלֹהִים עִמָּדִי:

j וְהִנֵּה אָנֹכִי עִמָּךְ וּשְׁמַרְתִּיךָ בְּכֹל אֲשֶׁר־תֵּלֵךְ⁹:

---

4. See lesson 19 footnote 3.

5. אֹכֵל is an imperfect form, 1 c. sg., which happens to be identical in form to the active participle.

6. חַיִּים is the plural of adjective חַי (vocabulary item 185), used as a noun meaning 'life,' here in shortened form with a suffix pronoun.

7. This perfect form should be translated here as present tense.

8. מֶה = מַה.

9. Suggested translation: 'wherever you go' (lit. 'in all that you go').

3. Write a short conversation in Hebrew using the material studied in this lesson. These phrases may also be useful:

'Greetings, peace' (to a group)	שָׁלוֹם אֲלֵיכֶם
'Greetings, peace' (to a man/woman)	שָׁלוֹם לְךָ/לָךְ
'How are you?' (to a man/woman)	מָה שְׁלוֹמְךָ/שְׁלוֹמֵךְ
'Good morning'	בֹּקֶר טוֹב
'Good evening'	עֶרֶב טוֹב
'Thank you very much'	תּוֹדָה רַבָּה
'Goodbye, see you later' (lit. 'to see again')	לְהִתְרָאוֹת

4. Practise the Hebrew song *Adonay Yishmorkha*.

Figure 12. Manhole Cover in English, Hebrew, Arabic, and Russian.[10]

---

10. Photo 'Optical cable manhole' by Hyrdlak / CC0 1.0.

Complex Stems 1

We have already seen that most Hebrew verbs have three-letter roots (e.g. שׁמר). When vowels are added to a root, it becomes a stem (e.g. שָׁמַר). This simple stem is called qal (קַל 'light, quick').

There are also several complex stems. They are often called 'derived stems' because they appear to be derived from the qal stem, though it may be more accurate to see them as alternative stems to the qal. Some books call them 'verb patterns' rather than stems. The Modern Hebrew term is בִּנְיָן (lit. 'building,' from root בנה). In this lesson, we study three complex stems: niphal, hiphil, and hophal. The names are taken from the corresponding forms of the verb פָּעַל (pa'al) 'do, make,' for example נִפְעַל (nif'al, commonly written 'niphal').

21.1 Niphal

The niphal stem (נִפְעַל) is formed from a three-letter root by adding the prefix נ (n), often followed by the vowels i and a. It usually has a passive meaning. For example:

Niphal			Qal		
'be kept'	nishmar	נִשְׁמַר	'keep'	shamar	שָׁמַר
'be heard'	nishma	נִשְׁמַע	'hear'	shama	שָׁמַע
'be found'	nimtsa	נִמְצָא	'find'	matsa	מָצָא

This pattern is followed by strong verbs, but there are variations in some weak verbs. Three of these variations should be noted.

a. Verbs with an initial guttural usually have a short e vowel on the niphal prefix instead of i, followed by a compound shewa on the guttural letter. For example:

'be said'	neᵉmar	נֶאֱמַר	'say'	amar	אָמַר
'be gathered'	neᵉsaf	נֶאֱסַף	'gather'	asaf	אָסַף

b. Initial **י** usually becomes **וֹ** in the niphal stem. For example:

'be known'	*noda*	נוֹדַע	'know'	*yada*	יָדַע
'be born'	*nolad*	נוֹלַד	'give birth to'	*yalad*	יָלַד

c. Initial **נ** merges with the following letter to make a double letter. For example:

'be lifted'	*nissa*	נִשָּׂא	'lift'	*nasa*	נָשָׂא
'be given'	*nittan*	נִתַּן	'give'	*natan*	נָתַן

21.2 Hiphil

The most common stem, apart from qal, is formed with the prefix **ה** (*h*), usually with a short *i* vowel and infix **ִי** (*i*). This stem is called 'hiphil' (הִפְעִיל). It often has a causative meaning (making something happen). For example:

Hiphil			Qal		
'bring near'	*hiqriv*	הִקְרִיב	'approach'	*qarav*	קָרַב
'make heard'	*hishmia*	הִשְׁמִיעַ	'hear'	*shama*	שָׁמַע

This pattern is followed by strong verbs, but there are variations in many weak verbs. The first three variations are similar to those for niphal stems mentioned above.

a. Verbs with an initial guttural have a short *e* vowel on the hiphil prefix instead of *i*, followed by a compound shewa on the guttural letter. For example:

'strengthen'	*hekhᵉziq*	הֶחֱזִיק	'be strong'	*khazaq*	חָזַק
'cause to stand'	*heᵉmid*	הֶעֱמִיד	'stand'	*amad*	עָמַד

b. Initial **י** usually becomes **וֹ** in the hiphil stem, though the vowel letter is sometimes omitted leaving just the vowel sign **ֹ**. For example:

'bring out'	*hotsi*	הוֹצִיא	'go out'	*yatsa*	יָצָא
'increase, do again'	*hosif*	הוֹסִיף	'add'	*yasaf*	יָסַף

c. Initial נ merges with the following letter to make a double letter. For example:

'make fall, cast'	*hippil*	הִפִּיל	'fall'	*nafal*	נָפַל
'tell'	*higgid*	הִגִּיד	(not used)	*n-g-d*	נגד

d. In hollow verbs, the middle vowel letter drops out and is replaced by the infix יִ. The prefix vowel is usually *e*. For example:

'bring in, carry'	*hevi*	הֵבִיא	'come, go in'	*bo*	בּוֹא
'kill, execute'	*hemit*	הֵמִית	'die'	*mut*	מוּת

e. Verbs with a final ה have a long *a* vowel instead of the infix יִ. For example:

'make many'	*hirba*	הִרְבָּה	'be many'	*rava*	רָבָה
'bring up, offer'	*heᵉla*	הֶעֱלָה	'go up'	*ala*	עָלָה

21.3 Hophal

The hophal stem (הָפְעַל) is the passive form of the hiphil. It is also formed with the prefix ה (*h*) but followed by different vowels: *o* or *u* in the first syllable, then *a* in the second. For example:

Hophal	Hiphil	Niphal	Qal
horᵃa הָרְאָה 'be shown'	*herᵃa* הֶרְאָה 'show'	*nirᵃa* נִרְאָה 'appear, be seen'	*raᵃ* רָאָה 'see'
hoᵃla הָעֳלָה 'be offered'	*heᵉla* הֶעֱלָה 'bring up, offer'	*naᵃla* נַעֲלָה [1] 'be led up'	*ala* עָלָה 'go up'
humat הוּמַת 'be killed'	*hemit* הֵמִית 'kill'	—	*mut* מוּת 'die'

The hophal is quite rare, so there is no need to learn the forms for every kind of verb. Any difficult forms will be explained as they appear.

---

1. This is an exception to the rule that the niphal prefix on verbs with an initial guttural has a short *e* vowel (21.1.a).

21.4 Perfect

The complex stems have the same conjugations as the qal, using prefixes, suffixes, and vowel changes to indicate the meaning more precisely. In this lesson, we begin with the perfect conjugation, which is quite straightforward. The simplest form is the third-person masculine singular, and this is given in the tables and vocabularies. Other forms have suffixes, following the usual patterns for person, gender, and number (see 9.1 and 9.4). For example, the niphal stem נִשְׁמַר ('be kept') and hiphil stem הִקְרִיב ('bring near') have the following perfect forms. Note that the hiphil infix יִ becomes a short *a* vowel in first- and second-person forms:

Singular		Niphal		Hiphil	
1	c.	nishm*a*rti	נִשְׁמַ֫ר תִּי	hiqr*a*vti	הִקְרַ֫ב תִּי
2	m.	nishm*a*rta	נִשְׁמַ֫ר תָּ	hiqr*a*vta	הִקְרַ֫ב תָּ
	f.	nishmart	נִשְׁמַ֫ר תְּ	hiqravt	הִקְרַ֫ב תְּ
3	m.	nishmar	נִשְׁמַ֫ר	hiqriv	הִקְרִיב
	f.	nishm^era	נִשְׁמְרָ ה	hiqriva	הִקְרִ֫יבָ ה
Plural					
1	c.	nishm*a*rnu	נִשְׁמַ֫ר נוּ	hiqr*a*vnu	הִקְרַ֫ב נוּ
2	m.	nishmartem	נִשְׁמַ֫ר תֶּם	hiqravtem	הִקְרַ֫ב תֶּם
	f.	nishmarten	נִשְׁמַ֫ר תֶּן	hiqravten	הִקְרַ֫ב תֶּן
3	c.	nishm^eru	נִשְׁמְר וּ	hiqrivu	הִקְרִ֫יב וּ

Vocabulary (21)

'Aaron'	ah^aron		אַהֲרֹן	217
'bring in, carry'	hevi	(hiphil בוא)	הֵבִיא	218
'bring up, offer'	he^ela	(hiphil עלה)	הֶעֱלָה	219
'make fall, cast'	hippil	(hiphil נפל)	הִפִּיל	220
'show' (verb)	her'a	(hiphil ראה)	הֶרְאָה	221
'be shown'	hor'a	(hophal ראה)	הָרְאָה	222

'make heard, announce'	hishmia	(hiphil שמע)	הִשְׁמִיעַ 223
'place' (noun)	maqom		מָקוֹם 224
'be said, be called'	neʼᵉmar	(niphal אמר)	נֶאֱמַר 225
'appear, be seen'	nirʼa	(niphal ראה)	נִרְאָה 226
'do, make'	paʼal		פָּעַל 227
'ask, request'	shaʼal		שָׁאַל 228

It may be helpful to have a reminder of three hiphil stems that have already been mentioned but not fully explained:

'separate'	hivdil	(hiphil בדל)	הִבְדִּיל 136
'tell'	higgid	(hiphil נגד)	הִגִּיד 196
'bring out'	hotsi	(hiphil יצא)	הוֹצִיא 174

Exercise (21)

1. Memorize the highlighted table above (21.3).

2. Analyse these verb forms, following the examples:

Form	Root	Stem and Conjugation	PGN	Extras
יִפְעַל	פעל	qal impf.	3 m. sg.	—
נִרְאָה	ראה	niphal pf.	3 m. sg.	—
הָרְאֵתָ	ראה	hophal pf.	2 m. sg.	—
אֲשִׂימְךָ				
נָשָׂא				
נוֹדַע				
נִרְאוּ				
הִבְדִּילוּ				

הֻבְדַּלְתָּ				
הִשְׁמִיעֲךָ				
הוֹצֵאתָ				
הֵבֵיאתִי				
הֶעֱלוּ				
הֶרְאֲךָ				
הוּמַת				

3. Translate and practise reading:

a וַיֹּאמֶר נָתָן אֶל־הַמֶּלֶךְ כֹּל אֲשֶׁר בִּלְבָבְךָ לֵךְ עֲשֵׂה כִּי יְהוָה עִמָּךְ[2]:

b וַיְהִי בַּלַּיְלָה הַהוּא וַיְהִי דְּבַר־יְהוָה אֶל־נָתָן לֵאמֹר: לֵךְ וְאָמַרְתָּ
אֶל־עַבְדִּי אֶל־דָּוִד כֹּה אָמַר[3] יְהוָה הַאַתָּה[4] תִּבְנֶה־לִּי בַיִת לְשִׁבְתִּי:

c כִּי לֹא יָשַׁבְתִּי בְּבַיִת לְמִיּוֹם הַעֲלֹתִי[5] אֶת־בְּנֵי יִשְׂרָאֵל מִמִּצְרַיִם
וְעַד הַיּוֹם הַזֶּה:

d נִרְאָה יְהוָה אֶל־שְׁלֹמֹה בַּלָּיְלָה וַיֹּאמֶר אֱלֹהִים שְׁאַל מָה אֶתֶּן־לָךְ:

e אַתָּה הָרְאֵתָ לָדַעַת כִּי יְהוָה הוּא הָאֱלֹהִים אֵין עוֹד:

f מִן־הַשָּׁמַיִם הִשְׁמִיעֲךָ אֶת־קֹלוֹ וְעַל־הָאָרֶץ הֶרְאֲךָ אֶת־אִשּׁוֹ[6] הַגְּדוֹלָה
וּדְבָרָיו שָׁמַעְתָּ מִתּוֹךְ הָאֵשׁ:

g אַתָּה הִבְדַּלְתָּ אֶת־עַמְּךָ יִשְׂרָאֵל מִכֹּל עַמֵּי הָאָרֶץ:

h יְהוָה לִי לֹא אִירָא מַה־יַּעֲשֶׂה לִי אָדָם:

i אֲנִי יְהוָה הוּא שְׁמִי וּכְבוֹדִי לְאַחֵר לֹא־אֶתֵּן:

j אֲנִי יְהוָה קְדוֹשְׁכֶם בּוֹרֵא יִשְׂרָאֵל מַלְכְּכֶם:

---

2. The suffix pronoun looks like the 2 f. sg. form, but is actually 2 m. sg. with a vowel change because of the end-of-sentence pause.

3. The perfect is best translated as present tense in this expression.

4. The prefix is an interrogative marker, not definite article.

5. Root עלה, hiphil inf. cstr., suffix pronoun (1 c. sg.).

6. Noun אֵשׁ with suffix pronoun.

k מִי הִשְׁמִיעַ זֹאת הֲלֹא אֲנִי יְהוָה וְאֵין־עוֹד אֱלֹהִים:

l הוֹדוּ לַיהוָה כִּי־טוֹב   כִּי לְעוֹלָם חַסְדּוֹ:

יֹאמַר־נָא [7] יִשְׂרָאֵל   כִּי לְעוֹלָם חַסְדּוֹ:

m יֹאמְרוּ־נָא בֵית־אַהֲרֹן   כִּי לְעוֹלָם חַסְדּוֹ:

יֹאמְרוּ־נָא יִרְאֵי יְהוָה   כִּי לְעוֹלָם חַסְדּוֹ:

Figure 13. Seal of Shema (replica). An eighth-century seal, found in Megiddo, that reads:

לשמע עבד ירבעם
'[belonging] to Shema, servant of Jeroboam'

**This was probably Jeroboam II, king of northern Israel (785–745 BC).
The lion was a symbol of strength (Judg 14:18) and symbolised
both Judah (Gen 49:9) and Dan (Deut 33:22).[8]**

---

7. The imperfect with particle נָא is jussive in meaning (third-person impv.), so it may be translated 'Let Israel say.' The next two lines are similar.

8. Photo by Ferrell Jenkins, ferrelljenkins.blog. Used by permission.

Complex Stems 2

22.1 Imperfect

The imperfect conjugation of complex stems is more complicated than the perfect because there are two prefixes: the imperfect prefix (see 13.1) and the stem prefix (נ or ה).

a. With *niphal* stems, adding the imperfect prefix normally causes the stem prefix נ to merge with the first letter of the root, making a double letter. The following vowels are usually *a* and *e*. For example:

Imperfect		←			Niphal stem	Qal
tishshamer תִּשָּׁמֵר 'you will be kept'	←	נ שׁמר	תִּ	←	*nishmar* נִשְׁמַר 'be kept'	שָׁמַר 'keep'
yimmatse יִמָּצֵא 'he will be found'	←	נ מצא	יִ	←	*nimtsa* נִמְצָא 'be found'	מָצָא 'find'

b. If the root begins with a guttural or ר, this letter cannot be doubled. The stem prefix נ drops out and the short *i* vowel on the imperfect prefix is lengthened to long *e* instead. The following vowels are usually *a* and *e*. For example:

		←				
ye'amer יֵאָמֵר 'it will be said'	←	נ אמר	יִ	←	*ne'emar* נֶאֱמַר 'be said'	אָמַר 'say'
yera'u יֵרָאוּ 'they will be seen'	←	נ ראה	יִ	←	*nir'a* נִרְאָה 'be seen'	רָאָה 'see'

c. With *hiphil* stems, the stem prefix ה drops out and the vowel on the imperfect prefix becomes *a*. For example:

Imperfect		←			←	Hiphil stem	Qal
yaqriv יַקְרִיב 'he will bring near'	←	הַקְרִיב	יַ		←	*hiqriv* הִקְרִיב 'bring near'	קָרַב 'approach'
yaggid יַגִּיד 'he will tell'	←	הַגִּיד	יַ		←	*higgid* הִגִּיד 'tell'	נגד (not used)
avi אָבִיא 'I will bring in'	←	הַבִיא	אָ		←	*hevi* הֵבִיא 'bring in'	בּוֹא 'go in'
taᵃlu תַּעֲלוּ 'you will bring up'	←	הַעֲלָה	תַ		←	*heᵉla* הֶעֱלָה 'bring up'	עָלָה 'go up'

d. There is one exception to this rule. Hiphil stems from roots with initial י begin with a long *o* vowel, and this vowel does not become *a* in the imperfect. For example:

yotsi יוֹצִיא 'he will bring out'	←	הוֹצִיא	יֹ	←	*hotsi* הוֹצִיא 'bring out'	יָצָא 'go out'

e. With *hophal* stems, the stem prefix ה drops out when imperfect prefixes are added. The stem can be recognized by the distinctive hophal vowels *o/u* and *a*. For example:

Imperfect		←			←	Hophal stem	Qal
yumat יוּמַת 'he will be killed'	←	הוּמַת	יֹ		←	*humat* הוּמַת 'be killed'	מוּת 'die'

22.2 Imperative

a. *Niphal* imperatives are formed by removing the prefix from the second-person imperfect form, like qal imperatives. However, the resulting form begins with a double letter, and this is unacceptable in Hebrew. To remedy this, the prefix ה is added to make it pronounceable, usually with a short *i* vowel. For example:

Imperative		Imperfect		Niphal stem
hishshamer הִשָּׁמֵר 'be careful!'	←	תִּשָּׁמֵר 'you will be kept'	←	נִשְׁמַר 'be kept'

b. *Hiphil* imperatives are also formed by removing the prefix from the second-person imperfect form. When this happens, the stem prefix ה that dropped out in the imperfect is reinstated, normally with a short *a* vowel. Usually, the infix ִי drops out and the second vowel becomes *e* instead of *i*. For example:

Imperative		Imperfect		Hiphil stem
haqrev הַקְרֵב 'bring near!'	←	תַּקְרִיב 'you will bring near'	←	הִקְרִיב 'bring near'
hotse הוֹצֵא 'bring out!'	←	תּוֹצִיא 'you will bring out'	←	הוֹצִיא 'bring out'

c. Imperatives of complex stems have four forms to indicate gender and number, with the same suffixes as the qal (see 18.1.b). For example, these are the forms for הוֹצִיא (hiphil):

Imperative forms						Imperfect
2	m. sg.	'bring out!'	*hotse*	הוֹצֵא	←	תּוֹצִיא
	f. sg.	'bring out!'	*hotsi'i*	הוֹצִיאִי	←	תּוֹצִיאִי
2	m. pl.	'bring out!'	*hotsi'u*	הוֹצִיאוּ	←	תּוֹצִיאוּ
	f. pl.	'bring out!'	*hotsena*	הוֹצֶאנָה	←	תּוֹצֶאנָה

הוֹדוּ (vocabulary item 160) is hiphil impv., 2 m. pl., from root ידה.

d. *Hophal* imperatives are very rare and not studied here.

22.3 Participle

As already explained, there are two kinds of qal participle: active (18.2) and passive (18.3). However, each complex stem has only one participle, either active or passive. Generally, hiphil participles are active, whereas niphal and hophal participles are passive.

a. *Niphal* participles are the same or similar to the stem. For example:

Participle				Niphal stem	
'kept'	nishmar	נִשְׁמָר	←	'be kept'	נִשְׁמַר
'seen'	nir'e	נִרְאֶה	←	'be seen'	נִרְאָה
'found'	nimtsa	נִמְצָא	←	'be found'	נִמְצָא

b. *Hiphil* participles are formed with the prefix מ, that replaces the stem prefix ה. The prefix vowel is usually *a*. For example:

Participle				Hiphil stem	
'bringing near'	maqriv	מַקְרִיב	←	'bring near'	הִקְרִיב
'telling'	maggid	מַגִּיד	←	'tell'	הִגִּיד
'showing'	mar'e	מַרְאֶה	←	'show'	הֶרְאָה

c. *Hophal* participles are formed with the prefix מ, like the hiphil, but the prefix vowel is *o* or *u*. For example:

Participle				Hophal stem	
'shown'	more	מָרְאֶה	←	'be shown'	הָרְאָה
'killed'	mumat	מוּמָת	←	'be killed'	הוּמַת

d. Participles of complex stems have four forms to indicate gender and number, with the same suffixes as the qal (see 18.2.b). For example here are the forms for נִמְצָא (niphal):

Participle forms			
m. sg.	'found'	nimtsa	נִמְצָא
f. sg.	'found'	nimtsa'a	נִמְצָאָה
m. pl.	'found'	nimts^e'im	נִמְצָאִים
f. pl.	'found'	nimtsa'ot	נִמְצָאוֹת

22.4 Infinitives

a. The *niphal* infinitive absolute has two forms: one keeps the stem prefix נ; the other has ה instead, with doubling of the first root letter, like the imperative. Both have an *o* vowel on the last syllable. The infinitive construct is the same as the imperative, 2 m. sg. For example:

Infinitive construct	Infinitive absolute	Imperative 2 m. sg.	Niphal stem
הִשָּׁמֵר *hishshamer* 'to be kept'	*nishmor* נִשְׁמֹר *hishshamor* הִשָּׁמֹר (meaning depends on context)	הִשָּׁמֵר 'be careful!'	נִשְׁמַר 'be kept'

b. The *hiphil* infinitive absolute is the same as the imperative, 2 m. sg. The infinitive construct is similar to the stem form (pf., 3 m. sg.), but with a short *a* vowel in the first syllable.

Infinitive construct	Infinitive absolute	Imperative 2 m. sg.	Hiphil stem
haqriv הַקְרִיב 'to bring near'	*haqrev* הַקְרֵב (meaning depends on context)	הַקְרֵב 'bring near!'	הִקְרִיב 'bring near'

c. *Hophal* infinitives are very rare and not studied here.

Vocabulary (22)

'or'	*o*		אוֹ	229
'marry, rule'	*ba'al*		בָּעַל	230
'be killed, executed'	*humat*	(hophal מות)	הוּמַת	231
'strengthen, hold, seize'	*hekh^eziq*	(hiphil חזק)	הֶחֱזִיק	232
'break, frustrate'	*hefer*	(hiphil פרר)	הֵפֵר¹	233
'be found'	*nimtsa*	(niphal מצא)	נִמְצָא	234
'pass [over/through/by]'	*avar*		עָבַר	235

---

1. פרר is a geminate verb (see 15.3), so the final root letter drops out in many forms.

'witness' (noun)	ed	עֵד	236
'mouth, opening, speech'	pe/pi	פֶּה/פִּי	237
'three' (pl. 'thirty')	shalosh	שָׁלֹשׁ	238
'two'	sh^enayim	שְׁנַיִם	239
'gate'[2]	sha'ar	שַׁעַר	240

Exercise (22)

1. Analyse these verb forms:

Form	Root	Stem and Conjugation	PGN	Extras
יֵאָמֵר	אמר	niphal impf.	3 m. sg.	—
לַהֲבִיאֲךָ	בוא	hiphil inf. cstr.	—	preposition לְ; suffix pronoun (2 m. sg.)
יִמָּצֵא				
אָבִיא				
וְהוֹצֵאתָ				
אַעֲלֶה				
מַעֲלִים				
יַגִּידוּ				
יַשְׁמִיעַ				
מַשְׁמִיעַ				
מַרְאֶה				
מָרְאֶה				
וַיּוֹצִיאֲךָ				
יוּמַת				

2. שַׁעַר may also refer to a city with gates.

2. Translate and practise reading:

a וַיֹּאמֶר אֵלָיו מַה־שְּׁמֶךָ וַיֹּאמֶר יַעֲקֹב: וַיֹּאמֶר לֹא יַעֲקֹב יֵאָמֵר עוֹד שִׁמְךָ
כִּי אִם־יִשְׂרָאֵל:

b וַיִּשְׁאַל יַעֲקֹב וַיֹּאמֶר הַגִּידָה־נָּא שְׁמֶךָ וַיֹּאמֶר לָמָּה־זֶּה³ תִּשְׁאַל לִשְׁמִי
וַיְבָרֶךְ אֹתוֹ שָׁם:

c וַיִּקְרָא יַעֲקֹב שֵׁם הַמָּקוֹם פְּנִיאֵל⁴ כִּי־רָאִיתִי אֱלֹהִים פָּנִים אֶל־פָּנִים:

d יְהוָה אֱלֹהֵי אֲבֹתֵיכֶם נִרְאָה אֵלַי לֵאמֹר אַעֲלֶה אֶתְכֶם מִמִּצְרָיִם:

e אַתֶּם רְאִיתֶם אֲשֶׁר עָשִׂיתִי לְמִצְרָיִם וָאֶשָּׂא אֶתְכֶם וָאָבִיא אֶתְכֶם אֵלָי:

f אָהַב יְהוָה אֶת־אֲבֹתֶיךָ וַיּוֹצִאֲךָ בְּכֹחוֹ הַגָּדֹל מִמִּצְרָיִם
לַהֲבִיאֲךָ לָתֶת־לְךָ אֶת־הָאָרֶץ:

g כִּי־יִמָּצֵא בְקִרְבְּךָ בְּאַחַד שְׁעָרֶיךָ אֲשֶׁר־יְהוָה אֱלֹהֶיךָ נֹתֵן לָךְ⁵
אִישׁ אוֹ־אִשָּׁה אֲשֶׁר יַעֲשֶׂה אֶת־הָרַע בְּעֵינֵי יְהוָה־אֱלֹהֶיךָ לַעֲבֹר⁶ בְּרִיתוֹ:⁷
וַיֵּלֶךְ וַיַּעֲבֹד אֱלֹהִים אֲחֵרִים אֲשֶׁר לֹא־צִוִּיתִי: וְהוֹצֵאתָ אֶת־הָאִישׁ הַהוּא
אוֹ אֶת־הָאִשָּׁה הַהִיא אֲשֶׁר עָשׂוּ אֶת־הַדָּבָר הָרַע הַזֶּה אֶל־שְׁעָרֶיךָ וָמֵתוּ:

h עַל־פִּי⁸ שְׁנַיִם עֵדִים אוֹ שְׁלֹשָׁה עֵדִים יוּמַת הַמֵּת⁹
לֹא יוּמַת עַל־פִּי עֵד אֶחָד:

i וַיִּירָא יַעֲקֹב וַיֹּאמַר אֵין הַמָּקוֹם הַזֶּה כִּי אִם־בֵּית אֱלֹהִים
וְזֶה שַׁעַר הַשָּׁמָיִם:

---

3. Combination of לְ and מָה, that means 'why?' (lit. 'for what?').

4. The place name פְּנִיאֵל (pᵉniʾel) 'Peniel' means 'face of God.' There is a play on words with Jacob's declaration that he had seen God 'face to face.'

5. The suffix pronoun looks like the 2 f. sg. form, but is actually 2 m. sg. with a vowel change because of the mid-sentence pause.

6. The verb עָבַר means 'transgress' here.

7. In terms of meaning, these three sentences are really one long conditional sentence: כִּי ('if' or 'when') introduces the condition; the second sentence begins with waw consecutive ('and') to give more details of the condition; the third sentence begins with a waw conjunction ('then') to state the consequence.

8. פִּי here means 'testimony.'

9. Root מות, qal pt., m. sg., definite article: 'the one who dies,' i.e. 'the one who is to die.'

Complex Stems 3

In this lesson, we study three more complex stems: piel, pual, and hithpael. They are characterized by doubling of the middle root letter and are sometimes called 'intensive' because they often refer to an action that is more intense than the related qal stem. For example, the root שׁבר means 'break' in the qal (shavar שָׁבַר) and 'shatter' or 'smash into pieces' in the piel (shibber שִׁבֵּר).

23.1 Piel

The commonest of these three stems is called 'piel' (פִּעֵל). It is formed by doubling the middle letter of the root. This doubling is not visible in the name פִּעֵל because the letter ע cannot be doubled. The two vowels in piel verbs are usually *i* and *e,* or *i* and *a*.

a. The piel stem is always *active* in meaning, but apart from that it is difficult to be precise about its function. There is no parallel form in English, so it is best to learn the meaning of each piel stem as it is encountered. For example:

Piel			Qal	
'speak'	*dibber*	דִּבֵּר	'speak'	דָּבַר
'teach'	*limmad*	לִמַּד	'learn'	לָמַד
'command'	*tsiwwa*	צִוָּה	(not used)	צוה
'praise'	*hillel*	הִלֵּל	(not used)	הלל

b. When the middle letter of a root is a guttural or ר, that letter cannot be doubled, so the piel stem can only be distinguished from the qal by its vowels. The qal stem usually has *a* vowels, whereas the piel has at least one *i* or *e* vowel. For example:

Piel			Qal	
'show mercy, take pity'	*rikham*	רִחַם	'love'	רָחַם
'bless'	*berakh*	בֵּרַךְ	'bless'	בָּרַךְ

23.2 Pual

The *passive* form of the piel stem is called 'pual' (פֻּעַל). It is also formed by doubling the middle root letter, unless it is a guttural or ר. The vowels are usually *u* and *a*. For example:

Pual	Piel	Qal
kuppar כֻּפַּר 'be atoned for'	*kipper* כִּפֵּר 'atone'	*kafar* כָּפַר 'cover'
shullakh שֻׁלַּח 'be sent away'	*shillakh* שִׁלַּח 'send away, set free'	*shalakh* שָׁלַח 'send'

23.3 Hithpael

The third stem is the hithpael (הִתְפַּעֵל), which is formed by doubling the middle root letter and adding the prefix הִתְ (*hit*).

a. Hithpael stems are often *reflexive* in meaning, having the same subject and object, as may be seen in these examples:

Hithpael	Pual	Piel	Qal
הִתְקַדֵּשׁ *hitqaddesh* 'make oneself holy'	קֻדַּשׁ *quddash* 'be made holy'	קִדַּשׁ *qiddash* 'make holy'	קָדַשׁ *qadash* 'be holy'
הִתְגַּדֵּל *hitgaddel* 'boast'	גֻּדַּל *guddal* 'be grown'	גִּדַּל *giddal* 'make great, grow'	גָּדַל *gadal* 'be great'
הִתְיַלֵּד *hityalled* 'register genealogy'	יֻלַּד *yullad* 'be born'	יִלֵּד *yilled* 'act as midwife'	יָלַד *yalad* 'give birth to'

b. Hithpael stems sometimes describe actions that are *repetitive* or *reciprocal*. For example:

Hithpael			Qal	
'walk about'	*hithallekh*	הִתְהַלֵּךְ	'walk'	הָלַךְ
'see again, look at each other'	*hitra'a*	הִתְרָאָה	'see'	רָאָה

23.4 Conjugations

a. The *perfect* conjugation of piel, pual, and hithpael stems is formed with the usual suffixes, so needs no further explanation.

b. The *imperfect* conjugation of piel and pual stems is formed with the usual prefixes and suffixes, but the prefixes have a shewa rather than a full vowel. The following vowels are usually *a* and *e* for piel, and *u* and *a* for pual. For example:

Imperfect				Stem	
'I will speak'	ᵃdabber	אֲדַבֵּר	←	דִּבֵּר	piel
'they will speak'	yᵉdabbᵉru	יְדַבְּרוּ	←	דִּבֵּר	piel
'it will be atoned for'	tᵉkhuppar	תְכֻפַּר	←	כֻּפַּר	pual

Because the third-person prefix has a shewa (יְ), the י is not doubled after waw consecutive (13.2.d). For example: וַיְדַבְּרוּ ('and they spoke').

In the imperfect of the hithpael, the ה of the stem prefix drops out and is replaced by the imperfect prefix. For example:

Imperfect				Stem
'he will pray'	yitpallel	יִתְפַּלֵּל	←	הִתְפַּלֵּל
'they will make themselves holy'	yitqaddᵉshu	יִתְקַדְּשׁוּ	←	הִתְקַדֵּשׁ

c. *Imperatives* of piel stems are formed as usual by removing the prefix from the second-person imperfect form. For example:

Imperative				Imperfect		Stem
2 m. sg.	'speak!'	dabber	דַּבֵּר	←	תְּדַבֵּר	←	דִּבֵּר
2 f. pl.	'teach'	lammᵉdna	לַמֵּדְנָה	←	תְּלַמֵּדְנָה	←	לִמַּד

The hithpael imperative (2 m. sg.) is the same as the stem form (e.g. הִתְקַדֵּשׁ). Pual imperatives are very rare and not studied here.

d. *Participles* of these stems are formed with the prefix מ, like hiphil and hophal. For hithpael, מ replaces the ה. Vowels are similar to the imperfect. For example:

Participle				Stem	
'commanding'	*me tsawwe*	מְצַוֶּה	←	צִוָּה	piel
'teacher'	*me lammed*	מְלַמֵּד	←	לִמַּד	piel
'sent away'	*me shullakh*	מְשֻׁלָּח	←	שֻׁלַּח	pual
'praying'	*mitpallel*	מִתְפַּלֵּל	←	הִתְפַּלֵּל	hithpael

Gender and number are indicated with the same suffixes as qal (18.2.b). מְרַחֶפֶת (vocabulary item 92) is piel pt., f. sg., from root רחף.

e. *Infinitives* of piel and hithpael stems have the same form as the imperative, 2 m. sg. Pual infinitives are very rare and not studied here.

23.5 Summary of Stems

The seven stems we have studied may be summarized as follows:

Stem	Characteristics	Meaning
Qal	vowel *a* + *a*	active
Niphal	prefix נ; vowel *i* + *a*	passive
Hiphil	prefix ה; infix יָ	active causative
Hophal	prefix ה; vowel *o/u* + *a*	passive causative
Piel	middle letter doubled; vowel *i* + *e*	active [intensive]
Pual	middle letter doubled; vowel *u* + *a*	passive [intensive]
Hithpael	middle letter doubled; prefix הִתְ	reflexive

There are several more stems, but they are rare and not studied here.

Vocabulary (23)

'four' (pl. 'forty')	*arba*		אַרְבַּע 241
'redeem'	*ga'al*		גָּאַל 242
'make oneself holy'	*hitqaddesh*	(hithpael קדש)	הִתְקַדֵּשׁ 243

'be born'	yullad	(pual ילד)	יֻלַּד	244
'Canaan'	kᵉnaʿan		כְּנַעַן	245
'teach'	limmad	(piel למד)	לִמַּד	246
'birthplace, relatives'	moledet		מוֹלֶדֶת	247
'forgive'	salakh		סָלַח	248
'assembly, congregation'	eda/ᵃdat		עֵדָה/עֲדַת	249
'small, young'	qatan/qaton		קָטָן/קָטֹן	250
'show mercy, take pity'	rikham	(piel רחם)	רִחַם	251
'seven' (pl. 'seventy')	sheva		שֶׁבַע	252

Three piel stems have already been mentioned but not fully explained:

'bless'	berakh	(piel ברך)	בֵּרַךְ	158
'speak'	dibber	(piel דבר)	דִּבֶּר	159
'command' (verb)	tsiwwa	(piel צוה)	צִוָּה	203

Exercise (23)

1. Memorize the summary of stems in the highlighted table (23.5).

2. Analyse these verb forms:

Form	Root	Stem and Conjugation	PGN	Extras
דִּבֶּר				
וַיְדַבֵּר				
יְבָרֶךְ				
יָלְדוּ				
תְּכַפֵּר				
הִתְקַדִּשְׁתֶּם				
יִתְקַדֵּשׁ				

רִחַם				
יְלַמֵּד				
אֲצַוְּךָ				
וְהוֹצֵאתִי				
אַרְאֶךָּ				

3. Translate and practise reading:

a וַיְדַבֵּר יְהוָה אֶל־מֹשֶׁה לֵּאמֹר: דַּבֵּר אֶל־כָּל־עֲדַת בְּנֵי־יִשְׂרָאֵל וְאָמַרְתָּ
אֲלֵהֶם קְדֹשִׁים תִּהְיוּ כִּי קָדוֹשׁ אֲנִי יְהוָה אֱלֹהֵיכֶם:

b וְהִתְקַדִּשְׁתֶּם וִהְיִיתֶם קְדֹשִׁים כִּי אֲנִי יְהוָה אֱלֹהֵיכֶם:

c וַיֹּאמֶר יְהוָה אֶל־אַבְרָם¹ לֶךְ־לְךָ² מֵאַרְצְךָ וּמִמּוֹלַדְתְּךָ וּמִבֵּית אָבִיךָ
אֶל־הָאָרֶץ אֲשֶׁר אַרְאֶךָּ:

d וַיֵּלֶךְ אַבְרָם כַּאֲשֶׁר דִּבֶּר אֵלָיו יְהוָה וַיֵּלֶךְ אִתּוֹ לוֹט³ וְאַבְרָם בֶּן־חָמֵשׁ
שָׁנִים וְשִׁבְעִים שָׁנָה⁴ בְּצֵאתוֹ מֵחָרָן⁵:

e וַיֹּאמֶר יְהוָה אֶל־מֹשֶׁה רְאֵה נְתַתִּיךָ אֱלֹהִים לְפַרְעֹה
וְאַהֲרֹן אָחִיךָ יִהְיֶה נְבִיאֶךָ: אַתָּה תְדַבֵּר אֵת כָּל־אֲשֶׁר אֲצַוֶּךָּ
וְאַהֲרֹן אָחִיךָ יְדַבֵּר אֶל־פַּרְעֹה:

f וְלֹא־יִשְׁמַע אֲלֵכֶם פַּרְעֹה וְנָתַתִּי אֶת־יָדִי בְּמִצְרָיִם⁶ וְהוֹצֵאתִי אֶת־עַמִּי
בְנֵי־יִשְׂרָאֵל מֵאֶרֶץ מִצְרָיִם:

g וְיָדְעוּ מִצְרַיִם כִּי־אֲנִי יְהוָה וְהוֹצֵאתִי אֶת־בְּנֵי־יִשְׂרָאֵל מִתּוֹכָם:

h וַיַּעַשׂ מֹשֶׁה וְאַהֲרֹן כַּאֲשֶׁר צִוָּה יְהוָה אֹתָם כֵּן עָשׂוּ:

---

1. אַבְרָם (*avram*) is the original name of אַבְרָהָם, written 'Abram' in English (see Gen 17:5).

2. Lit. 'Go for you.' This form emphasizes the significance of the action for the subject. It has no equivalent in English, so may be simply translated 'Go!'

3. לוֹט (*lot*) is a personal name: 'Lot.'

4. Lit. 'son of five years and seventy years' = 'seventy-five years old.'

5. חָרָן (*kharan*) is a place name. The usual spelling in English is 'Haran,' though NIV 2011 has 'Harran.' It is spelt differently in Hebrew from the name of Abraham's brother Haran: הָרָן (*haran*).

6. The preposition בְּ here may be translated 'on' or 'against.'

i   אֵלֶּה בְּנֵי עֵשָׂו אֲשֶׁר יֻלְּדוּ־לוֹ בְּאֶרֶץ כְּנָעַן:

j   שְׁמַע יִשְׂרָאֵל יְהוָה אֱלֹהֵינוּ יְהוָה אֶחָד: וְאָהַבְתָּ אֵת יְהוָה אֱלֹהֶיךָ
בְּכָל־לְבָבְךָ וּבְכָל־נַפְשְׁךָ וּבְכָל־מְאֹדֶךָ:[7]

k   וְהָיוּ הַדְּבָרִים הָאֵלֶּה אֲשֶׁר אָנֹכִי מְצַוְּךָ הַיּוֹם עַל־לְבָבֶךָ: וְדִבַּרְתָּ בָּם[8]
בְּשִׁבְתְּךָ בְּבֵיתֶךָ וּבְלֶכְתְּךָ בַדֶּרֶךְ:

l   כְּרַחֵם[9] אָב עַל־בָּנִים רִחַם[10] יְהוָה עַל־יְרֵאָיו:

**Figure 14. Jewish Prayer Shawl (*Tallit*). Try to understand the Hebrew. The letter ד׳ denotes
the number 4 and replaces the four-letter name of God (יהוה). The last two words mean 'to
wrap oneself with tassels' (cf. Num 15:38). Note the hithpael verb with reflexive meaning.[11]**

---

7. The adverb מְאֹד is used here as a noun meaning 'strength.'
8. The preposition בְּ here may be translated 'about.'
9. Piel inf. cstr. with preposition.
10. The perfect with a verb signifying attitude may be translated with the present tense (see 9.2.c).
11. Photo by Ben Burton, pixabay. Used by Permission.

Reading 4
Jeremiah 31:31–34

The expression 'new covenant' is found only once in the Old Testament, in Jeremiah 31:31–34, so this prophecy is important for understanding the relationship between the Old Testament (literally 'old covenant') and New Testament ('new covenant'). The prophecy has two parts:

- God's promise to make a new covenant (vv. 31–32)
- the essence of the new covenant (vv. 33–34).

Let us now read Jeremiah 31:31–34 in Hebrew!

24.1 A New Covenant (Jer 31:31)

הִנֵּה יָמִים בָּאִים נְאֻם־יְהוָה וְכָרַתִּי אֶת־בֵּית יִשְׂרָאֵל וְאֶת־בֵּית
יְהוּדָה בְּרִית חֲדָשָׁה׃

יָמִים: literally 'days,' perhaps better translated here as 'time' (NET; CEB; NJPS). This word is easy to confuse with יַמִּים ('seas').

בָּאִים: participle, m. pl., matching the noun יָמִים.

נְאֻם־יְהוָה: This distinctive expression accompanies many Old Testament prophecies.

וְכָרַתִּי: The full form would be וְכָרַתְתִּי but the final ת of the root merges with the ת of the perfect suffix to make a double letter. It was common in the ancient world for an animal to be slaughtered ('cut') in a covenant-making ceremony (e.g. Gen 15:7–21), which is probably the origin of the expression כָּרַת בְּרִית ('make a covenant,' lit. 'cut a covenant'). The modern expression 'cut a deal' is apparently similar but probably unrelated.

בֵּית יִשְׂרָאֵל וּבֵית יְהוּדָה: The new covenant is to be made with both Israel and Judah, in other words the whole people of Israel. It is clear from this expression that the prophecy was spoken after the kingdom divided in two.

בְּרִית חֲדָשָׁה: The feminine form of the adjective **חָדָשׁ** is used with the feminine noun **בְּרִית**. Several covenants between God and human beings are recorded in the Old Testament, especially with Noah (Gen 9:8–17), Abraham (Gen 17), and David (Ps 89:3; cf. 2 Sam 7). Here Jeremiah announces God's plan to make a new covenant in the future.

24.2 Old Covenant Broken (Jer 31:32)

לֹא כַבְּרִית אֲשֶׁר כָּרַתִּי אֶת־אֲבוֹתָם בְּיוֹם הֶחֱזִיקִי בְיָדָם לְהוֹצִיאָם מֵאֶרֶץ מִצְרָיִם אֲשֶׁר־הֵמָּה הֵפֵרוּ אֶת־בְּרִיתִי וְאָנֹכִי בָּעַלְתִּי בָם נְאֻם־יְהוָה:

הֶחֱזִיקִי: root **חזק**, hiphil inf. cstr., suffix pronoun (1 c. sg.), lit. 'my holding.' It is probably best translated here as 'I held' (see 19.3.e).

לְהוֹצִיאָם: root **יצא**, hiphil inf. cstr., preposition **לְ**, suffix pronoun (3 m. pl.), meaning 'to bring them out.'

הֵפֵרוּ: root **פרר**, hiphil pf., 3 c. pl. The qal stem is not used in the Old Testament, but the hiphil is quite common and means 'break' or 'frustrate.' The history of Israel since the time of Moses has demonstrated their repeated failure to keep the covenant.

אֲשֶׁר ... בְּרִיתִי: the Hebrew word order seems strange to an English reader, so the phrase may be translated 'my covenant that they broke.'

וְאָנֹכִי: The conjunction here may be translated 'though' or 'whereas.'

בָּעַלְתִּי בָם: The verb **בָּעַל** ('marry, rule') is related to the noun **בַּעַל** (baʿal) that means 'husband' or 'owner,' and is well-known as the name of the Canaanite storm god. Either meaning of the verb is possible here, so it may be translated 'I was a husband to them' (NIV; cf. NRSV, ESV, NET) or 'I was their Master' (NJB). Perhaps both are intended since both are appropriate in terms of God's relationship to his people.

24.3 Relationship with God (Jer 31:33)

כִּי זֹאת הַבְּרִית אֲשֶׁר אֶכְרֹת אֶת־בֵּית יִשְׂרָאֵל אַחֲרֵי הַיָּמִים הָהֵם נְאֻם־יְהוָה

וְעַל־לִבָּם אֶכְתֲּבֶנָּה   נָתַתִּי אֶת־תּוֹרָתִי בְּקִרְבָּם

וְהֵמָּה יִהְיוּ־לִי לְעָם: וְהָיִיתִי לָהֶם לֵאלֹהִים

The second part of the prophecy is introduced in prose (v. 33a). Then the essence of the new covenant is set out in two lines of poetry:

- internalization of the law (v. 33b)
- relationship between God and his people (v. 33c).

נָתַתִּי: root נתן, qal pf., 1 c. sg. The final נ of the root is a weak letter, so merges with the perfect suffix. This is an example of a 'prophetic perfect,' where the perfect conjugation is used with reference to a future event because the prophet is confident that God's plan will be accomplished.

בְּקִרְבָּם: noun קֶרֶב with preposition and suffix pronoun.

לִבָּם: note the double ב and vowel change when לֵב takes a suffix pronoun.

אֶכְתֲּבֶנָּה: root כתב, qal impf., 1 c. sg., suffix pronoun (3 f. sg. – see 16.1).

Inner renewal is designed to achieve the goal of the covenant: the LORD as Israel's God and Israel as God's people. This 'covenant formula' was already well-known in Israel (see Exod 6:7; Lev 26:12; cf. Jer 7:23; Ezek 11:20) but was far from being a reality in their lives. On the contrary, the relationship between God and Israel was broken (Hos 1:9) because they had abandoned him (Jer 2:19). As a result, God plans to really make Israel his people by a plan that would be fulfilled through the Messiah (cf. 1 Pet 2:9–10).

24.4 Knowing God (Jer 31:34)

וְלֹא יְלַמְּדוּ עוֹד אִישׁ אֶת־רֵעֵהוּ וְאִישׁ אֶת־אָחִיו לֵאמֹר דְּעוּ

אֶת־יְהוָה כִּי־כוּלָּם יֵדְעוּ אוֹתִי לְמִקְטַנָּם וְעַד־גְּדוֹלָם נְאֻם־יְהוָה

כִּי אֶסְלַח לַעֲוֹנָם   וּלְחַטָּאתָם לֹא אֶזְכָּר־עוֹד:

Finally, in a mixture of prose and poetry, it is revealed that this new covenant will make it possible to know God in a new way.

יְלַמְּדוּ: note the plural verb with a singular noun (אִישׁ), following the meaning (several people teaching each other) rather than strict grammar.

רֵעֵהוּ: noun רֵעַ ('friend, neighbour'), with alternative suffix pronoun (3 m. sg. – 16.1).

דְּעוּ: root יָדַע, qal impv., 2 m. pl. The weak initial letter drops out in the imperfect (תֵּדְעוּ), then this form is shortened further to make the imperative. This verb is plural like יִלְמְדוּ, rather than singular which would be strictly correct.

כֻּלָּם = כֹּל + כֻּלָּם: כֹּל with suffix pronoun.

יֵדְעוּ: root יָדַע, qal impf., 3 m. pl.

אוֹתִי = אֹתִי: the object marker with suffix pronoun (1 c. sg.) becomes an independent pronoun indicating the object of a verb, i.e. 'me.'

לְמִקְטַנָּם (from מִן + קָטָן + ם): 'from the small/young among them' (lit. 'to from their small/young').

לַעֲוֺנָם: noun עָוֺן ('iniquity, guilt') with suffix pronoun. The preposition לְ indicates the object of the verb סָלַח and does not need to be translated into English.

וּלְחַטָּאתָם: noun חַטָּאת ('sin') with waw conjunction, preposition, and suffix pronoun.

אֶזְכָּר (ezkor): the verb זָכַר means 'remember.'

In the old covenant, Israel was repeatedly taught to know the Lord (see Exod 7:17; 10:2; Ps 46:10; 100:3; Isa 45:3; Ezek 7:4, 9). But in the new covenant, the law will be understood and appreciated in their inmost being. God's relationship with his people will be renewed. They will no longer be taught to know him because they will know him instinctively. The Hebrew word יָדַע ('know') is concerned not merely with knowledge but with relationships, sometimes the most intimate of human relationships (e.g. Gen 4:1). So, when the new covenant takes effect, God and human beings will have a truly close relationship, without mediation by Moses or the priests. There is only one mediator of the new covenant – Jesus Christ (Heb 7–9). Through faith in him and by the power of his indwelling Spirit, it is possible to know God as Father (Rom 8:9–11, 15; Heb 4:16). In such an intimate relationship, there is divine assurance that the past will be forgiven and forgotten:

$$\text{אֶסְלַח לַעֲוֺנָם וּלְחַטָּאתָם לֹא אֶזְכָּר־עוֹד:}$$

Vocabulary (24)

'sign'	ot		אוֹת 253
'generation'	dor		דּוֹר/דֹּר 254
'save, help'	hoshia	(hiphil יָשַׁע)	הוֹשִׁיעַ 255

'pray'	hitpallel	(hithpael פלל)	הִתְפַּלֵּל 256
'remember'	zakhar		זָכַר 257
'remembrance, memorial'	zekher		זֵכֶר 258
'sin' (noun)	khattat		חַטָּאת 259
'be gathered'	neʾesaf	(niphal אסף)	נֶאֱסַף 260
'be forgiven'	nislakh	(niphal סלח)	נִסְלַח 261
'iniquity, guilt'	awon		עָוֹן 262
'answer, reply' (verb)	ana		עָנָה 263
'friend, neighbour'	rea		רֵעַ 264

Exercise (24)

1. Analyse these verb forms:

Form	Root	Stem and Conjugation	PGN	Extras
דִּבַּרְתָּ				
שֹׁמְעִים				
עָשֹׂה				
בְּשִׁבְתְּךָ	יָשַׁב			
אֶשְׁלָחֲךָ				
וַיֵּאָסֵף				
לְכָה				
אוֹצִיא				
שְׁלַחְתִּיךָ				
שְׁלָחַנִי		qal pf.		
אֶתְפַּלֵּל				
הוֹשִׁיעוּ				

2. Practise reading Jeremiah 31:31–34 in Hebrew and translate it into English, using the notes here but without consulting Bible translations.

3. Translate and practise reading:

a עַתָּה לְכָה וְאֶשְׁלָחֲךָ אֶל־פַּרְעֹה וְהוֹצֵא¹ אֶת־עַמִּי בְנֵי־יִשְׂרָאֵל מִמִּצְרָיִם:

b וַיֹּאמֶר מֹשֶׁה אֶל־הָאֱלֹהִים מִי אָנֹכִי כִּי אֵלֵךְ אֶל־פַּרְעֹה
וְכִי אוֹצִיא אֶת־בְּנֵי יִשְׂרָאֵל מִמִּצְרָיִם:

c וַיֹּאמֶר כִּי־אֶהְיֶה עִמָּךְ וְזֶה־לְּךָ הָאוֹת כִּי אָנֹכִי שְׁלַחְתִּיךָ בְּהוֹצִיאֲךָ אֶת־הָעָם
מִמִּצְרַיִם תַּעַבְדוּן² אֶת־הָאֱלֹהִים עַל הָהָר הַזֶּה:

d וַיֹּאמֶר מֹשֶׁה אֶל־הָאֱלֹהִים הִנֵּה³ אָנֹכִי בָא אֶל־בְּנֵי יִשְׂרָאֵל וְאָמַרְתִּי לָהֶם
אֱלֹהֵי אֲבוֹתֵיכֶם שְׁלָחַנִי אֲלֵיכֶם וְאָמְרוּ־לִי מַה־שְּׁמוֹ מָה אֹמַר אֲלֵהֶם:

e וַיֹּאמֶר אֱלֹהִים אֶל־מֹשֶׁה אֶהְיֶה אֲשֶׁר אֶהְיֶה וַיֹּאמֶר
כֹּה תֹאמַר לִבְנֵי יִשְׂרָאֵל אֶהְיֶה שְׁלָחַנִי אֲלֵיכֶם:

f וַיֹּאמֶר עוֹד אֱלֹהִים אֶל־מֹשֶׁה כֹּה־תֹאמַר אֶל־בְּנֵי יִשְׂרָאֵל
יְהוָה אֱלֹהֵי אֲבֹתֵיכֶם אֱלֹהֵי אַבְרָהָם אֱלֹהֵי יִצְחָק וֵאלֹהֵי יַעֲקֹב
שְׁלָחַנִי אֲלֵיכֶם זֶה־שְּׁמִי לְעֹלָם וְזֶה זִכְרִי לְדֹר דֹּר⁴:

g הֲדָּבָר אֲשֶׁר־דִּבַּרְתָּ אֵלֵינוּ בְּשֵׁם יְהוָה אֵינֶנּוּ⁵ שֹׁמְעִים אֵלֶיךָ:
כִּי עָשֹׂה נַעֲשֶׂה אֶת־כָּל־הַדָּבָר אֲשֶׁר־יָצָא מִפִּינוּ כַּאֲשֶׁר עָשִׂינוּ
אֲנַחְנוּ וַאֲבֹתֵינוּ וּמְלָכֵינוּ:

h וַיֵּאָסֵף כָּל־אִישׁ יִשְׂרָאֵל אֶל־הָעִיר כְּאִישׁ אֶחָד חֲבֵרִים:

i וַיַּעַן וַיֹּאמֶר אֵלַי לֵאמֹר זֶה דְּבַר־יְהוָה אֶל־זְרֻבָּבֶל⁶ לֵאמֹר
לֹא בְחַיִל וְלֹא בְכֹחַ כִּי אִם־בְּרוּחִי אָמַר יְהוָה צְבָאוֹת:

---

1. Hiphil impv., 2 m. sg., waw conjunction.

2. The וֹ on the imperfect suffix does not affect the meaning (see 13.1.b).

3. הִנֵּה may mean 'if' or 'when' before a conditional clause.

4. Translate 'from generation to generation' (NIV, NET). Hebrew nouns, adjectives, and adverbs are often repeated for emphasis, e.g. שָׁלוֹם שָׁלוֹם (Jer 6:14); קָדוֹשׁ קָדוֹשׁ קָדוֹשׁ (Isa 6:3); מְאֹד מְאֹד ('greatly, mightily,' Gen 7:19).

5. אַיִן with suffix pronoun (1 c. pl.). It may be translated 'we are not' or 'we will not' (lit. 'there is not us').

6. זְרֻבָּבֶל (zᵉrubbavel) is a personal name: 'Zerubbabel.'

Summary of Word Forms

25.1 Verbs

To complete our study of Hebrew verbs, here is a summary of key forms, based on the roots שמר and קדש:

Form	Perfect	Imperfect	Imperative	Participle	Infinitive Absolute	Infinitive Construct
Qal	שָׁמַר	יִשְׁמֹר	שְׁמֹר	שֹׁמֵר	שָׁמוֹר	שְׁמֹר
Niphal	נִשְׁמַר	יִשָּׁמֵר	הִשָּׁמֵר	נִשְׁמָר	נִשְׁמֹר	הִשָּׁמֵר
Hiphil	הִשְׁמִיר	יַשְׁמִיר	הַשְׁמֵר	מַשְׁמִיר	הַשְׁמֵר	הַשְׁמִיר
Hophal	הָשְׁמַר	יָשְׁמַר	—	מָשְׁמָר	—	—
Piel	שִׁמֵּר	יְשַׁמֵּר	שַׁמֵּר	מְשַׁמֵּר	שַׁמֵּר	שַׁמֵּר
Pual	שֻׁמַּר	יְשֻׁמַּר	—	מְשֻׁמָּר	—	—
Hithpael	הִתְקַדֵּשׁ	יִתְקַדֵּשׁ	הִתְקַדֵּשׁ	מִתְקַדֵּשׁ	הִתְקַדֵּשׁ	הִתְקַדֵּשׁ

Notes

a. There are nine *perfect* forms of each verb, with suffixes to indicate the subject, differentiated by person, gender, and number (see 9.1).

b. There are ten *imperfect* forms, with prefixes to indicate the subject, differentiated by person, gender, and number (see 13.1).

c. *Imperatives* are generally addressed to another person (second person), with suffixes to indicate gender and number (see 18.1). Hophal and pual imperatives are very rare because commands are usually active rather than passive.

d. *Participles* have suffixes to indicate gender and number (see 18.2). The standard form of the qal participle given here is active, but there is also a passive participle following the pattern שָׁמוּר (see 18.3). Participles of complex stems are either active (hiphil, piel, hithpael) or passive (niphal, hophal, pual).

e. The *infinitive absolute* has no distinctions for person, gender, or number (see 19.1). The niphal infinitive absolute has an alternative form (הִשָּׁמֹר), likewise the piel (שַׁמֹּר). Hophal and pual infinitives are rare.

f. The *infinitive construct* has only one form, but it is often prefixed with prepositions like לְ and may also have suffix pronouns (see 19.2, 3).

g. The *niphal* stem (see 21.1) is characterized by the prefix נ, which merges with the first letter of the root in several forms; and it takes the prefix ה for the imperative and infinitives.

h. The *hiphil* stem (see 21.2) has a short *a* vowel in the first syllable of every form, except the perfect.

i. The *hophal* stem (see 21.3) has an *o* vowel (or sometimes *u*) in the first syllable.

j. The *piel, pual,* and *hithpael* stems (see 23.1, 2, 3) are characterized by doubling of the middle root letter.

k. These examples are strong verbs. There are many variations in weak verbs, as explained in Lesson 15 and elsewhere. It is beyond the scope of this book to go into more detail, but tables of various forms can be found in larger introductions (e.g. Kelley; Lambdin; Pratico and Van Pelt).

25.2 Nouns and Adjectives

The forms of nouns and adjectives depend on gender and number, and whether they are in the absolute or construct state. Here is a summary, based on the noun סוּס (*sus* 'horse'):

Form	Singular	Dual	Plural
Masculine absolute	סוּס	סוּסַיִם	סוּסִים
Masculine construct	סוּס	סוּסֵי	סוּסֵי
Feminine absolute	סוּסָה	סוּסָתַיִם	סוּסוֹת
Feminine construct	סוּסַת	סוּסָתֵי	סוּסוֹת

Notes

a. Adjectives have the same forms as nouns.

b. The vowels of nouns and adjectives often change when suffixes are added to indicate gender and number.

c. For more details of noun and adjective forms, see Lessons 11–12.

25.3 Numbers

Hebrew numbers were explained briefly in Lesson 12. Here is a summary of key forms with some further explanations:

		Basic Form	Secondary Form	Letter
1		(m.) אֶחָד	(f.) אַחַת	א׳
2	(m.) (sheᵊnayim) שְׁנַיִם		(f.) (shtayim¹) שְׁתַּיִם	ב׳
3		(f.) שָׁלֹשׁ	(m.) שְׁלֹשָׁה	ג׳
4		(f.) אַרְבַּע	(m.) אַרְבָּעָה	ד׳
5		(f.) חָמֵשׁ	(m.) חֲמִשָּׁה	ה׳
6		(f.) שֵׁשׁ	(m.) שִׁשָּׁה	ו׳
7		(f.) (sheva) שֶׁבַע	(m.) שִׁבְעָה	ז׳
8		(f.) שְׁמֹנֶה	(m.) שְׁמֹנָה	ח׳
9		(f.) (tesha) תֵּשַׁע	(m.) תִּשְׁעָה	ט׳
10		(f.) (eser) עֶשֶׂר	(m.) עֲשָׂרָה	י׳
11		(m.) אַחַד עָשָׂר	(f.) אַחַת עֶשְׂרֵה	י״א
12		(m.) שְׁנֵים עָשָׂר	(f.) שְׁתֵּים עֶשְׂרֵה	י״ב
13		(f.) שְׁלֹשׁ עֶשְׂרֵה	(m.) שְׁלֹשָׁה עָשָׂר	י״ג
20		(c.) עֶשְׂרִים		כ׳

---

1. This is probably the correct pronunciation of this unusual form, taking the shewa to be silent and the dagesh as weak.

כ״א	עֶשְׂרִים וְאַחַת (f.)	עֶשְׂרִים וְאֶחָד (m.)	21
כ״ב	עֶשְׂרִים וּשְׁתַּיִם (f.)	עֶשְׂרִים וּשְׁנַיִם (m.)	22
ל׳	שְׁלֹשִׁים (c.)		30
מ׳	אַרְבָּעִים (c.)		40
נ׳	חֲמִשִּׁים (c.)		50
ק׳	מֵאָה (c.)		100
ר׳	מָאתַיִם (c.) (*matayim*)		200
ש׳	שְׁלֹשׁ מֵאוֹת (c.)		300
ת׳	אַרְבַּע מֵאוֹת (c.)		400
—	אֶלֶף (c.) (*elef*)		1,000
—	אַלְפַּיִם (c.) (*alpayim*)		2,000
—	שְׁלֹשֶׁת אֲלָפִים (c.)		3,000
—	רִבּוֹ/רְבָבָה (c.)		10,000

Notes

a. Number 1 follows the noun it qualifies, like an adjective; other numbers normally come before the noun.

b. With numbers 2–10, nouns are always plural; with other numbers, they may be singular or plural.

c. Numbers 3–10 are unusual: the basic form is used with feminine nouns; the form with suffix הָ appears to be feminine but is used with masculine nouns.

d. Numbers 11–19 are combinations of 1–9 with a distinctive form of 10 (עָשָׂר or עֶשְׂרֵה), like 'teen' in English.

e. Number 20 is a plural form of 10. Numbers 30–90 are plurals of 3–9.

f. Numbers have construct forms. They may be used instead of the absolute forms, with no apparent difference in meaning. For example:

Construct		Absolute
אַחַד	←	אֶחָד
שְׁנֵי	←	שְׁנַיִם
שְׁלֹשֶׁת	←	שְׁלֹשָׁה

g. So far, we have focused on cardinal numbers. There are also ordinal numbers. For example, ordinals are formed from cardinal numbers 2–10 with the suffix יִ ִ (-i): שֵׁנִי ('second'), שְׁלִישִׁי ('third'), etc. There is a separate word meaning 'first': רִאשׁוֹן (rishon; cf. אַחֲרוֹן 'last').

25.4 Hebrew Song 6 (*Hevenu Shalom*)

הֵבֵאנוּ שָׁלוֹם עֲלֵיכֶם, (x3)
הֵבֵאנוּ שָׁלוֹם שָׁלוֹם שָׁלוֹם עֲלֵיכֶם!

See mini songbook for music

We bring peace to you,

we bring peace, peace, peace to you! (Traditional song)

Vocabulary (25)

'flesh, meat'[2]	basar		בָּשָׂר	265
'strike' (verb)	hikka	(hiphil נכה)	הִכָּה[3]	266
'live, be alive' (verb)	khaya		חָיָה	267
'go down'	yarad		יָרַד	268
'seat, throne'	kisse		כִּסֵּא	269
'atone'	kipper	(piel כפר)	כִּפֶּר	270
'in order that, for the sake of'	lᵉma'an		לְמַעַן	271

---

2. The word בָּשָׂר is often used figuratively to mean 'human being.'

3. The root נכה is doubly weak, with an initial נ and final ה. See 21.2.c, e.

'altar'	mizbeakh	מִזְבֵּחַ	272
'messenger, angel'	mal'akh	מַלְאָךְ	273
'time'	et	עֵת	274
'bury'	qavar	קָבַר	275
'judge' (verb)	shafat	שָׁפַט	276

Exercise (25)

1. Analyse these verb forms:

Form	Root	Stem and Conjugation	PGN	Extras
מִתְקַדֵּשׁ				
מְלַמֵּד				
מוֹשִׁיעֶךָ				
הִכִּיתָ				
עָלִינוּ				
מְדַבֵּר				
יָרֹד				
תֵּרֶד				
רֶדֶת				
רֵד				
רְדָה⁴				
יָלַדְתִּי				

2. Practise counting from 1 to 10 in Hebrew, both orally and in writing, using the basic forms given above (25.3).

---

4. See 18.1.c.

3. Translate and practise reading the following sentences. Several personal names are not in the vocabularies, but they should be easy to recognize: Hagar, Ishmael, Saul, Laban, Nahor, Rachel, Jeremiah, and Zedekiah.

a וַיִּמְצָא אֶת־הָגָר מַלְאַךְ יְהוָה עַל־עֵין⁵ הַמַּיִם בַּמִּדְבָּר:

b אֵלֶּה יְמֵי שְׁנֵי־חַיֵּי אַבְרָהָם מְאַת שָׁנָה וְשִׁבְעִים שָׁנָה וְחָמֵשׁ שָׁנִים:

וַיָּמָת אַבְרָהָם וַיֵּאָסֶף אֶל־עַמָּיו וַיִּקְבְּרוּ אֹתוֹ יִצְחָק וְיִשְׁמָעֵאל בָּנָיו:

c וְכִפֶּר עַל־הַמִּזְבֵּחַ הַכֹּהֵן עַל־חַטַּאת הָאִישׁ אֲשֶׁר־חָטָא וְנִסְלַח לוֹ⁶:

d שָׁמְעוּ כָל־יִשְׂרָאֵל לֵאמֹר הִכָּה שָׁאוּל אֶת־פְּלִשְׁתִּים:

e אָרוּר הַיּוֹם אֲשֶׁר יֻלַּדְתִּי בּוֹ יוֹם אֲשֶׁר־יְלָדַתְנִי⁷ אִמִּי אַל־יְהִי⁸ בָרוּךְ:

f וַיֹּאמֶר לָהֶם יַעֲקֹב אַחַי מֵאַיִן אַתֶּם וַיֹּאמְרוּ מֵחָרָן⁹ אֲנָחְנוּ:

וַיֹּאמֶר לָהֶם הַיְדַעְתֶּם אֶת־לָבָן בֶּן־נָחוֹר וַיֹּאמְרוּ יָדָעְנוּ:

וַיֹּאמֶר לָהֶם הֲשָׁלוֹם לוֹ וַיֹּאמְרוּ שָׁלוֹם וְהִנֵּה רָחֵל בִּתּוֹ בָּאָה עִם־הַצֹּאן:

g וְיָדְעוּ כָל־בָּשָׂר כִּי אֲנִי יְהוָה מוֹשִׁיעֵךְ וְגֹאֲלֵךְ:

h יְבָרֵךְ יְהוָה אֶת־עַמּוֹ בַשָּׁלוֹם:

i אָנֹכִי עֹמֵד בֵּין־יְהוָה וּבֵינֵיכֶם בָּעֵת הַהוא¹⁰ לְהַגִּיד לָכֶם אֶת־דְּבַר יְהוָה כִּי יְרֵאתֶם מִפְּנֵי¹¹ הָאֵשׁ וְלֹא־עֲלִיתֶם בָּהָר:

j וַיֹּאמֶר יִרְמְיָהוּ אֶל־צִדְקִיָּהוּ כֹּה־אָמַר יְהוָה אֱלֹהֵי צְבָאוֹת אֱלֹהֵי יִשְׂרָאֵל:

4. Practise the Hebrew song *Hevenu Shalom*.

---

5. This preposition has many meanings; here it may be translated 'by' or 'beside'.

6. Translate 'and he will be forgiven' (lit. 'and it will be forgiven to him').

7. See 16.3.a.

8. Jussive (cf. Gen 1:3, see above: 14.1).

9. See lesson 23, footnote 5.

10. This is an example of a distinctive Hebrew way of correcting errors. Scribes were reluctant to change the sacred text, so they left the consonants unchanged (*kᵉtiv* 'written') and added vowels from the correct reading (*qᵉre* 'read'). Here the *kᵉtiv* is הוא (= הוּא), which is masculine whereas the noun it qualifies (עֵת) is feminine, so the feminine form הִיא is read (*qᵉre*). To indicate this, the scribes wrote הַהוא. The terms *kᵉtiv* and *qᵉre* are Aramaic forms from the roots כתב and קרא.

11. Translate 'on account of' or simply 'of' (lit. 'from the face of').

Dictionaries

26.1 Using a Hebrew Dictionary

The next step in learning Hebrew is to learn how to use a dictionary (sometimes called a 'lexicon'). Two dictionaries are recommended at this stage of study: *The Concise Dictionary of Classical Hebrew* (*CDCH* – ed. David Clines, 2009) and *A Concise Hebrew and Aramaic Lexicon of the Old Testament* (*CHALOT* – ed. William Holladay, 1971). Both are short versions of multi-volume works that are essential for advanced study. There is also an older dictionary that is still widely used, partly because it is cheaper to buy and often included with Bible software: *A Hebrew and English Lexicon of the Old Testament* (BDB – ed. Francis Brown, S. R. Driver, & Charles A. Briggs, 1907). The bibliography at the end of this book gives further details of these and other dictionaries.

a. Nouns and Adjectives

Nouns, adjectives, and similar words are listed in modern dictionaries by their basic form (lemma), without prefixes or suffixes. For example:

- הַשַּׁבָּת consists of הַ + שַׁבָּת, so is listed by שַׁבָּת
- שְׂכָרָה consists of שָׂכָר + ָה, so is listed by שָׂכָר
- הַגְּדוֹלָה consists of הַ + גָּדוֹל + ָה, so is listed by גָּדוֹל.

In BDB, however, they are usually listed under the three-letter roots that they are thought to come from. For example: the noun שַׁבָּת is listed under the root שבת and the adjective גָּדוֹל is under גדל.

When the basic form is found in a dictionary, several pieces of information are given (with some variations between dictionaries):

- statistics (usage in Old Testament; *CDCH* adds usage in other Hebrew texts)
- part of speech (noun, adjective, etc.)

- morphology (common forms of the word)
- meaning in English
- examples of texts where the word is used.

b. Verbs

To find a verb in a Hebrew dictionary, it is necessary to identify its root. For example, here are three verbs with qal stems:

- לִבְרֹחַ is listed under the root ברח
- וַיִּזְעָקוּ is listed under the root זעק
- וַיֵּרֶד is listed under the root ירד

CDCH gives the roots without vowels (e.g. שמר), whereas *CHALOT* and BDB add the vowels of the perfect, 3 m. sg., as in the vocabularies of this book (e.g. שָׁמַר).

Verbs with complex stems are also listed under their three-letter roots. For example:

- גִּדַּלְתּוֹ (piel) is listed under the root גדל
- הֵטִיל (hiphil) is listed under the root טול
- לְהִשָּׁבֵר (niphal) is listed under the root שבר

When a root is used in several different stems, there are sub-entries for each stem with morphology, meaning, and examples.

c. Particles

Most particles in Hebrew have only one form, so they can be found directly in a dictionary.

26.2 Summary of Prefixes

As already explained, before looking up a word in a Hebrew dictionary, it is necessary to remove any prefixes or suffixes to identify the simplest form of the word. The analysis exercises in this book are designed to give practice in doing this. Many prefixes and suffixes are similar to each other, so a list of common prefixes is given here to help identify and distinguish them. A list of suffixes is given in the following section.

Lesson	Explanation	Meaning	Prefix
13.1	imperfect, 1 c. sg.; vowel *e* or *a*	'I'	אֶ
8.1 8.2	preposition, used with nouns, infinitive construct, and suffix pronouns; sometimes shewa is replaced by vowel *a*, *e*, or *i*	'in, at, with, by'	בְּ
7.2	definite article; following letter doubled (except gutturals and ר); also הָ or הֶ	'the'	הַ
7.4	interrogative marker; also הַ or הֶ	'?'	הֲ
21.2 22.2 22.4	hiphil perfect, imperative, and infinitive; vowel *a*, *e*, *i*, or *o*	—	ה
21.3	hophal perfect; vowel *o* or *u*	—	ה
22.2 22.4	niphal imperative and some infinitives	—	הִ
23.3	hithpael perfect, imperative, and infinitive	—	הִתְ
6.5	waw conjunction; also וּ or וָ	'and, but, or, then'	וְ
13.2	waw consecutive; used with imperfect; following letter doubled (except 1 c. sg. → וָ)	'and, but, or, then'	וַ
13.1	imperfect, 3 m.; vowel *i*, *a*, or *e*	'he, they'	י
8.1 8.2	preposition, used with nouns and infinitive construct; sometimes shewa is replaced by vowel *a*, *e*, or *i*	'as, like, according to'	כְּ
16.3	alternative form of preposition כְּ, often used with suffix pronouns	'as, like, according to'	כְּמוֹ
8.1 8.2	preposition, used with nouns, infinitive construct, and suffix pronouns; sometimes shewa is replaced by vowel *a*, *e*, or *i*	'to, for'	לְ
11.2	forms a noun from a root	—	מ
22.3	participle of complex stems (except niphal)	—	מ

Lesson	Explanation	Meaning	Prefix
8.3	short form of preposition מִן, used with nouns and infinitive construct; first letter of following word doubled (with guttural becomes מֵ)	'from'	מִ
16.3	alternative form of preposition מִן, sometimes used with suffix pronouns	'from'	מִמֶּ
13.1	imperfect, 1 c. pl.; vowel *i*, *a*, or *e*	'we'	נ
21.1 22.3 22.4	niphal perfect, participle, and some infinitives	—	נ
27.3	short form of אֲשֶׁר	'who, which, what, that'	שֶׁ
13.1	imperfect, 2 m. & f.; vowel *i*, *a*, or *e*	'you'	תּ
13.1	imperfect, 3 f.; vowel *i*, *a*, or *e*	'she, they'	תּ

26.3 Summary of Suffixes

Suffix	Meaning	Explanation	Lesson
ה ָ	'she'	perfect, 3 f. sg.	9.1
ה ָ	—	noun, adjective, and participle ending, f. sg. absolute	11.1
ה ָ	—	with imperative, 2 m. sg.	18.1
ה ָ	'let me/us'	with imperfect, 1 c. sg. and pl., to form cohortative	18.1
ה ָ	'to, toward'	direction marker; used with nouns and pronouns; unstressed	27.1
ה ָ	'her'	suffix pronoun (3 f. sg.); also הָ	16.1
הוּ	'him, his'	alternative suffix pronoun (3 m. sg.)	16.1
הֶם	'them, their'	suffix pronoun (3 m. pl.)	16.1
הֶן	'them, their'	suffix pronoun (3 f. pl.)	16.1

Suffix	Meaning	Explanation	Lesson
וֹ	'him, his'	suffix pronoun (3 m. sg.); also וֹ (-w)	16.1
יו	'his'	suffix pronoun (3 m. sg.) with plural nouns and some prepositions (pronounced -aw)	16.2
וּ	'they'	perfect, 3 c. pl.	9.1
וּ	—	imperfect, 2 & 3 m. pl.; imperative, 2 m. pl.; also וּן	13.1 18.1
י	—	imperfect and imperative, 2 f. sg.; also יִן.	13.1 18.1
י	'me, my'	suffix pronoun (1 c. sg.)	16.1
ִי	'me, my'	suffix pronoun (1 c. sg.) with plural nouns and some prepositions	16.2 16.3
ֵי	—	m. pl. construct of noun, adjective, and participle	12.1
ִים	—	m. pl. absolute of noun, adjective, and participle	12.1
ַיִם	—	dual noun	12.4
ךָ	'you, your'	suffix pronoun (2 m. sg.); also כָה. or ךְ.	16.1
ךְ	'you, your'	suffix pronoun (2 f. sg.; sometimes pausal form of 2 m. sg.)	16.1
כֶם	'you, your'	suffix pronoun (2 m. pl.)	16.1
כֶן	'you, your'	suffix pronoun (2 f. pl.)	16.1
ם	'them, their'	alternative suffix pronoun (3 m. pl.); also מוֹ	16.1
ן	'them, their'	alternative suffix pronoun (3 f. pl.)	16.1
נָה	—	imperfect, 2 and 3 f. pl.; imperative, 2 f. pl.	13.1 18.1
נָּה.	'her'	alternative suffix pronoun (3 f. sg.)	16.1
נוּ	'we'	perfect, 1 c. pl.	9.1
נוּ	'us, our'	suffix pronoun (1 c. pl.)	16.1
נּוּ.	'him, his'	alternative suffix pronoun (3 m. sg.)	16.1

Suffix	Meaning	Explanation	Lesson
נִי	'me, my'	alternative suffix pronoun (1 c. sg.); also נִּ ָ	16.1
ת	—	f. sg. construct of noun, adjective, and participle	11.2
ת	—	infinitive construct of root with weak initial letter	19.2
וֹת	—	f. pl. absolute of noun, adjective, and participle	12.2
וֹת	—	infinitive construct of root with final ה	19.2
תָּ	'you'	perfect, 2 m. sg.	9.1
תְּ	'you'	perfect, 2 f. sg.	9.1
תִּי	'I'	perfect, 1 c. sg.	9.1
תֶּם	'you'	perfect, 2 m. pl.	9.1
תֶּן	'you'	perfect, 2 f. pl.	9.1

26.4 Homonyms

English has many homonyms (words that are pronounced or written the same but have different meanings), for example 'to,' 'too,' and 'two.' When these words are written, they can be distinguished by their spelling; but when spoken, they sound the same and the meaning must be deduced from the context. The same thing happens in Hebrew, and it is important to distinguish such words carefully. Here are some common homonyms:

'serve, work, worship'	עָבַד	'perish, be lost'	אָבַד
object marker (with suffix pronoun)	אֹת/אֵת	'sign'	אוֹת
'eye, spring'	עַיִן	'there is/are not'	אַיִן[1]
'to, toward'	אֶל-	'God, god'	אֵל
'on, over, against, about'	עַל	'not'	אַל
'with'	עִם	'if'	אִם
'with'	אֵת	object marker	אֵת
'time'	עֵת		

---

1. Cf. מֵאַיִן 'from where?'

'now'	עַתָּה	'you' (m. sg.)	אַתָּה
'come, go in'	בּוֹא	'in/with him'	בּוֹ
'herdsman'	בּוֹקֵר	'morning'	בֹּקֶר
'between'	בֵּין	'son, child'	בֵּן
'voice, sound'	קוֹל	'all, every'	כֹּל
'to him'	לוֹ	'no, not'	לֹא
'go!'	לְכָה	'to you' (m. sg.)	לְךָ
'Nathan'	נָתָן	'give'	נָתַן
'bad, evil, disaster' (f.)	רָעָה (I)	'see'	רָאָה
'tend, graze'	רָעָה (II)		
'two' (m. cstr.)	שְׁנֵי	'years' (pl. cstr.)	שְׁנֵי

Vocabulary (26)

Look up these words in a standard dictionary, then memorize them. There is a mini dictionary at the end of this book for quick reference, but you should use a full dictionary for this and the following exercises.

ulay		אוּלַי[2]	277
barakh		בָּרַח	278
hetil	(hiphil טול)	הֵטִיל	279
hiqhil	(hiphil קהל)	הִקְהִיל	280
zahav		זָהָב	281
za'aq		זָעַק	282
kesef		כֶּסֶף	283
nishbar	(niphal שבר)	נִשְׁבַּר	284
petakh		פֶּתַח	285

---

2. Adverb (not the homonym that is the name of a river). If there is more than one homonym for the following words, give the meaning of the most common one.

tsᵉdaqa	צְדָקָה	286
rishon	רִאשׁוֹן	287
shakhav	שָׁכַב	288

Exercise (26)

Translate and practise reading:

a הַקְהֵל אֶת־הָעָם לְמַעַן יִשְׁמְעוּ וּלְמַעַן יִלְמְדוּ וְיָרְאוּ³ אֶת־יְהוָה אֱלֹהֵיכֶם
וְשָׁמְרוּ לַעֲשׂוֹת אֶת־כָּל־דִּבְרֵי הַתּוֹרָה הַזֹּאת:

b כֹּה אָמַר יְהוָה רֵד בֵּית־מֶלֶךְ יְהוּדָה וְדִבַּרְתָּ שָׁם אֶת־הַדָּבָר הַזֶּה:
וְאָמַרְתָּ שְׁמַע דְּבַר־יְהוָה מֶלֶךְ יְהוּדָה הַיֹּשֵׁב עַל־כִּסֵּא דָוִד אַתָּה וַעֲבָדֶיךָ
וְעַמְּךָ הַבָּאִים בַּשְּׁעָרִים הָאֵלֶּה:

c כֹּה אָמַר יְהוָה עֲשׂוּ מִשְׁפָּט וּצְדָקָה: אִם⁴־עָשׂוֹ תַּעֲשׂוּ אֶת־הַדָּבָר הַזֶּה
וּבָאוּ⁵ בְשַׁעֲרֵי הַבַּיִת הַזֶּה מְלָכִים יֹשְׁבִים לְדָוִד עַל־כִּסְאוֹ:

d לִי הַכֶּסֶף⁶ וְלִי הַזָּהָב נְאֻם יְהוָה צְבָאוֹת: גָּדוֹל⁷ יִהְיֶה כְּבוֹד הַבַּיִת הַזֶּה
הָאַחֲרוֹן מִן־הָרִאשׁוֹן אָמַר יְהוָה צְבָאוֹת וּבַמָּקוֹם הַזֶּה אֶתֵּן שָׁלוֹם
נְאֻם יְהוָה צְבָאוֹת:

e כֹּה אָמַר יְהוָה צְבָאוֹת שְׁאַל־נָא אֶת־הַכֹּהֲנִים תּוֹרָה:

f שְׂאוּ שְׁעָרִים רָאשֵׁיכֶם   וּשְׂאוּ פִּתְחֵי עוֹלָם⁸   וְיָבוֹא מֶלֶךְ הַכָּבוֹד:
מִי זֶה מֶלֶךְ הַכָּבוֹד   יְהוָה צְבָאוֹת   הוּא מֶלֶךְ הַכָּבוֹד:

---

3. Root ירא, not ראה.

4. The first clause of this conditional sentence begins with אִם ('if') to state the condition; the second begins with a waw conjunction ('then') and states the consequence.

5. The subject of the verb is after the short pause (מְלָכִים).

6. 'The silver is mine' (lit. 'for me the silver'); likewise the following phrase.

7. The adjective גָּדוֹל followed by preposition מִן has a comparative meaning: 'greater than.'

8. עוֹלָם ('eternity') can also mean 'ancient time.' This genitive expression may be translated 'eternal doors' (NET; cf. NJPS) or 'ancient doors' (NIV, NRSV, ESV, cf. NJB).

g יְהוָה אֱלֹהֵיכֶם הוּא אֱלֹהֵי הָאֱלֹהִים הָאֵל הַגָּדוֹל אֲשֶׁר לֹא־יִשָּׂא פָנִים:[9]

h וְעַתָּה כֹּה־אָמַר יְהוָה אֶל־יִשְׂרָאֵל קָרָאתִי בְשִׁמְךָ לִי אַתָּה
כִּי־תֵלֵךְ בַּמַּיִם אִתְּךָ־אָנִי:

i לְךָ חָטָאתִי וְהָרַע בְּעֵינֶיךָ עָשִׂיתִי:

j וַיַּעַשׂ נֹחַ כְּכֹל אֲשֶׁר צִוָּה אֹתוֹ אֱלֹהִים כֵּן עָשָׂה:

k וַיָּשֻׁבוּ הַמַּיִם מֵעַל הָאָרֶץ אַחֲרֵי חֲמִשִּׁים וּמְאַת יוֹם:

כִּי כֹּה אָהַב אֱלֹהִים אֶת הָעוֹלָם[10] עַד כִּי נָתַן
אֶת בְּנוֹ יְחִידוֹ לְמַעַן לֹא יֹאבַד כָּל הַמַּאֲמִין בּוֹ
אֶלָּא יִנְחַל חַיֵּי עוֹלָם

Can you work out what the text above means?

---

9. This idiom is explained on p. 97, footnote 3.

10. The word עוֹלָם ('eternity') also means 'world' in modern Hebrew.

Reading 5
Jonah 1:1–7

The goal of this Hebrew introduction is to begin reading the Old Testament in its original language as soon as possible. For that reason, we will not spend further time on systematic study of grammar and syntax but focus on reading the text of the Hebrew Bible. Most essentials of Hebrew grammar have already been covered, and a few additional points will be explained when encountered. Many short texts have already been studied, both in the four readings (Lessons 10, 14, 17, 24) and in the exercises. Now we begin to study a whole biblical book – Jonah – except for a poetic section where the language is rather difficult (Jonah 2:3–10). The language of the prose narrative is quite straightforward, and several key words are used repeatedly, which is helpful for study. In addition, it is an enjoyable story with a message that is still relevant today.

The notes here are intended to help students read Jonah in Hebrew by explaining difficult words and forms, not to give a complete analysis of word forms. With gradually decreasing assistance, students are encouraged to read and understand Hebrew texts for themselves, accompanied by a dictionary when necessary. Some more common words are included in the vocabularies, while others are simply mentioned as they occur in the reading. It is not necessary to memorize these other words, so long as you understand them in their context.

The text of Jonah is not printed here. You should be able to use a standard Hebrew Bible by now. If that is not available, you can use the text at the end of this book, which is set out as a dramatic reading.

27.1 Jonah's Call (Jonah 1:1–3)
Verse 1

יוֹנָה: Jonah's name means 'dove.' Some interpreters think this is the key to understanding the book because the dove is a symbol of the Jewish people (cf. Gen 8:9; Ps 55:6; 74:19; Hos

11:11 – also mentioned in the Talmud). They see Jonah as a symbol of Israel and interpret the book allegorically. Other scholars interpret the book historically or as an extended parable. In any case, Jonah is the name of a prophet mentioned in Old Testament history (2 Kgs 14:25) who lived during the reign of Jeroboam II (c. 793–753 BC), but it is likely that the book of Jonah was written later. For this study, we focus on the story as told and what we can learn from that, without discussing its historicity or genre.

Verse 2

קוּם לֵךְ: two short imperatives from familiar verbs.

עָלֶיהָ: preposition עַל with suffix pronoun (3 f. sg.).

רָעָתָם: noun רָעָה with suffix pronoun (3 m. pl.).

לְפָנָי: preposition לִפְנֵי with suffix pronoun (1 c. sg.).

Verse 3

וַיָּקָם: note accent on second syllable, indicating that this syllable is stressed rather than the final one. Because the final syllable is closed and unstressed, its vowel must be short *o*, not long *a*, so the word is pronounced *wayyaqom*.

לִבְרֹחַ: inf. cstr., preposition לְ.

תַּרְשִׁישָׁה: a suffix הָ is sometimes added to nouns to indicate direction or place, with a similar meaning to the preposition לְ ('to, toward'). It may be called a *direction marker*. Unlike similar suffixes (see 26.3), it is unstressed. Tarshish was probably in Spain, about the furthest possible destination for Jonah in the opposite direction to Nineveh!

וַיֵּרֶד: note the accent, indicating stress on the second syllable instead of the last one. The root is יָרַד, qal impf. with waw consecutive. The Hebrew words equivalent to 'go up' and 'go down' are often used for journeys, as in English 'go up to London' and 'go down to the sea.' In Genesis, for example, Abram goes down to Egypt (יָרַד, 12:10) then goes up to Canaan (עָלָה, 13:1).

יָפוֹ: 'Joppa,' a city with a natural harbour on the Mediterranean coast of central Palestine.

אֳנִיָּה (°*niyya*): 'ship.'

בָּאָה: root בוא, qal pt., f. sg. This verb usually means 'go in' or 'come' but sometimes has the meaning 'go' (equivalent to הָלַךְ).

וַיִּתֵּן: root נתן.

שְׂכָרָה: noun שָׂכָר ('fare, wages') with suffix pronoun (3 f. sg. – here translated 'its' rather than 'her').

וַיֵּרֶד: this word has a different accent for its second occurrence in the verse, also on the second syllable. The literal meaning is 'go down,' but the English equivalent would be 'go aboard.'

מִלִּפְנֵי יְהוָה: this expression is repeated for emphasis.

27.2 The Great Storm (Jonah 1:4–5)
Verse 4

Note the unusual word order. The subject comes before the verb and is therefore emphasized: 'But the LORD – he threw …'

סַעַר (saʿar): 'storm.'

חִשְּׁבָה: piel stem חָשַׁב ('threaten'), pf., 3 f. sg.

לְהִשָּׁבֵר: niphal stem נִשְׁבַּר, inf. cstr., preposition לְ.

Verse 5

הַמַּלָּחִים: noun מַלָּח (mallakh) 'sailor.'

אִישׁ: '[each] person.'

אֱלֹהָיו: 'his god.' The plural form אֱלֹהִים usually means 'God' or 'gods,' but the construct form with a suffix pronoun may mean 'god.'

וַיָּטִלוּ: hiphil stem הֵטִיל.

הַכֵּלִים: noun כְּלִי (vocabulary item 212). The plural form means 'cargo' in this context.

לְהָקֵל: hiphil stem הֵקַל (root קלל), inf. cstr., preposition לְ, meaning 'to lighten' (cf. קַל 'light').

וְיוֹנָה יָרַד: note the word order that emphasizes the name Jonah ('but Jonah – he had gone down …'). Cf. v. 4 (וַיהוָה הֵטִיל).

יַרְכְּתֵי: noun יְרֵכָה ('inner part, rear'), cstr. pl.

הַסְּפִינָה: 'ship,' a word that comes from Aramaic and is only found here in the Old Testament.

וַיֵּרָדַם: niphal stem נִרְדָּם ('be sound asleep'), impf., 3 m. sg., waw consecutive.

27.3 Jonah Found Guilty (Jonah 1:6–7)
Verse 6

רַב: this word may be used as an adjective ('many, much, great') or a noun ('chief, master'). In later Hebrew, it is a term of respect for Jewish teachers and interpreters of the Law. With a 1 c. sg. suffix pronoun, it becomes רַבִּי (*rabbi*, lit. 'my master').

הַחֹבֵל:חֹבֵל means 'sailor,' here used collectively for 'crew,' so רַב הַחֹבֵל is the captain.

נִרְדָּם: niphal stem נִרְדָּם, pt. m. sg., that means 'sleeper' or 'sound asleep.'

אֱלֹהֶיךָ: 'your god' (see note above on אֱלֹהָיו).

יִתְעַשֵּׁת: hithpael stem הִתְעַשֵּׁת ('give a thought, take notice'), a word of Aramaic origin that occurs only here in the Old Testament.

הָאֱלֹהִים: in the light of אֱלֹהֶיךָ earlier in the sentence (explained above), this may be translated 'the god.'

Verse 7

אִישׁ אֶל־רֵעֵהוּ: cf. Jeremiah 31:34.

לְכוּ: root הלך, qal impv., 2 m. pl.; lit. 'Go' but here means 'Come on!'

וְנַפִּילָה: hiphil stem הִפִּיל (root נפל), cohortative, 1 c. pl. The cohortative is a first-person imperfect form with suffix הָ‎ ָ, which serves as a first-person imperative (see 18.1.h). Here it expresses a command or wish addressed to a group of people including the speaker ('let us …'). The waw conjunction does not affect the tense in this form.

גּוֹרָלוֹת: the noun גּוֹרָל (*goral*) is masculine but has a f. pl. ending (cf. אָבוֹת). It means 'lot,' either one of the stones used to determine something or the portion allotted in this way (cf. Num 26:55–56; Neh 10:34; Prov 16:33; Mic 2:5). The portion allotted to Jonah here is the responsibility for angering the gods, so that they sent the great storm.

וְנֵדְעָה: root ידע, qal cohortative, 1 c. pl.

בְּשֶׁלְּמִי: combination of בְּ + שֶׁ + לְ + מִי (lit. 'by what to who?'). שֶׁ is a short form of אֲשֶׁר that is prefixed to the following word. Various translations of the combination are suggested, e.g. 'who is responsible for' (NIV); 'who is to blame for' (NJB); 'whose fault it is' (NET).

וַיַּפִּלוּ: second occurrence of נפל hiphil in the verse. This time it is impf. 3 m. pl. with waw consecutive.

וַיִּפֹּל: the root נפל occurs for a third time in the verse.

Vocabulary (27)

Look up these words in a dictionary, then memorize them:

		af	אַף[1]	289
		bala	בָּלַע	290
		dag	דָּג	291
		dam	דָּם	292
		heshiv	(hiphil שׁוב) הֵשִׁיב	293
(verb)		*zavakh*	זָבַח	294
(noun)		*zevakh*	זֶבַח	295
(verb)		*khafets*	חָפֵץ	296
		yakhol	יָכֹל	297
		yir'a	יִרְאָה	298
		kaf	כַּף	299
		ma'ᵃse	מַעֲשֶׂה	300

---

1. Noun (not the particle that is spelt the same and means 'also, even').

Exercise (27)

1. Practise reading Jonah 1:1–7 until you can do so fluently, either from a Hebrew Bible or from the text for dramatic reading at the end of this book.

2. Identify the prefixes and suffixes in the words from Jonah 1:1–7 listed below, plus the basic form that would be listed in a dictionary, following the examples:

Word	Prefix	Suffix	Basic form
הַגְּדוֹלָה	definite article	adjective f. sg.	גָּדוֹל
עָלֶיהָ	—	suffix pronoun 3 f. sg.	עַל
וַיָּקָם	waw consecutive; impf. 3 m. sg.	—	קום
עָלְתָה			
רָעָתָם			
לְפָנַי			
תַּרְשִׁישָׁה			
מִלְּפְנֵי			
שְׂכָרָהּ			
עִמָּהֶם			
וַיִּירְאוּ			
הַמַּלָּחִים			
אֱלֹהָיו			
נֵדְעָה			
גּוֹרָלוֹת			

3. Translate Jonah 1:1–7 into English, using the notes from this lesson and a Hebrew dictionary, *without* consulting an English Bible. If you give a dynamic equivalent for a word or phrase, give the literal meaning in brackets.

4. Compare your translation with NIV (or NRSV or ESV). If you discover errors in your translation, correct them; if there are interesting alternatives to your translation, note them but do not change your own.

5. Reflect on the meaning of this text today. How would we respond if God called us to preach his message in a foreign country? Should we wake those who are sleeping in a quiet place, ignoring the storm that is raging in the world outside?

Figure 15. The Story of Jonah.[2]

---

2. Azaria Mbatha. Source unknown.

Reading 6
Jonah 1:8–2:2

28.1 Confession of Faith (Jonah 1:8–9)

Verse 8

בְּשֶׁלְּמִי = בַּאֲשֶׁר לְמִי (v. 7).

For notes on the rest of vv. 8–9, see 20.2.

28.2 Confession of Sin (Jonah 1:10–12)

Verse 10

מַה־זֹּאת עָשִׂיתָ: This question is not asking for information. The sailors know quite well what Jonah has done because he has just told them. Rather, it is a rhetorical question asking him to take responsibility for his wrongdoing. Similar questions are common in the Old Testament, especially in Genesis (e.g. 3:13; 4:10; 12:18).

בֹּרֵחַ: root ברח, qal active pt., m. sg.

Verse 11

מַה־נַּעֲשֶׂה לָּךְ (*mannaᵃsellakh*). The two double letters link מָה with נַעֲשֶׂה and נַעֲשֶׂה with לָךְ. The usual pronunciation of the last word is לָךְ, but it changes here because of the short pause (˙).

וְיִשְׁתֹּק: qal stem שָׁתַק ('become calm'). The imperfect with waw conjunction (not waw consecutive) has a jussive meaning here, indicating an action that is desired ('so that it may become calm').

מֵעָלֵינוּ: lit. 'from on us,' perhaps better translated here 'for us.'

הוֹלֵךְ וְסֹעֵר: the qal stem סָעַר means 'rage', specifically referring to a storm. Cf. the noun סַעַר ('storm') in v. 4. The pair of participles means literally 'going and raging'. NJPS translates them freely but conveys the meaning well: 'growing more and more stormy'.

Verse 12

שָׂאוּנִי וַהֲטִילֻנִי: impv., 2 m. pl., suffix pronoun (1 c. sg.).

כִּי ... כִּי: 'because ... that'.

בְּשֶׁלִּי: 'it is my fault' (lit. 'by what to me'). Cf. בְּשֶׁלְמִי (v. 7).

28.3 Salvation for the Sailors (Jonah 1:13–15)

Verse 13

וַיַּחְתְּרוּ: qal stem חָתַר ('row').

לְהָשִׁיב: hiphil stem הֵשִׁיב, inf. cstr.

Verse 14

אָנָּה (anna): interjection meaning 'oh' or 'please'.

נֹאבְדָה: cohortative, 1 c. pl., here with a negative, expressing a wish that something should not happen (cf. v. 7).

בְּנֶפֶשׁ: בְּ here means 'on account of' and נֶפֶשׁ may be translated 'life'.

תִּתֵּן: root נתן. The meaning here is 'lay [on us]' (ESV; cf. KJV), i.e. 'hold accountable' (NIV) or 'make guilty' (NRSV).

נָקִיא: 'innocent'.

Verse 15

וַיִּשְׂאוּ: root נשא. The initial נ usually merges with the letter שׂ to become שׂ in the imperfect, but here the strong dagesh is missing.

וַיְטִלֻהוּ: וַ + יָטִילוּ + הוּ (cf. v. 5).

מִזַּעְפּוֹ: זַעַף (za'af) is a noun according to DCH and BDB; but HALOT lists it as inf. cstr. of the verb זָעַף. Either way, it means 'anger'.

28.4 Repentance of the Sailors (Jonah 1:16)

Verse 16

The first four words are the same as the first four of v. 10, here supplemented with
אֶת־יְהוָה (direct object of וַיִּֽירְאוּ).

וַיִּדְּרוּ: qal stem נָדַר ('vow').

נְדָרִים: noun נֶדֶר (ne̲der) 'vow.'

28.5 Lesson from the Fish (Jonah 2:1–2)

The verse numbers of chapter 2 in Hebrew are different from those in many English
translations, as shown for the first two verses.

Verse 1 (English 1:17)

וַיְמַן: piel stem מִנָּה ('appoint, send'). The final ה drops out in this imperfect form, so the
strong dagesh in the middle root letter is omitted.

בִּמְעֵי: noun מֵעִים ('belly'), cstr. with preposition.

שְׁלֹשָׁה: This form is used with masculine nouns (25.3). The noun לֵילוֹת appears to be
feminine but is actually masculine.

Verse 2 (English 2:1)

הַדָּגָה: feminine form of דָּג, with definite article.

Vocabulary (28)

o̲rekh		אֹרֶךְ	301
b^ehema		בְּהֵמָה	302
baqar		בָּקָר	303
giddal	(piel גדל)	גִּדֵּל	304
he^emin	(hiphil אמן)	הֶאֱמִין	305
hekhel	(hiphil חלל)	הֵחֵל¹	306

---

1. חלל is a geminate verb, so the final root letter drops out in many forms.

harbe	הַרְבֵּה	307
khara	חָרָה	308
naga	נָגַע	309
sukka	סֻכָּה	310
shemesh	שֶׁמֶשׁ	311
shata	שָׁתָה	312

Exercise (28)

1. Practise reading Jonah 1:8–2:2 until you can do so fluently.

2. Identify the root of each verb in Jonah 1:8–2:2 listed below:

Verb	Root	Verb	Root
וַיֹּאמְרוּ		וַהֲטִילֵנִי	
הַגִּידָה		יוֹדֵעַ	
וַיִּירְאוּ		וַיַּחְתְּרוּ	
עָשִׂיתָ		לְהָשִׁיב	
יָדְעוּ		יָכְלוּ	
וַיָּמָן		וַיִּקְרְאוּ	
וְיִשְׁתֹּק		נֹאבְדָה	
הוֹלֵךְ		תִּתֵּן	
שָׂאוּנִי		חָפַצְתָּ	
וַיִּדְּרוּ		וַיַּעֲמֹד	

3. Translate Jonah 1:8–2:2 into English, using the notes from this lesson and a Hebrew dictionary.

4. Compare with NIV, NRSV, or ESV and note significant differences.

5. Reflect on the contrast between Jonah and the sailors in this story. Jonah has a good intellectual knowledge of God (Jonah 1:8–9) but disobeys his command and tries to run away from him. The pagan sailors hardly know God, but they work and pray to tackle their problem (vv. 13–14; cf. v. 5), then remember to thank God after he answers their prayer (vv. 15b–16). What can we learn from this?

Figure 16. Jonah in the Belly of the Fish.[2]

---

2. Source unknown.

Reading 7
Jonah 2:11–3:10

Read Jonah's prayer of repentance in 2:3–10 (English: vv. 2–9) in English, before continuing with the following reading.

29.1 Salvation for Jonah (Jonah 2:11)

Verse 11

וַיָּקֵא: hiphil stem הֵקִיא (root קיא), meaning 'vomit.'

29.2 Jonah's Second Call (Jonah 3:1–3)

Verse 1

שֵׁנִית: feminine form of שֵׁנִי.

Verse 2

וּקְרָא: it is printed וּקְרָא in BHS, following the Leningrad codex, with the first letter a combination of ו and ו. The correct form is probably ו (as in BFBS and BHS footnote).

קְרִיאָה: 'message, proclamation,' noun from root קרא ('call, proclaim'). The content of the message is not given here, but it is presumably the same as in Jonah 1:2 (cf. 3:4).

דֹּבֵר: qal stem דָּבַר ('speak'). The same word is used in a similar expression referring to Moses' call (Exod 6:29). The qal stem דָּבַר occurs forty-two times in the Old Testament, almost always as a participle. Its meaning is similar to the piel stem דִּבֵּר.

Verse 3

וַיָּקָם: pronounced *wayyaqom*.

לֵאלֹהִים: This expression is often used to describe something extraordinary by human standards (cf. Gen 10:9; Pss 36:7; 80:11). It may be translated 'very' or 'exceedingly.'

מַהֲלַךְ: noun meaning 'walk, journey,' from root הלך ('walk, go').

שְׁלֹשֶׁת: construct form of שְׁלֹשָׁה.

29.3 Repentance of Nineveh (Jonah 3:4–5)

Verse 4

וַיָּחֶל: hiphil stem הֵחֵל, from root חלל.

נֶהְפָּכֶת: niphal stem נֶהְפַּךְ ('overturned, overthrown'), pt. f. The participle here indicates something that will happen very soon.

Verse 5

וַיַּאֲמִינוּ: hiphil stem הֶאֱמִין.

צוֹם: noun meaning 'fast.'

וַיִּלְבְּשׁוּ: qal stem לָבַשׁ ('put on').

שַׂקִּים: plural of שַׂק ('sack, sackcloth').

מִגְּדוֹלָם וְעַד־קְטַנָּם: cf. Jeremiah 31:34.

29.4 The King's Command (Jonah 3:6–9)

Verse 6

וַיִּגַּע: qal stem נָגַע.

וַיָּקָם: *wayyaqom.*

מִכִּסְאוֹ: the double ס in כִּסֵּא becomes single ס with a suffix pronoun.

וַיַּעֲבֵר: hiphil stem הֶעֱבִיר ('make pass'), here meaning 'take off' or 'remove.'

אַדַּרְתּוֹ: noun אַדֶּרֶת (*adderet,* 'robe, splendour') with suffix pronoun.

וַיְכַס: piel stem כִּסָּה ('cover'), here implicitly 'oneself with.' The final ה and strong dagesh are omitted (cf. Jonah 2:1).

וַיֵּשֶׁב: root ישׁב.

הָאֵפֶר: noun אֵפֶר (*efer*) 'dust, ashes.'

Verse 7

וַיַּזְעֵק: hiphil stem הִזְעִיק ('issue a proclamation,' lit. 'make cry out').

מִטַּעַם: noun טַעַם (ta'am) 'taste, decree,' with preposition.

וּגְדֹלָיו: adjective גָּדוֹל, m. pl., suffix pronoun, vowel letter omitted, here used as a noun ('noble, official').

יִטְעֲמוּ: qal stem טָעַם ('taste'), impf. with jussive meaning. Here it is linked with the particle אַל to make a prohibition.

מְאוּמָה: indefinite pronoun meaning 'anything, something.'

יִשְׁתּוּ and יִרְעוּ: impf. with אַל expressing prohibition.

Verse 8

וְיִתְכַּסּוּ: hithpael stem הִתְכַּסָּה ('cover oneself'). The third-person impf. with waw conjunction (not waw consecutive) indicates a command, like the jussive. The same applies for וְיִקְרְאוּ. Cf. Jonah 1:11.

חָזְקָה (khozqa): noun meaning 'strength.'

וְיָשֻׁבוּ: root שׁוּב, not יָשַׁב (which would be יֵשְׁבוּ).

מִדַּרְכּוֹ: noun דֶּרֶךְ with prefix preposition and suffix pronoun.

הָרָעָה: feminine adjective with definite article ('evil').

הֶחָמָס: noun חָמָס ('violence').

בְּכַפֵּיהֶם: noun כַּף, cstr. pl., suffix pronoun.

Verse 9

וְנִחַם: niphal stem נָחַם, pf., meaning 'regret, change one's mind, have compassion.'

מֵחֲרוֹן: noun חָרוֹן ('anger, wrath').

אַפּוֹ: the noun אַף is used figuratively here for God's wrath. The genitive expression means literally 'the anger of his nose' and may be translated 'his fierce anger' (NIV, NRSV).

29.5 Salvation for Nineveh (Jonah 3:10)

Verse 10

וַיִּנָּחֶם: niphal stem נָחַם (cf. v. 9).

Vocabulary (29)

		ohel	אֹהֶל	313
		elef	אֶלֶף	314
	(piel בקשׁ)	biqqesh	בִּקֵּשׁ	315
	(hiphil נצל)	hitsil	הִצִּיל	316
		khodesh	חֹדֶשׁ	317
		kherev	חֶרֶב	318
		yamin	יָמִין	319
		yarash	יָרַשׁ	320
		lekhem	לֶחֶם	321
(verb)		qedem	קֶדֶם	322
		ra[1]	רעע/רַע	323
		semol	שְׂמֹאל	324

Tip: *Directions in Hebrew are often given from the perspective of someone facing east, so 'right' = 'south,' 'left = 'north,' 'in front' = 'east' (cf. Gen 13:9, 11).*

Exercise (29)

1. Practise reading Jonah 2:11–3:10 until you can do it fluently.

2. Identify each noun and adjective in Jonah 2:11–3:10 listed below in its basic form (the form by which it would be found in a dictionary):

Noun	Basic form	Noun	Basic form
לַדָּג		בְּחָזְקָה	
הַיַּבָּשָׁה		מַדְרְכֹּו	
כִּדְבַר		בְּכַפֵּיהֶם	

---

1. The root רעע is geminate (middle letter = final letter), so the final ע drops out in most forms. For example, the perfect, 3 m. sg., is רַע (ra).

יָמִים		מֶחָרוֹן	
שַׂקִּים		מַעֲשֵׂיהֶם	
קְטַנָּם		וּגְדֹלָיו	
מִכִּסְאוֹ		הַקְּרִיאָה	

3. Translate this text into English, using the notes from this lesson and a Hebrew dictionary if necessary.

4. Compare your translation with a published translation into your mother tongue or another language you know. Note any significant differences or points of interest.

5. Compare Jonah 3:1–3 with Jonah 1:1–3 in Hebrew. What are the key similarities and differences?

6. Reflect on this comparison. Has Jonah repented in chapter 3? Read chapter 4:1-3 in English to get a fuller picture.

Figure 17. Jonah Preaches in Nineveh.[2]

---

2. Azaria Mbatha. Source unknown.

Reading 8
Jonah 4:1–11

30.1 Jonah's Anger (Jonah 4:1–3)

Verse 1

וַיֵּרַע: root רעע, qal impf. This verb does not have a specific subject, so it is completed with the explanation אֶל־יוֹנָה. The phrase means literally 'It was bad to Jonah,' so may be translated 'this seemed wrong to Jonah' (cf. NIV) or 'this was displeasing to Jonah' (NRSV).

רָעָה: feminine noun meaning 'something that is bad, evil.' Together with the adjective גְדוֹלָה, it functions as an adverbial phrase to strengthen the verb וַיֵּרַע. It may be translated with an appropriate English adverb, such as 'very' or greatly.' Cf. וַיֵּרַע לָהֶם רָעָה גְדֹלָה (Neh 2:10).

וַיִּחַר: root חרה. This verb does not have a specific subject (like יֵרַע), so it is completed with the explanation לוֹ. The phrase may be translated 'he was angry' (lit. 'it was angry to him').

Verse 2

אָנָּה: see Jonah 1:14.

לוֹא: alternative spelling of לֹא, here with interrogative marker.

הֱיוֹתִי: root היה, qal inf. cstr., suffix pronoun. With preposition עַד it has a temporal meaning (cf. 19.3.c): 'while I was still' (lit. 'until my being').

אַדְמָתִי: noun אֲדָמָה, construct form with suffix pronoun.

עַל־כֵּן: 'that is why' (lit. 'on thus').

קִדַּמְתִּי: piel stem קָדַם ('do something before'). Here it functions as an auxiliary verb to introduce the inf. cstr. with prefix preposition לְ. The phrase is variously translated 'I fled at the beginning' (NRSV), 'I fled beforehand' (NJPS), and 'I first tried to flee' (NJB).

כִּי ... כִּי: 'because ... that.'

חַנּוּן וְרַחוּם: 'gracious and compassionate.' Cf. Exodus 34:6–7.

אֶרֶךְ אַפַּיִם: אַפַּיִם is the dual form of אַף ('nose, anger'). It means literally 'pair of nostrils,' but in this context the figurative meaning is intended ('anger'). The word אֶרֶךְ is the construct form of אָרֵךְ ('length'), so the genitive expression means 'length of [time before] anger,' expressed in English by 'slow to anger' or 'long-suffering.'

נִחָם: niphal stem נָחַם ('regret, change one's mind, have compassion'), pt., m. sg.

הָרָעָה: here means 'disaster.'

Verse 3

טוֹב מוֹתִי מֵחַיָּי: adjective followed by preposition מִן indicates a comparison ('better than').

30.2 Jonah Leaves the City (Jonah 4:4–5)

Verse 4

הַהֵיטֵב: hiphil stem הֵיטִיב ('do good, make good,' root יטב), inf. abs. with interrogative marker, meaning 'Is it good?' God's question to Jonah may be compared with his questions to Cain in Genesis 4:6–7, and the sailors' question in Jonah 1:10.

Verse 5

Some scholars suggest that this verse belongs after 3:4 (cf. BHS footnote). But there is really no problem with the text as it stands. Perhaps it should be understood as in NIV: 'Jonah had gone out ...'

מִקֶּדֶם לְ: 'to the east of' (lit. 'from east to').

תַּחְתֶּיהָ: preposition תַּחַת with suffix pronoun.

בַּצֵּל: noun צֵל ('shade') with prefix preposition בְּ (בְּ + הַ).

30.3 Lesson from the Plant (Jonah 4:6–8)

Verse 6

קִיקָיוֹן: it probably means 'castor-oil plant' (*DCH*; *HALOT*; NJB). However, the identification is uncertain so many translations choose a more general term, for example 'leafy plant' (NIV), 'bush' (NRSV), 'plant' (ESV), and 'shrub' (CEV).

וַיַּעַל: qal stem עָלָה, here meaning 'grow.'

מֵעַל לְ: 'over' (lit. 'from over to').

לְהַצִּיל: hiphil stem הִצִּיל, inf. cstr.

מֵרָעָתוֹ: רָעָה here may be translated 'discomfort' (NIV; NRSV), referring to Jonah's exposure to the hot sun; or 'ill-humour' (NJB), referring to Jonah's upset about the repentance of Nineveh (v. 1).

שִׂמְחָה: 'joy' (cf. verb שָׂמַח 'rejoice').

Verse 7

תּוֹלַעַת (*tola'at*): 'worm.'

בַּעֲלוֹת: root עלה, qal inf. cstr. It means literally 'at the going up.'

שַׁחַר (*shakhar*): 'dawn.' With the previous word, the phrase may be translated 'when dawn came up' (NRSV).

לַמָּחֳרָת: noun מָחֳרָת (*makhᵉrat*) 'morrow, next day' with preposition and definite article.

וַתַּךְ: hiphil stem הִכָּה ('strike'), impf., 3 f. sg., initial ה and final ה dropped. The strong dagesh has also dropped out. Here 'attack' may be a good translation.

וַיִּיבָשׁ: qal stem יָבֵשׁ ('be dry, wither'); cf. יַבָּשָׁה ('dry land').

Verse 8

כִּזְרֹחַ: qal stem זָרַח ('rise'), inf. cstr. The prefix preposition כְּ with inf. cstr. indicates time ('when').

קָדִים: 'east,' often referring to an east wind. Cf. קֶדֶם ('in front, east').

חֲרִישִׁית: 'sultry, scorching,' occurs only here in the Old Testament.

וַיִּתְעַלָּף: hithpael stem הִתְעַלֵּף ('be/become faint').

טוֹב מוֹתִי מֵחַיָּי: cf. note on v. 3.

30.4 God's Love (Jonah 4:9–11)

Verse 9

Compare with verse 4, where Jonah ignores God's question. Here, however, he replies by justifying himself.

Verse 10

חַסְתָּ: qal stem חוס ('pity, be concerned about').

עָמַלְתָּ: qal stem עָמַל ('labour, work').

גִּדַּלְתּוֹ: piel stem גָּדַל, pf., 2 m. sg., suffix pronoun.

שֶׁבִּן: combination of אֲשֶׁר and בֶּן. The latter is linked with לַיְלָה in a genitive relationship, so the phrase means literally 'which [is] son of a night.' With the verb הָיָה, it may be translated freely as 'it came into being in a night' (NRSV) or 'which appeared overnight' (NJPS).

Verse 11

There is no interrogative pronoun or marker, but it is clear from the context that this sentence is a question.

אָחוּס: qal stem חוס (see v. 10).

הַרְבֵּה מִ: adjective (vocabulary item 307) with preposition מִן to express comparative: 'more than' (lit. 'many from').

שְׁתֵּים־עֶשְׂרֵה רִבּוֹ: 'twelve ten-thousand' (= 120,000).

אֲשֶׁר לֹא־יָדַע בֵּין־יְמִינוֹ לִשְׂמֹאלוֹ: this could refer to inhabitants of Nineveh who are ignorant or to little children. The words יָמִין and שְׂמֹאל should be understood literally here, referring to right and left hands, not directions (south and north).

30.5 Hebrew Song 7 (*Hava Nagila*)

See mini
songbook
for music

הָבָה¹ נָגִילָה², הָבָה נָגִילָה, הָבָה נָגִילָה, וְנִשְׂמְחָה! (x2)
הָבָה נְרַנְּנָה³, הָבָה נְרַנְּנָה, הָבָה, הָבָה נְרַנְּנָה! (x2)
עוּרוּ⁴, עוּרוּ אַחִים,
עוּרוּ־נָא אַחִים בְּלֵב שָׂמֵחַ, (x4)
עוּרוּ־נָא אַחִים, עוּרוּ־נָא אַחִים, בְּלֵב שָׂמֵחַ!
הָבָה נָגִילָה, הָבָה נָגִילָה, הָבָה נָגִילָה, וְנִשְׂמְחָה! (x2)

Come let us shout for joy (three times), and let us rejoice!

Come let us sing, come let us sing, come, come let us sing!

Awake, awake brothers [and sisters],

awake brothers [and sisters] with a rejoicing heart … *(based on Ps 118:24)*

Vocabulary (30)

(verb)	*khazaq*	חָזַק	325
	khen	חֵן	326
(verb)	*male*	מָלֵא	327
	milkhama	מִלְחָמָה	328
	mashakh	מָשַׁח	329
	mashiakh	מָשִׁיחַ	330
	saviv	סָבִיב	331
	safar	סָפַר	332
	sefer	סֵפֶר	333
	paqad	פָּקַד	334
	sade	שָׂדֶה	335
	sar	שַׂר	336

---

1. Qal stem יָהַב ('give'), impv., 2 m. sg., used as interjection meaning 'Come!' or 'Come on!' (cf. Gen 11:3).
2. Qal stem גִּיל ('rejoice, shout for joy'), cohortative, 1 c. pl.
3. Piel stem רָנַן ('sing for joy'), cohortative, 1 c. pl.
4. Qal stem עוּר ('awake, rouse oneself'), impv., 2 m. pl.

Exercise (30)

1. Practise reading Jonah 4 until you can do it fluently.

2. Translate it into English using the notes from this lesson and a Hebrew dictionary if necessary.

3. Be careful to distinguish various words in the book of Jonah that contain the letters ר and either א or ע. Complete this table:

Word	Verses	Dictionary form	Dictionary meaning
רָעָתָם	1:2	רַע	'bad, evil'
וַיִּירְאוּ	1:5, 10, 16	ירא	'be afraid, fear'
רֵעֵהוּ	1:7		
הָרָעָה	1:7, 8; 3:8, 10, 10; 4:2		
יָרֵא	1:9		
יִרְאָה	1:10, 16		
יִרְעוּ	3:7		
וַיַּרְא	3:10		
וַיֵּרַע	4:1		
רָעָה	4:1		
יִרְאֶה	4:5		
מֵרָעָתוֹ	4:6		

4. The word גָּדוֹל occurs fourteen times in Jonah. Find each occurrence, giving the chapter and verse reference and stating what is 'great' in each case (in Hebrew, with English translation).

5. Read the whole book of Jonah in Hebrew (except 2:3–10) and try to understand it without using a dictionary or English Bible.

6. If you are studying Hebrew with a group or class, allocate the parts in the dramatic reading and read the whole book out loud together.

7. Practise the Hebrew song *Hava Nagila*.

Appendix

1. Prologue to Sirach

The book of Sirach (Ecclesiasticus) in the deuterocanonical books (Apocrypha) was written in Hebrew, then translated into Greek by the author's grandson. It begins with a prologue, written by the grandson, with interesting comments on translation method and the value of reading the original if possible:

> Many great teachings have been given to us through the Law and the Prophets and the others that followed them, and for these we should praise Israel for instruction and wisdom. Now, those who read the scriptures must not only themselves understand them, but must also as lovers of learning be able through the spoken and written word to help the outsiders. So my grandfather Jesus, who had devoted himself especially to the reading of the Law and the Prophets and the other books of our ancestors, and had acquired considerable proficiency in them, was himself also led to write something pertaining to instruction and wisdom, so that by becoming familiar also with his book those who love learning might make even greater progress in living according to the law. You are invited therefore to read it with goodwill and attention, and to be indulgent in cases where, despite our diligent labour in translating, we may seem to have rendered some phrases imperfectly. For what was originally expressed in Hebrew does not have exactly the same sense when translated into another language. Not only this book, but even the Law itself, the Prophecies, and the rest of the books differ not a little when read in the original. When I came to Egypt in the thirty-eighth year of the reign of Euergetes and stayed for some time, I found opportunity for no little instruction. It seemed highly necessary that I should myself devote some diligence and labour to the translation of this book. During that time I have applied my skill day and night to complete and publish the book for those living abroad who wished to gain learning and are disposed to live according to the law. (NRSV)

2. Luther and Languages

One of Martin Luther's greatest contributions to theology was his emphasis on studying the Bible in its original languages. He set out his arguments in a treatise on education entitled

To the Councilmen of All Cities in Germany That They Establish and Maintain Christian Schools (1524). Here are some excerpts:

Though the Gospel has come and daily comes through the Holy Spirit alone, we cannot deny that it has come by means of the languages, by which it was also spread abroad, and by which it must be preserved. For when God desired through the apostles to spread abroad the Gospel in all the world, He provided tongues for that purpose. And before that He had spread the Greek and Latin languages, by means of the Roman empire, throughout all lands, in order that His Gospel might the more speedily bear fruit far and wide ...

In proportion, then, as we prize the Gospel, let us guard the languages. For not in vain did God have His Scriptures set down in these two languages alone – the Old Testament in Hebrew, the New in Greek. The languages, therefore, that God did not despise but chose above all others for His Word, we too ought to honour above all others ...

And let us be sure of this: we shall not long preserve the Gospel without the languages. The languages are the sheath in which this sword of the Spirit is contained; they are the casket in which we carry this jewel; they are the vessel in which we hold this wine; they are the larder in which this food is stored; and as the Gospel itself says, they are the baskets in which we bear these loaves and fishes and fragments. If through our neglect we let the languages go (which may God forbid!), we shall ... lose the Gospel ...

This has been proved and is still shown by experience. Immediately after the days of the apostles, when languages ceased, the Gospel, the faith and the whole Church gradually declined ... On the other hand, since the languages have been restored, they bring with them so bright a light and accomplish such great things that the whole world wonders and is forced to confess that we have the Gospel quite as purely as the apostles had it, and that it has altogether attained to its original purity, far beyond what it was in the days of St. Jerome or St. Augustine ... "But," you say, "many of the fathers were saved and even became teachers without languages." That is true. But how do you account for the fact that they so frequently erred in the Scriptures? ... Was not St. Jerome obliged to make a revised translation of the Psalter from the Hebrew, because when we dispute with Jews on the basis of our Psalter they laugh at us and say our version does not agree with the Hebrew? Now the expositions of all the early fathers who treated the Scriptures without languages, even when their teaching is not wrong, are of such a nature that they very often employ uncertain, inconsistent and inappropriate language; they grope like a blind man along a wall, so that they very frequently miss the sense of their text … Even St. Augustine is obliged to confess … that a Christian teacher who is to expound the Scriptures must know, in addition to Latin, also Greek and Hebrew; otherwise it is impossible not to stumble constantly, nay, there is room enough for labour and toil even when one is well versed in the languages.

There is a great difference, therefore, between a simple preacher of the faith and an expositor of Scripture, or as St. Paul puts it, a prophet. A simple preacher, to be sure, is in possession of so many clear passages and texts from translations that he can know and teach Christ, lead a holy life and preach to others. But to interpret Scripture, to treat it independently, and to dispute with those who cite it incorrectly, to that he is unequal; that cannot be done without languages. Yet there must always be such prophets in the Church, who are able to treat and expound the Scriptures and also to dispute; a saintly life and correct doctrine are not enough. Hence languages are absolutely necessary in the Church, just as prophets or expositors are necessary, although not every Christian or preacher need be such a prophet, as St. Paul says in 1 Corinthians 12 and Ephesians 4 …

Since, then, it becomes Christians to use the Holy Scriptures as their own and only book, and it is a sin and shame not to know our own book nor to understand our God's speech and words, it is a still greater sin and loss if we do not study the languages, the more that God is now offering and giving us men and books and every aid and inducement to this study, and desires His Bible to be an open book …

Here belongs also what St. Paul says in 1 Corinthians 14:27, namely, that there should be in the Church those who will judge all teaching. To this end it is undoubtedly necessary to know the languages. For the preacher or teacher may expound the Bible from beginning to end after his own fashion, hit or miss, if there is no one present to judge whether his teaching be right or wrong. But in order to judge, men must know the languages, otherwise it is impossible. Therefore, though the faith and the Gospel may be proclaimed by simple preachers without the languages, such preaching is flat and tame … But when the preacher is versed in the languages, his discourse has freshness and force, the whole of Scripture is treated, and faith finds itself constantly renewed by a continual variety of words and works.[1]

---

1. http://www.godrules.net/library/luther/NEW1luther_d9.htm.

Dramatic Reading

Jonah 1:1–2:2; 2:11–4:11

מְסַפֵּר[1] וַיְהִי דְּבַר־יְהוָה אֶל־יוֹנָה בֶן־אֲמִתַּי לֵאמֹר: ¹:¹

אֱלֹהִים קוּם לֵךְ אֶל־נִינְוֵה הָעִיר הַגְּדוֹלָה וּקְרָא עָלֶיהָ ²

כִּי־עָלְתָה רָעָתָם לְפָנָי:

מְסַפֵּר וַיָּקָם יוֹנָה לִבְרֹחַ תַּרְשִׁישָׁה מִלִּפְנֵי יְהוָה וַיֵּרֶד יָפוֹ וַיִּמְצָא ³

אֳנִיָּה בָּאָה תַרְשִׁישׁ וַיִּתֵּן שְׂכָרָהּ וַיֵּרֶד בָּהּ לָבוֹא עִמָּהֶם

תַּרְשִׁישָׁה מִלִּפְנֵי יְהוָה:

וַיהוָה הֵטִיל רוּחַ־גְּדוֹלָה אֶל־הַיָּם וַיְהִי סַעַר־גָּדוֹל בַּיָּם ⁴

וְהָאֳנִיָּה חִשְּׁבָה לְהִשָּׁבֵר: וַיִּירְאוּ הַמַּלָּחִים וַיִּזְעֲקוּ אִישׁ ⁵

אֶל־אֱלֹהָיו וַיָּטִלוּ אֶת־הַכֵּלִים אֲשֶׁר בָּאֳנִיָּה אֶל־הַיָּם לְהָקֵל

מֵעֲלֵיהֶם וְיוֹנָה יָרַד אֶל־יַרְכְּתֵי הַסְּפִינָה וַיִּשְׁכַּב וַיֵּרָדַם:

וַיִּקְרַב אֵלָיו רַב הַחֹבֵל וַיֹּאמֶר לוֹ ⁶

רַב הַחֹבֵל מַה־לְּךָ נִרְדָּם קוּם קְרָא אֶל־אֱלֹהֶיךָ

אוּלַי יִתְעַשֵּׁת הָאֱלֹהִים לָנוּ וְלֹא נֹאבֵד:

מְסַפֵּר וַיֹּאמְרוּ אִישׁ אֶל־רֵעֵהוּ ⁷

מַלָּחִים לְכוּ וְנַפִּילָה גוֹרָלוֹת וְנֵדְעָה בְּשֶׁלְּמִי הָרָעָה הַזֹּאת לָנוּ

מְסַפֵּר וַיַּפִּלוּ גּוֹרָלוֹת וַיִּפֹּל הַגּוֹרָל עַל־יוֹנָה:

וַיֹּאמְרוּ אֵלָיו ⁸

---

1. מְסַפֵּר is a participle from the piel verb סִפֵּר ('recount, report, tell'), meaning 'narrator.' Cf. qal stem סָפַר ('count, write') and its participle סֹפֵר ('writer, scribe'); also noun סֵפֶר (*sefer* – 'book, scroll').

מַלָּחִים	הַגִּידָה־נָּא לָנוּ בַּאֲשֶׁר לְמִי־הָרָעָה הַזֹּאת לָנוּ מַה־מְּלַאכְתְּךָ
	וּמֵאַיִן תָּבוֹא מָה אַרְצֶךָ וְאֵי־מִזֶּה עַם אָתָּה:
מִסַּפֵּר	⁹וַיֹּאמֶר אֲלֵיהֶם
יוֹנָה	עִבְרִי אָנֹכִי וְאֶת־יְהוָה אֱלֹהֵי הַשָּׁמַיִם אֲנִי יָרֵא
	אֲשֶׁר־עָשָׂה אֶת־הַיָּם וְאֶת־הַיַּבָּשָׁה:
מִסַּפֵּר	¹⁰וַיִּירְאוּ הָאֲנָשִׁים יִרְאָה גְדוֹלָה וַיֹּאמְרוּ אֵלָיו
מַלָּחִים	מַה־זֹּאת עָשִׂיתָ
מִסַּפֵּר	כִּי־יָדְעוּ הָאֲנָשִׁים כִּי־מִלִּפְנֵי יְהוָה הוּא בֹרֵחַ
	כִּי הִגִּיד לָהֶם: ¹¹וַיֹּאמְרוּ אֵלָיו
מַלָּחִים	מַה־נַּעֲשֶׂה לָּךְ וְיִשְׁתֹּק הַיָּם מֵעָלֵינוּ
מִסַּפֵּר	כִּי הַיָּם הוֹלֵךְ וְסֹעֵר: ¹²וַיֹּאמֶר אֲלֵיהֶם
יוֹנָה	שָׂאוּנִי וַהֲטִילֻנִי אֶל־הַיָּם וְיִשְׁתֹּק הַיָּם מֵעֲלֵיכֶם
	כִּי יוֹדֵעַ אָנִי כִּי בְשֶׁלִּי הַסַּעַר הַגָּדוֹל הַזֶּה עֲלֵיכֶם:
מִסַּפֵּר	¹³וַיַּחְתְּרוּ הָאֲנָשִׁים לְהָשִׁיב אֶל־הַיַּבָּשָׁה וְלֹא יָכֹלוּ כִּי הַיָּם
	הוֹלֵךְ וְסֹעֵר עֲלֵיהֶם: ¹⁴וַיִּקְרְאוּ אֶל־יְהוָה וַיֹּאמְרוּ
מַלָּחִים	אָנָּה יְהוָה אַל־נָא נֹאבְדָה בְּנֶפֶשׁ הָאִישׁ הַזֶּה וְאַל־תִּתֵּן עָלֵינוּ
	דָם נָקִיא כִּי־אַתָּה יְהוָה כַּאֲשֶׁר חָפַצְתָּ עָשִׂיתָ:
מִסַּפֵּר	¹⁵וַיִּשְׂאוּ אֶת־יוֹנָה וַיְטִלֻהוּ אֶל־הַיָּם וַיַּעֲמֹד הַיָּם מִזַּעְפּוֹ:
	¹⁶וַיִּירְאוּ הָאֲנָשִׁים יִרְאָה גְדוֹלָה אֶת־יְהוָה וַיִּזְבְּחוּ־זֶבַח לַיהוָה
	וַיִּדְּרוּ נְדָרִים:
	²:¹וַיְמַן יְהוָה דָּג גָּדוֹל לִבְלֹעַ אֶת־יוֹנָה וַיְהִי יוֹנָה בִּמְעֵי הַדָּג
	שְׁלֹשָׁה יָמִים וּשְׁלֹשָׁה לֵילוֹת: ²וַיִּתְפַּלֵּל יוֹנָה אֶל־יְהוָה אֱלֹהָיו
	מִמְּעֵי הַדָּגָה: ...
	¹¹וַיֹּאמֶר יְהוָה לַדָּג וַיָּקֵא אֶת־יוֹנָה אֶל־הַיַּבָּשָׁה:

וַיְהִי דְבַר־יְהֹוָה אֶל־יוֹנָה שֵׁנִית לֵאמֹר: ³:¹

אֱלֹהִים קוּם לֵךְ אֶל־נִינְוֵה הָעִיר הַגְּדוֹלָה וּקְרָא אֵלֶיהָ ²

אֶת־הַקְּרִיאָה אֲשֶׁר אָנֹכִי דֹּבֵר אֵלֶיךָ:

מְסַפֵּר וַיָּקָם יוֹנָה וַיֵּלֶךְ אֶל־נִינְוֵה כִּדְבַר יְהֹוָה וְנִינְוֵה הָיְתָה ³

עִיר־גְּדוֹלָה לֵאלֹהִים מַהֲלַךְ שְׁלֹשֶׁת יָמִים: ⁴וַיָּחֶל יוֹנָה לָבוֹא

בָעִיר מַהֲלַךְ יוֹם אֶחָד וַיִּקְרָא וַיֹּאמַר

יוֹנָה עוֹד אַרְבָּעִים יוֹם וְנִינְוֵה נֶהְפָּכֶת:

מְסַפֵּר וַיַּאֲמִינוּ אַנְשֵׁי נִינְוֵה בֵּאלֹהִים וַיִּקְרְאוּ־צוֹם וַיִּלְבְּשׁוּ שַׂקִּים ⁵

מִגְּדוֹלָם וְעַד־קְטַנָּם: ⁶וַיִּגַּע הַדָּבָר אֶל־מֶלֶךְ נִינְוֵה וַיָּקָם

מִכִּסְאוֹ וַיַּעֲבֵר אַדַּרְתּוֹ מֵעָלָיו וַיְכַס שַׂק וַיֵּשֶׁב עַל־הָאֵפֶר:

⁷וַיַּזְעֵק וַיֹּאמֶר בְּנִינְוֵה מִטַּעַם הַמֶּלֶךְ וּגְדֹלָיו לֵאמֹר

מֶלֶךְ הָאָדָם וְהַבְּהֵמָה הַבָּקָר וְהַצֹּאן אַל־יִטְעֲמוּ מְאוּמָה אַל־יִרְעוּ

וּמַיִם אַל־יִשְׁתּוּ: ⁸וְיִתְכַּסּוּ שַׂקִּים הָאָדָם וְהַבְּהֵמָה וְיִקְרְאוּ

אֶל־אֱלֹהִים בְּחָזְקָה וְיָשֻׁבוּ אִישׁ מִדַּרְכּוֹ הָרָעָה וּמִן־הֶחָמָס

אֲשֶׁר בְּכַפֵּיהֶם: ⁹מִי־יוֹדֵעַ יָשׁוּב וְנִחַם הָאֱלֹהִים וְשָׁב מֵחֲרוֹן

אַפּוֹ וְלֹא נֹאבֵד:

מְסַפֵּר וַיַּרְא הָאֱלֹהִים אֶת־מַעֲשֵׂיהֶם כִּי־שָׁבוּ מִדַּרְכָּם הָרָעָה ¹⁰

וַיִּנָּחֶם הָאֱלֹהִים עַל־הָרָעָה אֲשֶׁר־דִּבֶּר לַעֲשׂוֹת־לָהֶם

וְלֹא עָשָׂה:

וַיֵּרַע אֶל־יוֹנָה רָעָה גְדוֹלָה וַיִּחַר לוֹ: ⁴:¹

וַיִּתְפַּלֵּל אֶל־יְהֹוָה וַיֹּאמַר ²

יוֹנָה	אָנָּה יְהוָה הֲלוֹא־זֶה דְבָרִי עַד־הֱיוֹתִי עַל־אַדְמָתִי עַל־כֵּן
	קִדַּמְתִּי לִבְרֹחַ תַּרְשִׁישָׁה כִּי יָדַעְתִּי כִּי אַתָּה אֵל־חַנּוּן וְרַחוּם
	אֶרֶךְ אַפַּיִם וְרַב־חֶסֶד וְנִחָם עַל־הָרָעָה: ³וְעַתָּה יְהוָה
	קַח־נָא אֶת־נַפְשִׁי מִמֶּנִּי כִּי טוֹב מוֹתִי מֵחַיָּי:
מְסַפֵּר	⁴וַיֹּאמֶר יְהוָה
אֱלֹהִים	הַהֵיטֵב חָרָה לָךְ:
מְסַפֵּר	⁵וַיֵּצֵא יוֹנָה מִן־הָעִיר וַיֵּשֶׁב מִקֶּדֶם לָעִיר וַיַּעַשׂ לוֹ שָׁם סֻכָּה
	וַיֵּשֶׁב תַּחְתֶּיהָ בַּצֵּל עַד אֲשֶׁר יִרְאֶה מַה־יִּהְיֶה בָּעִיר:
	⁶וַיְמַן יְהוָה־אֱלֹהִים קִיקָיוֹן וַיַּעַל מֵעַל לְיוֹנָה לִהְיוֹת צֵל
	עַל־רֹאשׁוֹ לְהַצִּיל לוֹ מֵרָעָתוֹ וַיִּשְׂמַח יוֹנָה עַל־הַקִּיקָיוֹן שִׂמְחָה
	גְדוֹלָה: ⁷וַיְמַן הָאֱלֹהִים תּוֹלַעַת בַּעֲלוֹת הַשַּׁחַר לַמָּחֳרָת וַתַּךְ
	אֶת־הַקִּיקָיוֹן וַיִּיבָשׁ: ⁸וַיְהִי כִּזְרֹחַ הַשֶּׁמֶשׁ וַיְמַן אֱלֹהִים רוּחַ
	קָדִים חֲרִישִׁית וַתַּךְ הַשֶּׁמֶשׁ עַל־רֹאשׁ יוֹנָה וַיִּתְעַלָּף וַיִּשְׁאַל
	אֶת־נַפְשׁוֹ לָמוּת וַיֹּאמֶר
יוֹנָה	טוֹב מוֹתִי מֵחַיָּי:
מְסַפֵּר	⁹וַיֹּאמֶר אֱלֹהִים אֶל־יוֹנָה
אֱלֹהִים	הַהֵיטֵב חָרָה־לְךָ עַל־הַקִּיקָיוֹן
מְסַפֵּר	וַיֹּאמֶר
יוֹנָה	הֵיטֵב חָרָה־לִי עַד־מָוֶת:
מְסַפֵּר	¹⁰וַיֹּאמֶר יְהוָה
אֱלֹהִים	אַתָּה חַסְתָּ עַל־הַקִּיקָיוֹן אֲשֶׁר לֹא־עָמַלְתָּ בּוֹ וְלֹא גִדַּלְתּוֹ
	שֶׁבִּן־לַיְלָה הָיָה וּבִן־לַיְלָה אָבָד: ¹¹וַאֲנִי לֹא אָחוּס עַל־נִינְוֵה
	הָעִיר הַגְּדוֹלָה אֲשֶׁר יֶשׁ־בָּהּ הַרְבֵּה מִשְׁתֵּים־עֶשְׂרֵה רִבּוֹ
	אָדָם אֲשֶׁר לֹא־יָדַע בֵּין־יְמִינוֹ לִשְׂמֹאלוֹ וּבְהֵמָה רַבָּה:

Mini Dictionary

This mini dictionary contains all the words in the lessons, readings, vocabularies, and exercises of this book. It is designed for quick reference and memorization, and only gives the most common meanings of words. Students are encouraged to use the standard dictionaries for fuller information.

א

אָב/אֲבִי *av/ᵃvi* 'father, ancestor'

אבד – qal אָבַד *avad* 'perish, be lost'

אַבְרָהָם *avraham* 'Abraham'

אַבְרָם *avram* 'Abram'

אָדָם *adam* 'man, mankind, Adam'

אֲדָמָה *ᵃdama* 'land, ground'

אֲדֹנָי *ᵃdonay* 'Lord'

אַדֶּרֶת *adderet* 'robe, splendour'

אהב – qal אָהַב *ahav* 'love' (verb)

אֹהֶל *ohel* 'tent'

אַהֲרֹן *ahᵃron* 'Aaron'

אוֹ *o* 'or'

אוּלַי *ulay* 'perhaps'

אוֹר *or* 'light'

אוֹת *ot* 'sign'

אָחִי/אָח *akh/ᵃkhi* 'brother'

אַחַת/אֶחָד *ekhad/akhat* 'one'

אַחֵר *akher* 'other, another'

אַחֲרֵי/אַחַר *akhar/akhᵃre* 'after, behind'

אַחֲרוֹן *akhᵃron* 'last, latter, behind'

אַיֵּה/אֵי *e/ayye* 'where? which?'; with מִן, it becomes מֵאַיִן ('from where?')

אַיִן/אֵין *ayin/en* 'there is/are not'

אִישׁ *ish* 'man, husband, person'; pl. אֲנָשִׁים

אכל – qal אָכַל *akhal* 'eat'

אַל *al* 'not'

אֵל *el* 'God, god'

אֶל- *el-* 'to, toward'

אֶלָּא *ella* 'but' (mod.)

אֵלֶּה *elle* 'these' (pl.)

אֱלֹהִים *ᵉlohim* 'God, gods'

אֱלוֹהַ *ᵉloah* 'God, god'

אֱלִישָׁע *ᵉlisha* 'Elisha'

אֶלֶף *elef* 'thousand, clan'

אִם *im* 'if'

אֵם *em* 'mother'; pl. אִמּוֹת; with suffix pronoun אִמִּי etc.

אמן – hiphil הֶאֱמִין *heᵉmin* 'believe'

אָמֵן *amen* 'amen, truly'

אמר – qal אָמַר *amar* 'say' niphal נֶאֱמַר *neᵉmar* 'be said, be called'

אֱמֶת *ᵉmet* 'truth'

אַנְגְּלִיָּה *angᵉliyya* 'England' (mod.)

אָנָּא/אָנָּה *anna* 'oh, please'

אֲנַחְנוּ *ᵃnakhnu* 'we'

אָנֹכִי/אֲנִי *ᵃni/anokhi* 'I'

אֳנִיָּה *ᵒniyya* 'ship'

אסף – qal אָסַף *asaf* 'gather' niphal נֶאֱסַף *neᵉsaf* 'be gathered'

אֶסְתֵּר *ester* 'Esther'

אַף *af* 'nose, anger'

אֵפֶר *efer* 'dust, ashes'

אֵצֶל *etsel* 'beside, with'

אַרְבַּע *arba* 'four' (pl. 'forty')

אָרוֹן ^a*ron* 'ark, chest'

אֹרֶךְ *orekh* 'length'

אֲרָם ^a*ram* 'Aram'

אֲרַמִּי ^a*rammi* 'Aramean'

אֲרָמִית ^a*ramit* 'Aramaic' (language)

אֶרֶץ *erets* 'land, earth'

ארר – qal אָרַר *arar* 'curse'

אֵשׁ *esh* 'fire'; with suffix pronoun אִשּׁוֹ
etc.

אִשָּׁה *ishsha* 'woman, wife'; pl. נָשִׁים

אַשּׁוּר *ashshur* 'Assyria'

אֲשֶׁר ^a*sher* 'who, which, what, that'

אָשֵׁר *asher* 'Asher'

אֶת/אֵת *et* 'with'

אֶת/אֵת *et* object marker

אוֹת/אֹת *ot* object marker with suffix
pronoun

אַתְּ *att* 'you' (f. sg.)

אַתָּה *atta* 'you' (m. sg.)

אַתֶּם *attem* 'you' (m. pl.)

אַתֵּן *atten* 'you' (f. pl.)

ב

בְּ *b^e* 'in, at, with, by'

בָּבֶל *bavel* 'Babylon'

בדל – hiphil הִבְדִּיל *hivdil* 'separate'

בְּהֵמָה *b^ehema* 'animal, animals'

בחר – qal בָּחַר *bakhar* 'choose'

בוא – qal בָּא/בּוֹא *bo/ba* 'come, go in'
hiphil הֵבִיא *hevi* 'bring in, carry'

בּוֹקֵר *boqer* 'herdsman'

בֵּין *ben* 'between'

בין – qal בִּין *bin* 'understand'

בַּיִת/בֵּית *bayit/bet* 'house, household'

בֵּית־אֵל *bet-el* 'Bethel'

בלע – qal בָּלַע *bala* 'swallow'

בִּלְתִּי *bilti* 'not, except'

בֵּן/בֶּן *ben* 'son, child, person'

בֶּן־חוּר *ben-khur* 'Ben-Hur'

בנה – qal בָּנָה *bana* 'build'

בעל – qal בָּעַל *ba'al* 'marry, rule'

בַּעַל *ba'al* 'husband, owner, Baal'

בִּנְיָן *binyan* 'building'; also 'stem' (mod.)

בָּקָר *baqar* 'cattle'

בֹּקֶר *boqer* 'morning'

בקש – piel בִּקֵּשׁ *biqqesh* 'seek'

ברא – qal בָּרָא *bara* 'create'

ברח – qal בָּרַח *barakh* 'run, flee'

בְּרִית *b^erit* 'covenant'

ברך – qal בָּרַךְ *barakh* 'bless'
piel בֵּרַךְ *berakh* 'bless'

בָּשָׂר *basar* 'flesh, meat'; used figuratively
to mean 'human being'

בַּת *bat* 'daughter'; pl. בָּנוֹת ; with suffix
pronoun בִּתִּי etc.

בַּת־שֶׁבַע *bat-sheva* 'Bathsheba'

ג

גאל – qal גָּאַל *ga'al* 'redeem'

גִּבּוֹר *gibbor* 'hero, warrior'

גָּדוֹל/גְּדֹל *gadol* 'great'

גדל – qal גָּדַל *gadal* 'be great'
piel גִּדַּל *giddal* 'make great, make grow,
bring up'
pual גֻּדַּל *guddal* 'be grown'
hithpael הִתְגַּדֵּל *hitgaddel* 'boast'

גּוֹי *goy* 'nation, people'

גּוֹרָל *goral* 'lot' (one of the stones used
  to determine something or the
  portion allotted in this way)

גיל – qal גָּל/גִּיל *gil/gal* 'rejoice, shout for
  joy'

גַּם *gam* 'also, even' (adds emphasis to the
  following word)

גַּת הַחֵפֶר *gat hakhefer* 'Gath Hepher'

ד

דבר – qal דָּבַר *davar* 'speak'
  piel דִּבֶּר *dibber* 'speak'

דָּבָר *davar* 'word, thing'

דָּג *dag* 'fish'

דָּוִד *dawid* 'David'

דֹּר/דּוֹר *dor* 'generation'

דָּם *dam* 'blood'

דָּן *dan* 'Dan'

דֶּרֶךְ *derekh* 'way, road'

ה

הַ *ha* 'the' (definite article)

הֲ *ha* interrogative marker

הֶבֶל *hevel* 'Abel'

הָגָר *hagar* 'Hagar'

הוּא *hu* 'he, it, that'

הִיא *hi* 'she, it, that'

היה – qal הָיָה *haya* 'be, become, happen'

הלך – qal הָלַךְ *halakh* 'walk, go'
  hithpael הִתְהַלֵּךְ *hithallekh* 'walk
  about'

הלל – piel הִלֵּל *hillel* 'praise'

הֵמָּה/הֵם *hem/hemma* 'they, those' (m.)

הֵנָּה *henna* 'they, those' (f.)

הִנֵּה *hinne* 'behold! look!'

הפך – niphal נֶהְפַּךְ *nehpakh*
  'overturned, overthrown'

הִפְעִיל *hif'il* 'hiphil' stem (mod.)

הָפְעַל *hof'al* 'hophal' stem (mod.)

הַר *har* 'mountain'

הַרְבֵּה *harbe* 'many, much'

הָרָן *haran* 'Haran' (person)

הִתְפַּעֵל *hitpa'el* 'hithpael' stem (mod.)

ו

וְ *we* 'and, but, or, then'
  (waw conjunction)

ז

זֹאת *zot* 'this' (f. sg.)

זבח – qal זָבַח *zavakh* 'slaughter,
  sacrifice' (verb)

זֶבַח *zevakh* 'sacrifice' (noun)

זֶה *ze* 'this'

זָהָב *zahav* 'gold'

זכר – qal זָכַר *zakhar* 'remember'

זֵכֶר *zekher* 'remembrance, memorial'

זמר – piel זִמֵּר *zimmer* 'sing, praise'

זַעַף *za'af* 'anger'

זעק – qal זָעַק *za'aq* 'cry, call for help'
  hiphil הִזְעִיק *hiz'iq* 'issue a
  proclamation'

זְרֻבָּבֶל *zerubbavel* 'Zerubbabel'

זרח – qal זָרַח *zarakh* 'rise'

ח

חֹבֵל *khovel* 'sailor'

חָבֵר *khaver* 'companion, partner'

חָדָשׁ *khadash* 'new'

חֹדֶשׁ *khodesh* 'month, new moon'

חַוָּה *khawwa* 'Eve'

חוס – qal חָס/חוּס *khus/khas* 'pity, be concerned about'

חזק – qal חָזַק *khazaq* 'be strong'
hiphil הֶחֱזִיק *hekhᵉziq* 'strengthen, hold, seize'

חָזְקָה *khozqa* 'strength'

חטא – qal חָטָא *khata* 'sin' (verb)

חַטָּאת *khattat* 'sin' (noun)

חַי *khay* 'living, alive' (adj.); oath formula חַי־יְהוָה = '[as] the Lord is alive'; pl. form חַיִּים can be noun meaning 'life, lifetime'

חיה – qal חָיָה *khaya* 'live, be alive'

חַיִל *khayil* 'power, wealth, army'

חָכָם *khakham* 'wise, wise person'

חָכְמָה *khokhma* 'wisdom'

חלל – hiphil הֵחֵל *hekhel* 'begin'

חָמָס *khamas* 'violence'

חָמֵשׁ *khamesh* 'five' (pl. 'fifty')

חֵן *khen* 'favour, grace'

חַנּוּן *khannun* 'gracious'

חֶסֶד *khesed* 'loyalty, steadfast love'

חפץ – qal חָפֵץ *khafets* 'desire, delight'

חֶרֶב *kherev* 'sword'

חרה – qal חָרָה *khara* 'be hot, angry'

חָרוֹן *kharon* 'anger, wrath'

חֲרִישִׁית *khᵃrishit* 'sultry, scorching'

חָרָן *kharan* 'Haran' (place); or 'Harran' (NIV 2011).

חָרָשׁ *kharash* 'skilled worker'

חשב – piel חִשֵּׁב *khishshev* 'threaten'

חֹשֶׁךְ *khoshekh* 'darkness'

חתר – qal חָתַר *khatar* 'row' (verb)

ט

טוֹב *tov* 'good'

טול – hiphil הֵטִיל *hetil* 'throw'

טעם – qal טָעַם *ta'am* 'taste' (verb)

טַעַם *ta'am* 'taste, decree' (noun)

י

יבש – qal יָבֵשׁ *yavesh* 'be dry, wither'

יַבָּשָׁה *yabbasha* 'dry land'

יָד *yad* 'hand, arm'

ידה – hiphil impv., 2 m. pl. הוֹדוּ *hodu* 'praise! give thanks!'

ידע – qal יָדַע *yada* 'know'
niphal נוֹדַע *noda* 'be known'

יָהּ *yah* 'Yah' (short form of Yhwh)

יהב – qal יָהַב 'give'

יָהוּ *yahu* 'Yahu' (short form of Yhwh)

יְהוּדָה *yᵉhuda* 'Judah'

יְהוָה *ᵃdonay* 'Lord, the Lord' (Yhwh)

יוֹבֵל *yovel* 'ram, ram's horn, jubilee'

יוֹם *yom* 'day'; pl. יָמִים (*yamim*)

יוֹנָה *yona* 'dove, Jonah'

יוֹסֵף *yosef* 'Joseph'

יַחַד *yakhad* 'unity, together'

יָחִיד *yakhid* 'only'

יטב – hiphil הֵיטִיב *hetiv* 'do good, make good'

יכל – qal יָכֹל *yakhol* 'be able'

ילד – qal יָלַד *yalad* 'give birth to, beget'
niphal נוֹלַד *nolad* 'be born'
piel יִלֵּד *yilled* 'act as midwife'
pual יֻלַּד *yullad* 'be born'
hithpael הִתְיַלֵּד *hityalled* 'register genealogy'

יָם *yam* 'sea'; pl. יַמִּים (*yammim*)

יָמִין *yamin* 'right, right hand, south'

יסף – qal יָסַף *yasaf* 'add'

   hiphil הֹסִיף *hosif* 'increase, do again'

יַעֲקֹב *ya'aqov* 'Jacob'

יָפוֹ *yafo* 'Joppa'

יצא – qal יָצָא *yatsa* 'go out'

   hiphil הוֹצִיא *hotsi* 'bring out'

יִצְחָק *yitskhaq* 'Isaac'

יצר – qal יָצַר *yatsar* 'form, shape' (verb)

ירא – qal יָרֵא *yare* 'be afraid, fear'

   niphal נוֹרָא *nora* 'be feared, awesome'

יִרְאָה *yir'a* 'fear' (noun):

יָרָבְעָם *yarov'am* 'Jeroboam'

ירד – qal יָרַד *yarad* 'go down'

יְרוּשָׁלַםִ *y^erushalaim* 'Jerusalem'; also

   יְרוּשָׁלַיִם (*y^erushalayim*), especially

   in Modern Hebrew

יְרֵכָה *y^erekha* 'inner part, rear'

יִרְמְיָהוּ *yirm^eyahu* 'Jeremiah'

ירש – qal יָרַשׁ *yarash* 'inherit, take

   possession of'

יִשְׂרָאֵל *yisra'el* 'Israel'

יִשְׂרְאֵלִי *yisr^eeli* 'Israelite'

יֵשׁ/יֶשׁ *yesh* 'there is' or 'there are'

   (similar to French *il y a*)

ישב – qal יָשַׁב *yashav* 'sit, dwell, live'

יִשְׁמָעֵאל *yishma'el* 'Ishmael'

ישע – hiphil הוֹשִׁיעַ *hoshia* 'save, help'

יְשַׁעְיָהוּ *y^esha'yahu* 'Isaiah'

כ

כְּ *k^e* 'as, like, according to'

כָּבוֹד *kavod* 'glory, honour'

כֹּה *ko* 'thus, so'

כֹּהֵן *kohen* 'priest'

כֹּחַ *koakh* 'strength, power'

כִּי *ki* 'because, that, when, truly'; כִּי אִם

   ki im 'but, unless, nevertheless'

כָּל-/כֹּל *kol* 'all, every, the whole'

כְּלִי *k^eli* 'thing, vessel, utensil'

כֵּן *ken* 'thus, so'; also 'yes' (mod.)

כְּנַעַן *k^ena'an* 'Canaan'

כְּנַעֲנִי *k^ena'^ani* 'Canaanite'

כִּסֵּא *kisse* 'seat, throne'

כסה – piel כִּסָּה *kissa* 'cover'

   hithpael הִתְכַּסֶּה *hitkasse* 'cover

   oneself'

כֶּסֶף *kesef* 'silver, money'

כַּף *kaf* 'hand, palm'

כפר – qal כָּפַר *kafar* 'cover'

   piel כִּפֶּר *kipper* 'atone'

   pual כֻּפַּר *kuppar* 'be atoned for'

כרת – qal כָּרַת *karat* 'cut'; כָּרַת בְּרִית

   = 'make a covenant'

כתב – qal כָּתַב *katav* 'write'

ל

לְ *l^e* 'to, for'

לֹא *lo* 'no, not'

לֵבָב/לֵב *lev/levav* 'heart, mind'

לָבָן *lavan* 'Laban'

לבש – qal לָבַשׁ *lavash* 'put on'

לוֹט *lot* 'Lot'

לֶחֶם *lekhem* 'bread, food'

לַיְלָה *layla* 'night'

למד – qal לָמַד *lamad* 'learn'

   piel לִמַּד *limmad* 'teach'

לָמָה/לָמָּה *lamma/lama* 'why?' (lit. 'for

   what?')

לִמּוּד *limmud* 'student, disciple'

לְמַעַן *lᵉma'an* 'in order that, for the sake of'

לקח – qal לָקַח *laqakh* 'take'

מ

מְאֹד *mᵉ'od* 'very'

מֵאָה *me'a* 'hundred'

מְאוּמָה *mᵉ'uma* 'anything, something'

מִדְבָּר *midbar* 'desert, wilderness'

מָה *ma* 'what? how?'

מַהֲלָךְ *mahᵃlakh* 'walk, journey'

מוֹלֶדֶת *moledet* 'birthplace, relatives'

מות – qal מֵת/מוֹת *mut/met* 'die'
  hiphil הֵמִית *hemit* 'kill, execute'
  hophal הוּמַת *humat* 'be killed, executed'

מוֹת/מָוֶת *mawet/mot* 'death'

מִזְבֵּחַ *mizbeakh* 'altar'

מִזְמוֹר *mizmor* 'psalm'

מַחֲנֶה *makhᵃne* 'camp, army'

מָחֳרָת *makhᵒrat* 'morrow, next day'

מִי *mi* 'who?'

מַיִם *mayim* 'water'

מִין *min* 'kind'; also 'gender' (mod.)

מלא – qal מָלֵא *male* 'be full'

מַלְאָךְ *mal'akh* 'messenger, angel'

מְלָאכָה *mᵉlakha* 'work, occupation'

מִלָּה *milla* 'word'; also 'particle' (mod.)

מַלָּח *mallakh* 'sailor'

מִלְחָמָה *milkhama* 'war, battle'

מלך – qal מָלַךְ *malakh* 'become king, reign'

מֶלֶךְ *melekh* 'king'

מַלְכָּה *malka* 'queen'

מַמְלֶכֶת/מַמְלָכָה *mamlakha/mamlekhet* 'kingdom'

מִן *min* 'from'

מנה – piel מִנָּה *minna* 'appoint, send'

מִסְפָּר *mispar* 'number' (noun)

מֵעִים *me'im* 'belly'

מַעֲשֶׂה *ma'ᵃse* 'deed, product'

מצא – qal מָצָא *matsa* 'find'
  niphal נִמְצָא *nimtsa* 'be found'

מִצְוָה *mitsva* 'commandment'

מִצְרִי *mitsri* 'Egyptian'

מִצְרַיִם *mitsrayim* 'Egypt'

מִקְדָּשׁ *miqdash* 'holy place'

מָקוֹם *maqom* 'place' (noun)

מִקְרָא *miqra* 'assembly, reading'

מַרְאֶה *mar'e* 'appearance, sight'

מֹשֶׁה *moshe* 'Moses'

משח – qal מָשַׁח *mashakh* 'anoint'

מָשִׁיחַ *mashiakh* 'anointed one, messiah'

מִשְׁלַחַת *mishlakhat* 'deputation, mission'

מִשְׁמָר *mishmar* 'custody, guard'

מִשְׁמֶרֶת *mishmeret* 'guard-duty, watch'

מִשְׁפָּט *mishpat* 'judgement, justice'

נ

נָא *na* 'please'

נְאֻם *nᵉ'um* 'declaration'

נָבִיא *navi* 'prophet'

נְבִיאָה *nᵉvi'a* 'prophetess'

נגד – hiphil הִגִּיד *higgid* 'tell'

נגע – qal נָגַע *naga* 'touch, reach, hurt'

נדר – qal נָדַר *nadar* 'vow' (verb)

נֶדֶר *neder* 'vow' (noun)

נֹחַ *noakh* 'Noah'

נָחוֹר *nakhor* 'Nahor'

נחל – qal נָחַל *nakhal* 'obtain, inherit'

נַחֲלָה *nakhᵃla* 'inheritance, property'

נחם – niphal נִחַם *nikham* 'regret, change one's mind, have compassion'

נכה – hiphil הִכָּה *hikka* 'strike' (verb)

נָעִים *na'im* 'pleasant, lovely'

נפל – qal נָפַל *nafal* 'fall' (verb)
hiphil הִפִּיל *hippil* 'make fall, cast'

נִפְעַל *nif'al* 'niphal' stem (mod.)

נֶפֶשׁ *nefesh* 'soul, life, person'

נָקִיא *naqi* 'innocent'

נצל – hiphil הִצִּיל *hitsil* 'snatch away, deliver'

נשא – qal נָשָׂא *nasa* 'lift, carry'; נָשָׂא עֵינַיִם = 'look up'; נָשָׂא פָנִים = 'be favourable, show partiality'
niphal נִשָּׂא *nissa* 'be lifted, be carried'

נתן – qal נָתַן *natan* 'give, set'
niphal נִתַּן *nittan* 'be given, be set'

נָתָן *natan* 'Nathan'

ס

ס = סְתוּמָא *setuma* paragraph marker

סבב – qal סָבַב *savav* 'turn, go around'

סָבִיב *saviv* 'around'

סְגֻלָּה *segulla* 'personal property'

סוּס *sus* 'horse'

סוּסָה *susa* 'mare'

סִין *sin* 'China' (mod.)

סֻכָּה *sukka* 'hut, shelter'

סלח – qal סָלַח *salakh* 'forgive'
niphal נִסְלַח *nislakh* 'be forgiven'

סער – qal סָעַר *sa'ar* 'rage' (verb; about a storm)

סַעַר *sa'ar* 'storm'

סְפִינָה *sefina* 'ship'

ספר – qal סָפַר *safar* 'count, write'
piel סִפֵּר *sipper* 'recount, report, tell'

סֵפֶר *sefer* 'book, scroll'

ס = סְתוּמָא *setuma* paragraph marker

ע

עבד – qal עָבַד *avad* 'serve, work, worship'

עֶבֶד *eved* 'servant, slave'

עבר – qal עָבַר *avar* 'pass [over/through/by]'
hiphil הֶעֱבִיר *he'evir* 'make pass, take off'

עִבְרִי *ivri* 'Hebrew' (ethnicity)

עִבְרִית *ivrit* 'Hebrew' (language; mod.)

עַד *ad* 'until, as far as'

עֵד *ed* 'witness' (noun)

עֵדַת/עֵדָה *eda/ᵃdat* 'assembly, congregation'

עוֹד *od* 'again, still, more'

עוֹלָם *olam* 'long time, eternity'; also world (mod.)

עָוֹן *awon* 'iniquity, guilt'

עור – qal עָר/עוּר *ur/ar* 'awake, rouse oneself'

עֻזִּיָּהוּ *uzziyyahu* 'Uzziah'

עטף – hithpael הִתְעַטֵּף *hit'attef* 'wrap oneself'

עַיִן/עֵין *ayin/en* 'eye, spring [of water]'

עִיר *ir* 'town, city'; pl. עָרִים

עֵירֹם *erom* 'naked'

עַל *al* 'on, over, against, about'

עלה – qal עָלָה *ala* 'go up'

niphal נַעֲלָה *na'ala* 'be led up'

hiphil הֶעֱלָה *he'ela* 'bring up, offer'

hophal הָעֳלָה *ho'ala* 'be offered'

עֶלְיוֹן *elyon* 'high, highest, most high'

עלף – hithpael הִתְעַלֵּף *hit'allef* 'be/ become faint'

עַם *am* 'people'; pl. עַמִּים

עִם *im* 'with'; the מ is doubled with suffix pronouns, e.g. עִמִּי ; often ד is added too, e.g. עִמָּדִי

עמד – qal עָמַד *amad* 'stand'

hiphil הֶעֱמִיד *he'emid* 'cause to stand'

עמל – qal עָמַל *amal* 'labour, work' (verb)

עִמָּנוּ אֵל *immanu el* 'Immanuel'

ענה – qal עָנָה *ana* 'answer, reply' (verb)

עֵץ *ets* 'tree, wood'

עֶרֶב *erev* 'evening'

עשה – qal עָשָׂה *asa* 'do, make'

עֵשָׂו *esaw* 'Esau'

עֶשֶׂר *eser* 'ten' (pl. 'twenty')

עֶשְׂרֵה/עָשָׂר *asar/esre* 'teen' (forms of עֶשֶׂר that are combined with numbers 1–9 to make 11–19, e.g. שְׁלֹשָׁה עָשָׂר = 'thirteen')

עשת – hithpael הִתְעַשֵּׁת *hit'ashshet* 'give a thought'

עֵת *et* 'time'

עַתָּה *atta* 'now'

פ

פ = פְּתוּחָא *p'tukha* paragraph marker

פֶּה/פִּי *pe/pi* 'mouth, opening, speech'

פלל – hithpael הִתְפַּלֵּל *hitpallel* 'pray'

פְּלִשְׁתִּי *p'lishti* 'Philistine'

פְּנִיאֵל *p'ni'el* 'Peniel'

פָּנִים/פְּנֵי *panim/p'ne* 'face'; לִפְנֵי = 'before'

פעל – qal פָּעַל *pa'al* 'do, make'

פֹּעַל *po'al* 'deed, act'; also 'verb' (mod.)

פִּעֵל *pi'el* 'piel' stem (mod.)

פֻּעַל *pu'al* 'pual' stem (mod.)

פקד – qal פָּקַד *paqad* 'visit, appoint'

פַּרְעֹה *par'o* 'Pharaoh' (title)

פרר – hiphil הֵפֵר *hefer* 'break, frustrate'

פ = פְּתוּחָא *p'tukha* paragraph marker

פֶּתַח *petakh* 'opening, entrance, door'

צ

צֹאן *tson* 'sheep, goats, flock'

צְבָאוֹת *ts'va'ot* 'Almighty' (lit. 'armies')

צַדִּיק *tsaddiq* 'righteous, just'

צְדָקָה *ts'daqa* 'righteousness'

צִדְקִיָּהוּ *tsidqiyyahu* 'Zedekiah'

צוה – piel צִוָּה *tsiwwa* 'command' (verb)

צוֹם *tsom* 'fast' (noun)

צִיצִת *tsitsit* 'tassel'

צֵל *tsel* 'shade'

צֶלֶם *tselem* 'image'

ק

קבר – qal קָבַר *qavar* 'bury'

קָדוֹשׁ *qadosh* 'holy'

קָדִים *qadim* 'east, east wind'

קדם – piel קִדֵּם *qiddem* 'do something before'

קֶדֶם *qedem* 'in front, before, east'

קדש – qal קָדַשׁ *qadash* 'be holy'

piel קִדֵּשׁ *qiddash* 'make holy'

pual קֻדַּשׁ *quddash* 'be made holy'

hithpael הִתְקַדֵּשׁ *hitqaddesh* 'make oneself holy'

קֹדֶשׁ *qodesh* 'holiness'

קהל – niphal נִקְהַל *niqhal* 'assemble' (intransitive, i.e. when people assemble themselves)

hiphil הִקְהִיל *hiqhil* 'assemble' (transitive, i.e. when someone assembles other people or things)

קֹל/קוֹל *qol* 'voice, sound'

קום – qal קָם/קוּם *qum/qam* 'rise, stand'

קטל – qal קָטַל *qatal* 'kill'

קָטֹן/קָטָן *qatan/qaton* 'small, young'

קיא – hiphil הֵקִיא *heqi* 'vomit'

קַיִן *qayin* 'Cain'

קִיקָיוֹן *qiqayon* 'castor-oil plant'

קַל *qal* 'light, quick'; simple stem (mod.)

קלל – hiphil הֵקַל *heqal* 'lighten'

קָפֶה *qafe* 'coffee' (mod.)

קרא – qal קָרָא *qara* 'call, proclaim, read'

קרב – qal קָרַב *qarav* 'go near, approach'

hiphil הִקְרִיב *hiqriv* 'bring near'

קֶרֶב *qerev* 'midst, inward part'

קְרִיאָה *qᵉri'a* 'message, proclamation'

ר

ראה – qal רָאָה *ra'a* 'see'

niphal נִרְאָה *nir'a* 'appear, be seen'

hiphil הֶרְאָה *her'a* 'show'

hophal הָרְאָה *hor'a* 'be shown'

hithpael הִתְרָאָה *hitra'a* 'see again, look at each other'

רֹאשׁ *rosh* 'head'

רִאשׁוֹן *rishon* 'first, former'

רֵאשִׁית *reshit* 'beginning'

רַב *rav* 'many, much, great' (adj.)

רַב *rav* 'chief, master' (noun)

רבה – qal רָבָה *rava* 'be many'

hiphil הִרְבָּה *hirba* 'make many'

רִבּוֹ *ribbo* 'ten thousand'

רדם – niphal נִרְדָּם *nirdam* 'be sound asleep'

רוּחַ *ruakh* 'spirit, wind, breath'

רוּת *rut* 'Ruth'

רַחוּם *rakhum* 'compassionate'

רָחֵל *rakhel* 'Rachel'

רחם – qal רָחַם *rakham* 'love'

piel רִחַם *rikham* 'show mercy, take pity'

רחף – piel רִחֵף *rikhef* 'hover'

רנן – piel רִנֵּן *rinnen* 'sing for joy'

רֵעַ *rea* 'friend, neighbour'

רָעָה/רַע *ra/ra'a* 'bad, evil, disaster'

רעה – qal רָעָה *ra'a* 'tend, graze' (verb)

רעע – qal רַע *ra* 'be bad, evil'; the final ע of this root always drops out, so it is never pronounced in full

רָקִיעַ *raqia* 'dome, expanse'

שׂ

שָׂדֶה *sade* 'field, open country'

שׂיח – qal שָׂח/שִׂיחַ *siakh/sakh* 'meditate, talk'

שִׂיחָה *sikha* 'conversation' (mod.)

שׂים – qal שָׂם/שִׂים *sim/sam* 'put, place'

שָׂכָר *sakhar* 'fare, wages'

שְׂמֹאל *sᵉmol* 'left, left hand, north'

שמח – qal שָׂמַח *samakh* 'rejoice'

שִׂמְחָה *simkha* 'joy'

שַׂק *saq* 'sack, sackcloth'

שַׂר *sar* 'leader, chief, prince'

שָׂרָף *saraf* 'seraph'

שׁ

שֶׁ *she* short form of אֲשֶׁר

שׁאל – qal שָׁאַל *sha'al* 'ask, request'

שָׁאוּל *sha'ul* 'Saul'

שֶׁבַע *sheva* 'seven' (pl. 'seventy')

שׁבר – qal שָׁבַר *shavar* 'break'

   niphal נִשְׁבַּר *nishbar* 'be broken'

   piel שִׁבֵּר *shibber* 'shatter, smash into pieces'

שַׁבָּת *shabbat* 'sabbath'

שַׁדַּי *shadday* 'Almighty'

שׁוב – qal שָׁב/שׁוּב *shuv/shav* 'turn, return'

   hiphil הֵשִׁיב *heshiv* 'bring back, restore'

שַׁחַר *shakhar* 'dawn'

שׁכב – qal שָׁכַב *shakhav* 'lie down'

שָׁלוֹם *shalom* 'peace, prosperity, wholeness'

שׁלח – qal שָׁלַח *shalakh* 'send'

   piel שִׁלַּח *shillakh* 'send away, set free'

   pual שֻׁלַּח *shullakh* 'be sent away'

שָׁלֵם *shalem* 'Salem'

שְׁלֹמֹה *shelomo* 'Solomon'

שָׁלֹשׁ *shalosh* 'three' (pl. 'thirty')

שֵׁם *shem* 'name'; also 'noun' (mod.)

שָׁם *sham* 'there'

שְׁמוּאֵל *shemuel* 'Samuel'

שָׁמַיִם *shamayim* 'heaven, heavens, sky'

שְׁמֹנֶה *shemone* 'eight' (pl. 'eighty')

שׁמע – qal שָׁמַע *shama* 'hear, listen to'

niphal נִשְׁמַע *nishma* 'be heard'

hiphil הִשְׁמִיעַ *hishmia* 'make heard, announce'

שֶׁמַע *shema* 'Shema' (personal name)

שׁמר – qal שָׁמַר *shamar* 'keep, guard, watch'

niphal נִשְׁמַר *nishmar* 'be kept, be careful'

שֶׁמֶשׁ *shemesh* 'sun'

שָׁנָה *shana* 'year'

שֵׁנִי *sheni* 'second'

שְׁתַּיִם/שְׁנַיִם *shenayim/shtayim* 'two'

שִׁעוּר *shi'ur* 'lesson' (mod.)

שַׁעַר *sha'ar* 'gate'; may also refer to a city with gates

שׁפט – qal שָׁפַט *shafat* 'judge' (verb)

שֵׁשׁ *shesh* 'six' (pl. 'sixty')

שׁתה – qal שָׁתָה *shata* 'drink'

שׁתק – qal שָׁתַק *shataq* 'become calm'

ת

תֵּה *te* 'tea' (mod.)

תֹּהוּ וָבֹהוּ *tohu wavohu* 'formless void'

תְּהוֹם *tehom* 'the deep'

תּוֹדָה *toda* 'thanksgiving'; also 'thank you' (mod.)

תּוֹךְ/תָּוֶךְ *tawekh/tokh* 'middle, midst'

תּוֹלַעַת *tola'at* 'worm'

תּוֹרָה *tora* 'teaching, law'

תַּחַת *takhat* 'under, instead of'

תַּרְשִׁישׁ *tarshish* 'Tarshish'

תֵּשַׁע *tesha* 'nine' (pl. 'ninety')

Mini Songbook

This songbook provides musical accompaniment for the Hebrew songs learnt in this book. The words are transliterated to make them easier to sing. For the Hebrew text and English translation, see the lessons above, as given in brackets for each song. Most of the songs can be found on YouTube with accompanying videos. Be aware that some song titles are spelt differently from the transliteration used here, for example 'Shalom Chaverim' and 'Hinei Ma Tov.'

1. Shalom Khᵃverim (Lesson 1.5)

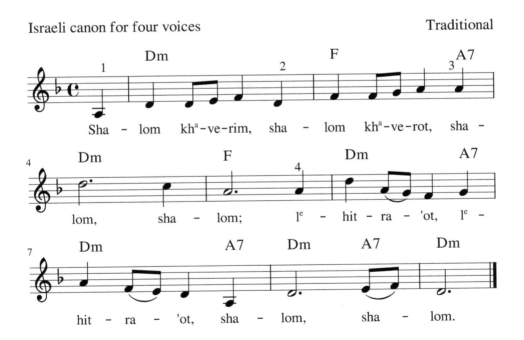

2. Lo V^ekhayil (5.5)

Lo Vekhayil

Zechariah 4:6

Peter van Woerden

3. Hinne Mattov (8.4)

Hinne Mattov

Psalm 133:1   Traditional

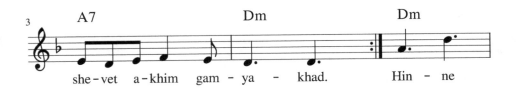

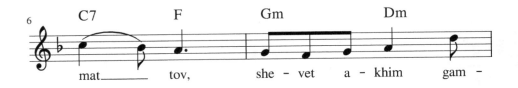

4. Barukh Habba (15.4)

Barukh Habba

Psalm 118: 26, 29

M. Chavez

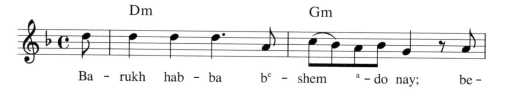

Ba - rukh   hab - ba   b^e - shem   ^a - do nay;   be -

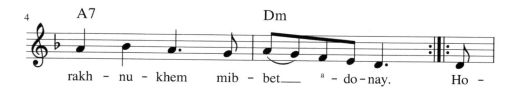

rakh - nu - khem   mib - bet___   ^a - do-nay.   Ho -

du   la-do-nay ki___   tov;   ki   l^e - 'o - lam_ khas - do.

5. Adonay Yishmorkha (20.3)

Adonay Yishmorkha

Psalm 121: 7-8

M. Chavez

6. Hevenu Shalom (25.4)

Hevenu Shalom

Traditional

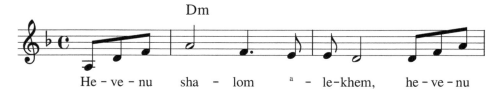

He - ve - nu   sha - lom   ᵃ - le-khem,   he - ve - nu

sha - lom   ᵃ - le-khem,   he - ve - nu   sha - lom   ᵃ -

le-khem,   he - ve - nu   sha-lom sha-lom   sha-lom ᵃ - le-khem!

7. Hava Nagila (30.5)

Hava Nagila

Eastern European folk dance

Abraham Zvi Idelsohn

13

u – ru – na   a – khim   beˉ - lev   sa – me – akh,

14

u – ru – na   a – khim   beˉ - lev   sa – me – akh,

15

u – ru – na   a – khim   beˉ - lev   sa – me – akh,

16

u – ru – na   a – khim   beˉ - lev   sa – me – akh,

17

u – ru – na   a – khim,   u – ru – na   a – khim,   beˉ -

18

D.C. al Fine

lev   sa – me – akh!

Bibliography

Hebrew Bibles

BFBS: *Hebrew Old Testament* (British & Foreign Bible Society, 1958).

BHQ: *Biblia Hebraica Quinta* (Deutsche Bibelgesellschaft, 2004–).

BHS: *Biblia Hebraica Stuttgartensia* (Deutsche Bibelgesellschaft, 1968–76; 5th edn, 1997).

JPS: *JPS Hebrew-English Tanakh: The Traditional Hebrew Text and the New JPS Translation – Second Edition*, ed. David E. Sulomm Stein (Philadelphia: Jewish Publication Society, 1999).

RHB: *A Reader's Hebrew Bible*, ed. A. Philip Brown, II, & Bryan W. Smith (Grand Rapids, Michigan: Zondervan, 2008).

Hebrew Dictionaries

BDB: *A Hebrew and English Lexicon of the Old Testament*. Edited by Francis Brown, S. R. Driver, and Charles A. Briggs. Oxford: Clarendon, 1907; repr. with corrections 1957.

CDCH: *The Concise Dictionary of Classical Hebrew*. Edited by David J. A. Clines. Sheffield: Sheffield Phoenix, 2009.

CHALOT: *A Concise Hebrew and Aramaic Lexicon of the Old Testament: Based Upon the Lexical Work of Ludwig Koehler and Walter Baumgartner*. Edited by William L. Holladay. Grand Rapids, MI: Eerdmans, 1971.

DCH: *The Dictionary of Classical Hebrew*. Edited by David J. A. Clines. 8 vols. Sheffield: Sheffield Academic, 1993–2011.

HALOT: *The Hebrew and Aramaic Lexicon of the Old Testament*. Edited by Ludwig Koehler, Walter Baumgartner, and Johann Jakob Stamm. 5 vols. Leiden: Brill, 1994–2000; translated from German, 1967–1996, edited for translation.

NIDOTTE: *New International Dictionary of Old Testament Theology and Exegesis*. Edited by Willem A. VanGemeren. 5 vols. Carlisle: Paternoster, 1997.

RHELOT: *A Reader's Hebrew-English Lexicon of the Old Testament: Four Volumes in One*. Edited by Terry A. Armstrong, Douglas L. Busby, and Cyril F. Carr. Grand Rapids, MI: Zondervan, 1989.

TDOT: *Theological Dictionary of the Old Testament*. Edited by G. Johannes Botterweck, and Helmer Ringgren. 15 vols. Grand Rapids, MI: Eerdmans, 1977–2006; translated from German, 1970–1995).

Hebrew Introductions (recommended for further study)

Kelley, Page H. *Biblical Hebrew: An Introductory Grammar*. Grand Rapids, MI: Eerdmans, 1992.

Lambdin, Thomas O. *Introduction to Biblical Hebrew*. London: Darton, Longman & Todd, 1973.

Pratico, Gary D., and Miles V. Van Pelt. *Basics of Biblical Hebrew Grammar*. 3rd ed. Grand Rapids, MI: Zondervan, 2019.

Simon, Ethelyn, Irene Resnikoff, and Linda Motzkin. *The First Hebrew Primer: The Adult Beginner's Path to Biblical Hebrew*. 3rd ed. Oakland, CA: EKS, 2005.

Advanced Hebrew

Groom, Susan Anne. *Linguistic Analysis of Biblical Hebrew*. Carlisle: Paternoster, 2003.
Joüon, Paul, and T. Muraoka. *A Grammar of Biblical Hebrew*. Rev. English ed. Subsidia Biblica, 27. Rome: Pontifical Biblical Institute, 2006; translated from French, 1923.
Kautzsch, E., and A. E. Cowley, eds. *Gesenius' Hebrew Grammar*. 2nd ed. Oxford: Clarendon, 1910; translated from German, 28th ed, 1909.
Waltke, Bruce K., and M. O'Connor. *An Introduction to Biblical Hebrew Syntax*. Winona Lake, IN: Eisenbrauns, 1990.
Watson, Wilfred G. E. *Classical Hebrew Poetry: A Guide to its Techniques*. 2nd ed. JSOTSup, 26. Sheffield: JSOT Press, 1986.

Other Works Used

Baker, David L. 'Which Hebrew Bible? Review of Biblia Hebraica Quinta, Hebrew University Bible, Oxford Hebrew Bible, and Other Modern Editions.' *Tyndale Bulletin* 61 (2010): 209–236.
Dobson, John H. *Learn Biblical Hebrew*. 2nd ed. Carlisle: Piquant, 2005.
Eaton, John H. *First Studies in Biblical Hebrew*. Birmingham: Birmingham University, 1980.
Even-Shoshan, Abraham, ed. *A New Concordance of the Bible*. 2nd ed. Jerusalem: Kiryat Sefer, 1989.
Futato, Mark D. *Beginning Biblical Hebrew*. Winona Lake, IN: Eisenbrauns, 2003.
Hackett, Jo Ann. *A Basic Introduction to Biblical Hebrew*. Peabody, MA: Hendrickson, 2010.
Levy, Harold. *Hebrew for All*. London: Vallentine Mitchell, 1976. (Introduction to modern conversational Hebrew).
Sawyer, John F. A. *A Modern Introduction to Biblical Hebrew*. Stocksfield: Oriel, 1976.
Tucker, W. Dennis, Jr. *Jonah: A Handbook on the Hebrew Text*. Baylor Handbook on the Hebrew Bible. Waco, TX: Baylor University Press, 2006.
Walker-Jones, Arthur. *Hebrew for Biblical Interpretation*. Resources for Biblical Study, 48. Atlanta, GA: Society of Biblical Literature, 2003.
Webster, Brian L. *The Cambridge Introduction to Biblical Hebrew*. Cambridge: Cambridge University Press, 2009.
Weingreen, J. *A Practical Grammar for Classical Hebrew*. 2nd ed. Oxford: Clarendon, 1959.

Langham Literature and its imprints are a ministry of Langham Partnership.

Langham Partnership is a global fellowship working in pursuit of the vision God entrusted to its founder John Stott –

to facilitate the growth of the church in maturity and Christ-likeness through raising the standards of biblical preaching and teaching.

Our vision is to see churches in the Majority World equipped for mission and growing to maturity in Christ through the ministry of pastors and leaders who believe, teach and live by the word of God.

Our mission is to strengthen the ministry of the word of God through:
- nurturing national movements for biblical preaching
- fostering the creation and distribution of evangelical literature
- enhancing evangelical theological education

especially in countries where churches are under-resourced.

Our ministry

Langham Preaching partners with national leaders to nurture indigenous biblical preaching movements for pastors and lay preachers all around the world. With the support of a team of trainers from many countries, a multi-level programme of seminars provides practical training, and is followed by a programme for training local facilitators. Local preachers' groups and national and regional networks ensure continuity and ongoing development, seeking to build vigorous movements committed to Bible exposition.

Langham Literature provides Majority World preachers, scholars and seminary libraries with evangelical books and electronic resources through publishing and distribution, grants and discounts. The programme also fosters the creation of indigenous evangelical books in many languages, through writer's grants, strengthening local evangelical publishing houses, and investment in major regional literature projects, such as one volume Bible commentaries like *The Africa Bible Commentary* and *The South Asia Bible Commentary*.

Langham Scholars provides financial support for evangelical doctoral students from the Majority World so that, when they return home, they may train pastors and other Christian leaders with sound, biblical and theological teaching. This programme equips those who equip others. Langham Scholars also works in partnership with Majority World seminaries in strengthening evangelical theological education. A growing number of Langham Scholars study in high quality doctoral programmes in the Majority World itself. As well as teaching the next generation of pastors, graduated Langham Scholars exercise significant influence through their writing and leadership.

To learn more about Langham Partnership and the work we do visit **langham.org**

CPSIA information can be obtained
at www.ICGtesting.com
Printed in the USA
LVHW061319180723
752727LV00014B/1247